D0948507

Constructing Test Items

Evaluation in Education and Human Services

Editors:

George F. Madaus, Boston College, Chestnut
  Hill, Massachusetts, U.S.A.
Daniel L. Stufflebeam, Western Michigan
  University, Kalamazoo, Michigan, U.S.A.

A selection of previously published books in the series:

Kelleghan, T., Madaus, G., and Airasian, P.:
  The Effects of Standardized Testing
Madaus, G. (editor):
  The Courts, Validity, and Minimum Competency Testing
Brinkerhoff, R., Brethower, D., Hluchyj, T., and Nowakowski, J.:
  Program Evaluation, Sourcebook/Casebook
Madaus, G., Scriven, M., Stufflebeam, D.:
  Evaluation Models: Viewpoints on Educational and Human Services Evaluation
Hambleton, R., Swaminathen, H.:
  Item Response Theory
Stufflebeam, D., Shrinkfield, A.:
  Systematic Evaluation
Cooley, W. and Bickel, W.:
  Decision-Oriented Educational Research
Gable, R.:
  Instrument Development in the Affective Domain
Sirotnik, K., and Oakes, J.:
  Critical Perspectives on the Organization and Improvement of Schooling
Wick, J.:
  *School-Based Evaluation: A Guide for Board Members, Superintendents, Principals,
  Department Heads, and Teachers*
Worthen, B. and White, K.:
  Evaluating Educational and Social Programs
McArthur, D.:
  Alternative Approaches to the Assessment of Achievement
May, L., Moore, C. and Zammit, S.:
  Evaluating Business and Industry Training
Glasman, N. and Nevo, D.:
  Evaluation in Decision Making: The Case of School Administration
Gephart, W. and Ayers, J.:
  Teacher Education Evaluation
Madaus, G. and Stufflebeam, D.:
  Educational Evaluation: Classic Works of Ralph W. Tyler
Gifford, B.:
  Test Policy and the Politics of Opportunity Allocation: The Workplace and the Law
Gifford, B.:
  Test Policy and Test Performance
Mertens, D.:
  Creative Ideas for Teaching Evaluation

Constructing Test Items

Steven J. Osterlind
University of Missouri-Columbia

Kluwer Academic Publishers
Boston/Dordrecht/London

Distributors for United States and Canada:
Kluwer Academic Publishers
101 Philip Drive,
Assinippi Park,
Norwell, MA 02061
USA

For all other countries:
Kluwer Academic Publishers Group
Distribution Centre
P. O. Box 322
3300 AH Dordrecht
The Netherlands

Library of Congress Cataloging-in-Publication Data

Osterlind, Steven J.
  Constructing test items.

  (Evaluation in education and human services series)
  Bibliography: p.
  Includes index.
  1. Examinations—Design and construction.   I. Title.
II. Series.
LB3060.65.O77   1989   371.2′61   89–8152
ISBN 0-7923-9012-1

ISBN 0-7923-9012-1

Copyright © 1989 by Kluwer Academic Publishers

Printed in the United States of America

Contents

List of Tables and Figures

Tables

Figures

Acknowledgements

Although the name of a single author appears on the frontpiece of this book, it could not have been produced without the manifold contributions of many people. I would like to cite the names of some of these persons, in appreciation of their effort. They are Dr. Ibrahim Khaleel, for his invaluable research assistance, and Drs. William R. Merz, Kathleen M. Wulf, Margret B. Jorgenson, and Thomas M. Haladyna, for reviewing drafts of the chapters. Without question, this book could not have been written without the loving support of my wife and children: Nancy, Alex, Janey, and Anna. To them I echo Wordsworth's sentiment:

> Enough of Science and Art;
> Close up those barren leaves;
> Come forth, and bring with you a heart
> That watches and receives.

Constructing Test Items

Chapter 1

What Is Constructing Test Items?

INTRODUCTION

Constructing test items for standardized tests of achievement, ability, and aptitude is a task of enormous importance—and one fraught with difficulty. The task is important because test items are the foundation of written tests of mental attributes, and the ideas they express must be articulated precisely and succinctly. Being able to draw valid and reliable inferences from a test's scores rests in great measure upon attention to the construction of test items. If a test's scores are to yield valid inferences about an examinee's mental attributes, its items must reflect a specific psychological construct or domain of content. Without a strong association between a test item and a psychological construct or domain of content, the test item lacks meaning and purpose, like a mere free-floating thought on a page with no rhyme or reason for being there at all.

Including only carefully crafted items on a test is also the primary method by which the skilled test developer reduces unwanted error variance, or errors of measurement, and increases a test score's reliability. The importance of constructing good test items is frequently manifest in a process of identifying, isolating, and minimizing sources of unwanted error variance in test scores.

The task of constructing good test items is difficult because writing precisely and succinctly is challenging. Since many test items are no more than a single sentence, there is often little opportunity to garner meaning from context. The grammar, diction, spelling, punctuation, and syntax must be correct and exact. It is distressingly easy for a test-item writer to inadvertently convey hints, biases, prejudices, opinions, or confusing information.

Also, gathering evidence for validity and reliability is demanding. One must establish a positive correlational relationship between a test item and a psychological construct or domain of content. And, reducing sources for error in measurement—whether random or systematic—requires constant diligence.

A further reason why constructing good test items is difficult is that the task challenges the writer to be creative. Imaginative and novel ways of expressing ideas can frequently be useful in test item construction. And, creativity includes an intuitive appreciation of how a particular test item may be perceived by examinees. Such rich understanding of test items will assist one in gaining a "sixth sense" about constructing them.

The perils of writing test items without adequate forethought are great. Decisions about persons, programs, projects, and materials are often made on the basis of test scores. If a test is made up of items haphazardly written by untutored persons, the resulting decisions could be erroneous. Such errors can sometimes have serious consequences for individuals. Programs, projects, and materials could be misjudged. Obviously, such a disservice to examinees as well as to the evaluation process should be avoided if at all possible.

Although there is abundant literature explaining measurement theory, test construction, and analysis of test results (see Anastasi, 1988; Cronbach, 1984; Ebel, 1979; Gulliksen, 1950; Hambleton & Swaminathan, 1985; Lord & Novick, 1968; Nunnally, 1978; Thorndike, 1982; Weiss & Davidson, 1981; Wright & Stone, 1979; and many others), there is woefully little information about planning, designing, and writing test items themselves. Cronbach observed in 1970 that "the design and construction of achievement test items have been given almost no scholarly attention" (p. 509). And

Bormuth (1970), remarking on the lack of concern for information about constructing test items, noted that most writers of test items have only their intuitive skills to rely upon. More recently, Nitko (1984a) lamented the dearth of item-writing research with gentle humor:

> *Elder item writers pass down to novices lists of rules and suggestions which they and their item-writing forefathers have learned through the process of applied art, empirical study, and practical experience. (p. 204)*

Even more disturbing is the conclusion of Haladyna and Downing (in press) after their scrutiny of 46 authoritative textbooks and other sources in the educational measurement literature: ". . . the body of knowledge about MC item writing seems not to be particularly well established, yet the practice of item writing is extensive and certainly warrants more scholarly attention than it appears to have received." Further, Wood (1977), in a report titled "Multiple Choice: A State of the Art Report," offers a comprehensive review of topics related to multiple-choice testing but offers little guidance about how to actually construct test items.

Other researchers—notably, Millman and Greene (in press), Roid and Haladyna (1982), and Wesman (1971)—have similarly commented about the lack of significant research or practical guidance on this subject. And, a 1984 survey of topics selected to be of interest to the membership of the prestigious National Council on Measurement in Education did not even include anything related to the problems associated with constructing test items, although it did cite issues related to test construction and even writing-skills assessment specifically (Berk and Boodoo, n.d.).

A sad testimony to the widespread neglect of this important part of testing is the fact that the single most popular introductory textbook to the field of psychological testing devotes only three paragraphs to effective item writing. This neglect is reinforced by the recent publication of an international handbook on educational research, methodology, and measurement which devotes only a scant, four-page article (out of over 800 pages) to item-writing techniques (Herman, 1988). Regretfully, it seems that Ebel's 1951 comment on the insufficiency of relevant research and guidance is still applicable today: "The problems of item writing have not received the attention they deserve in the literature on testing" (p. 188). Test-item writers are routinely left to their own devices because there is no comprehensive resource identifying the distinctive features and limitations of test items, the function of test items in measurement, or even basic editorial principles and stylistic guidelines.

The little guidance that is available to assist in constructing test items is frequently perfunctory or trivial, often consisting of a list of "dos" and "don'ts." A review of many of these lists reveals that they are predominantly comprised of idiosyncratically selected rules for achieving good writing (e.g., "avoid wordiness," "focus each item on a single idea," etc.). Further, typical lists of item-writing rules intermix with basic suggestions for good writing certain technical and editorial guidelines, such as "Avoid 'All of the Above,'" or "Keep options in a logical order." Although particular rules offered in such lists may be acceptable, a simple list neither captures the complexity of the task nor conveys why certain features are requisite to producing test items of merit.

This book does not suggest one list; rather, the emphasis here is on recognizing the importance of good writing generally in test-item construction and learning how it may be achieved. Additionally, two chapters are devoted specifically to communicating editorial rules for this type of technical writing. Working from this viewpoint, the skilled item writer will be both cognizant of good writing and sufficiently informed to employ whatever rule of writing or editorial style is appropriate to the particular item he or she is preparing.

Lest there be confusion on the point of not citing lists, one final comment. There is nothing wrong with lists of item-writing rules; however, I submit that it is more important to stress principles of good writing generally and to learn the specific editorial rules for this kind of technical writing than to attempt to identify just some particular rules that may apply to some test items. Certainly to list all applicable rules of writing style or of editorial mechanics for test items would be an enormously long compilation and of questionable utility.

Considering that test items are the backbone of most assessment instruments, the dearth of advice about how to construct them is remarkable. The old adage, "You can't build a good house without a solid foundation," is certainly apt. This book is a guide to building the foundation for tests: the test items.

WHAT THIS BOOK IS ABOUT

Four Major Issues in Item Construction

Constructing test items is a comprehensive field of endeavor which may be categorized by particular issues. This book addresses major issues included in constructing test items by focusing on four ideas. First, this book describes characteristics and functions of test items. Characteristics of test items involve classifying and describing test items by various item formats, that is, the depiction of test items as multiple-choice, true-false, matching, or some other type. It also includes problems of definition, terminology, and identification of relevant assumptions. Conjoined with characteristics of test items is an understanding of the various functions they serve in measurement, along with an awareness of their limitations and some familiarity with alternatives to test items in measurement. While this information is necessary background to constructing good test items, it is precursory to actually writing them.

A second feature of this book is the presentation of editorial guidelines for writing test items in all of the commonly used item formats. Editorial guidelines are prescriptive rules for style and form. They dictate the placement of punctuation, writing style, and many test-item protocols, such as where and how to place directions to test items, or when to use boldface type or italics.

The practice of measuring human attributes by means of test items is so common that style rules for writing test items in the various formats should be articulated, standardized, and accepted throughout the industry. There is a greater likelihood for a test item to do whatever it is intended to do if its conception and writing follow prescribed rules. Currently, there does not exist such a comprehensive or prescriptive set of editorial guidelines for writing test items. Clearly, this kind of guidance is needed.

A third aspect of this book is the presentation of methods for determining the quality of test items. Determining the quality of test items may be categorized into two interdependent issues: 1) procedures for gauging the proper content for test items, which revolve around concerns of validity, and 2) procedures for examining test items for either random errors or systematic bias, which reflect considerations of reliability. Both of these issues are addressed by judgmental procedures as well as statistical models. The methods described can be applied to making judgments about test items written by others as well as to test items written by the reader.

A fourth component of this book is the presentation of a compendium of important issues about test items. Some examples of issues discussed in this compendium are procedures for ordering items in a test, ethical and legal concerns for using copyrighted test items, item scoring schemes, and more. A compendium of subjects important to constructing test items could be very large, but this one is arbitrarily confined to cover only a few topics of paramount importance.

Type of Items Addressed

The issues discussed in this book are intended for test items that will be used in both standardized tests and many teacher-made tests. Standardized tests are tests whose initial construction, as well as conditions for administration and scoring, have a uniform procedure so that the scores yielded by the measure may be interpreted in a consistent manner from one administration to the next (Ebel & Frisbie, 1986; Mehrens & Lehmann, 1987; Wiersma & Jurs, 1985).

Teacher-made tests are typically not made according to specific and uniform procedures and the results from various administrations of a teacher-made test are difficult to compare. Regardless of the differences between standardized and teacher-made tests, the quality of the items is important to both kinds of tests.

Also, the material in this book applies to a variety of tests, regardless of whether they are administered to groups of examinees or to an individual. Such standardized or teacher-made tests of achievement, ability, or aptitude can be administered in a wide array of situations, including large- and small-scale assessment programs, clinical testing, educational and psychological testing in schools, tests used in counseling, employment testing, as well as professional and occupational licensing and certification testing. Also included are tests used in the evaluation of educational programs, projects, and materials. Additionally, the information in this book may be suited to tests used in special ways, as for example, testing people who have handicapping conditions, or testing linguistic minorities.

Furthermore, the information presented in this book describes test items as they may be used in tests of achievement, ability, or aptitude. Heavy emphasis, however, is given to test items found in achievement tests because achievement tests, as the most common type of test, are used for assessing many times the number of examinees tested with ability or aptitude measures.

Finally, this book does not differentiate between items that may be used in tests of psychological assessment and those incorporated into instruments designed for educational measurement. A word of explanation may be needed to clarify this point. Most test developers, psychometricians, and psychologists make a distinction between the assessment of psychological constructs and measuring educational achievement. For example, Messick (1980) wrote an influential paper emphasizing the importance of gathering evidence for valid interpretations in differing kinds of assessments, and urged persons to consider to consider both "evidential" and "consequential" basis for test interpretation and test use. These are useful distinctions for guiding one in judging the ethical grounds for a test's application as well as appraising potential social consequences of testing; however, the items to be included in these differing assessments are not different in kind. Items for both types of assessment instruments require the same degree of care and technical skill in their construction. Hence, the information presented in this book on constructing items will apply to either type of assessment.

Types of Items Not Covered

Since the description so far is of what is included in this book, it seems logical to also cite some kinds of test items and tests and measurement issues that are not covered. To begin, this book does not cover assessment done by essay, or writing sample. There are many and varied considerations when developing the essay prompt as well as an array of measurement problems to be dealt with in scoring essays; however, such issues are not addressed in this book. Also, some measures of personality and interest require questioning strategies beyond the scope of the material in this book. For example, this book does not directly address interview strategies, self-report measures, semantic differential, or Likert and Likert-type scales (i.e., scales that present a range of responses from "strongly agree" to "strongly disagree").

Further, many types of exercises used in intelligence testing are not included in this book, particularly questions and situations that involve inductive reasoning. Inductive reasoning is the ability to apply specific experiences to general rules. An example of an inductive-reasoning prompt may be the statement that a furry, four-legged animal that says "meow" is a cat, therefore, any furry, four-legged creature that makes the "meow" sound is a cat. These kinds of problems are commonly expressed as analogies. This book does not specifically address analogies.

Finally, there are manifold issues in measurement generally that are indirectly related to constructing test items but are not specifically addressed in this book. Some of these issues may contribute in some way to constructing good test items, but one simply cannot include everything about such a large topic as constructing test items in one book.

Criteria for Material Included

Two criteria were used in deciding whether to include a particular issue in this book. The first criterion was whether the issue related directly to test items as individual entities. Issues dealing with items assimilated into an entire test (e.g., generalizability of items, scaling items for various interpretations, etc.) are not included here. A second criterion for deciding what to include was the utility of the information. All of the information included in this book was selected because it has some potential for application in actual construction of test items. Sometimes this potential for application is very direct, such as when and how to incorporate a graphic in a test item; at other times, the information is more supportive and will enable one to understand more about test items generally, such as becoming aware of their proper role in measurement.

MAJOR PURPOSES OF THIS BOOK

Goal for This Book

The primary goal for this book is to contribute to the improvement of tests and measurement by aiding good test-item construction. It is hoped that this goal is accomplished in a number of ways. First, this book can make a significant contribution to the field by presenting complete and up-to-date information about test items and how to construct them. The information provided is of two types: information derived from the work of others and information that is original.

The review of the relevant literature will help in providing information by critiquing and synthesizing the best of what is currently known about test items and their construction. It will also serve as documentation of recent advances in knowledge about test items, item-writing technologies, and item-writing methods for commonly used types of tests. Nowhere else in the literature does there exist such a comprehensive review of information important to constructing test items.

Additionally, the author will contribute some new ideas about constructing test items. These new ideas are not mere guesses and speculation about strategies; rather, they represent useful ideas and successful item-writing techniques derived from the author's experience in planning and constructing items for a wide variety of tests. Providing this information—synthesis of existing information and original ideas—is perhaps the most important avenue used to reach the primary goal for this book.

Standardizing Editorial Guidelines for Writing Items

A principal feature of this book is to prescribe a uniform editorial style for particular test-item formats and a rationale for doing so. As far as the author is aware, nowhere else is such a suggested set of prescriptions put forth. Hence, this book represents a suggestion to test-item writers, test developers, and other interested persons to consider the development of a set of editorial guidelines for constructing test items as an industry standard.

Standardization will not stifle creativity in constructing test items; rather, it will provide a coherent framework for proven strategies as well as allow for new and untried approaches. This set of principles and standards for constructing test items will contribute significantly to the principal goal for this book.

Other Purposes

Still another major purpose for this book is to provide instruction in techniques and strategies for judging the quality of test items. An item merely written is unfinished; it should then be subjected to scrutiny to determine its worth. Poor test items should be discarded, salvageable items repaired, and good ones offered forth on tests.

Such a probe into particular test items should be guided by specific criteria for good test items, which this book offers. This close examination may be done by a variety of means, including subjective (but not arbitrary) reviews by knowledgeable persons making informed judgments about whether a particular test item meets the criteria for good test items. And, of course, there are manifold statistics, statistical procedures, and research methods available to lend assistance in the review of test items. Some of these will be described as well.

Yet another purpose for this book is to serve as both a text for instructing students and practitioners in constructing good test items as well as a reference source for a wide array of persons who have a need for information about test items and allied issues. Currently, neither a text nor a comprehensive reference source exists for the important enterprise of constructing test items. Students may gain from the book's organization into chapters of increasing sophistication, guiding them from an initial understanding of the necessary considerations when constructing test items and why they are important, to learning the mechanics of how to construct the items, to becoming familiar with a host of relevant issues. Practitioners who may require a reference source will appreciate the book's thoroughness. Serving the need for a text and reference source in this field is an important purpose for this book.

WHY THIS INFORMATION IS IMPORTANT

Unquestionably, the principal reason the information presented in this book is important is because it may contribute to better decision making, the *raison d'etre* for any testing. Knowing about constructing test items will assist persons in being better informed and, hence, more likely to make reasoned decisions, either as test developers, as test takers, or as test users. Of course, evaluative judgments about persons or programs made on the basis of scores derived from standardized examinations are common. Such decisions occur regularly in schools, counseling situations, business and industry, and elsewhere. It is estimated than annually over 25 million Americans take a standardized examination (Osterlind, 1986). In each instance, the examination was administered so that a decision of some kind could be made. The consequences of decisions made on the basis of test scores can range from innocuous to dramatic. But, regardless of how frequently such decisions occur or the significance of the consequences, it is ethically responsible to promote the notion that test items should be constructed by informed persons.

Another reason the information presented in this book is important is that standardization is called for in this burgeoning field. There are simply so many tests and so many people involved in developing them that it is not realistic to hope that quality test items will result each time, independently, without some generally accepted standards.

Haphazard approaches to constructing test items may or may not produce good items. More likely, lack of uniformity can lead to confusion about relevant information, with a resulting diminution in quality. Buros (1972), lamenting the generally poor quality of tests produced, has remarked that "at least half of the tests currently on the market should never have been published" (p. xxvii). One hopes that with accurate, readily available information, the problem expressed in Buros' sad lament will be gradually alleviated. To that end, this book standardizes a core of basic information about test items.

Further, the guides and editorial rules for constructing particular test-item formats set down in this book could eventually—after review, deliberation, discussion, and appropriate modification—become industry standards for constructing test items. In this book they can serve as a first-draft model insofar as they may generate public discussion and deliberation among professionals in the field. Just as the *Standards for Educational and Psychological Testing* (American Educational Research Association, American Psychological Association, and National Council on Measurement in Education, 1985) and the *Standards for Evaluations of Educational*

Programs, Projects, and Materials (Joint Committee, 1981) serve professionals as guides by articulating important, shared information that promotes quality work in the field, the standards offered in this book may serve a similar purpose.

Another reason the information described here is important is that this book documents a significant amount of information about test items, both recent advances and traditionally accepted knowledge. In doing so this book will, in some measure, alleviate the paucity of scholarly materials about test items mentioned above. Additionally, disseminating the information will diminish myths and other inaccuracies about constructing good test items.

Yet a further reason for the importance of this book is the timeliness of the information. With the recent surge of interest in assessment, an enormous number of tests are currently used. The *Mental Measurements Yearbook* (Mitchell, 1985) lists over 1,409 tests and *Tests in Print* (Mitchell, 1983) includes 2,672 citations of currently available tests. The most recent edition of *Tests* (Sweetland & Keyser, 1986) presents the tests of 437 publishers, in addition to a description of over 600 new and revised tests. Certainly, there are many times these numbers of tests not formally published but devised for use in classrooms and elsewhere. It is obvious that the number of tests developed will continue to grow in the coming years.

While not all of the instruments catalogued in the reference books are currently used, nor do all of them contain the item formats addressed in this book, those books do cite thousands of tests used widely and regularly that employ the kinds of test items addressed in this book. Given these facts, the need for information about constructing test items is current.

A final reason this book is important is that nowhere else is such a complete collection of information about test items gathered under one cover. While much of the information presented in this book is described piecemeal in other publications, it is worthwhile to assimilate, critique, and synthesize these topics in one comprehensive reference. This book serves as such a reference.

PERSONS FOR WHOM THIS BOOK IS INTENDED

This book is intended for a variety of audiences. Of course, primary audiences for whom this book is intended are all of the direct participants in the testing process: the test developer, who develops or writes the test and who may administer the test; the test user, who requires the information yielded for some decision; and the examinee, who takes the test by choice or mandate. Each has a stake in learning about test-item construction. The information may be especially helpful to test developers as they may assume the role of test-item writers.

Two Groups of Item Writers

Test-item writers may be loosely categorized into two groups: professional test-item writers and casual test-item writers. Professionals may find this book helpful as a resource book for current information as well as a guide for following a uniform style for the most commonly used item formats. Casual item writers (a group which can include many classroom teachers and others who occasionally need to develop a single test instrument) may find the entire contents of the book useful as a learning tool. Both groups may follow the prescriptive set of editorial rules.

Other Groups Who May Use This Information

A second group of persons for whom this information may be useful is educational researchers and other social scientists, including evaluators of curricula, programs, and projects. These persons regularly use test instruments in their work, and frequently must evaluate existing instruments or develop original instruments to meet particular needs. Knowing the "hows, whys, and wherefores" of constructing test items and judging them for quality may contribute substantially to their ability to evaluate the tests they use or develop.

Of course, students wishing to learn about issues related to test items as well as strategies for constructing them and evaluating them may find this book especially helpful. In addition to serving a basic heuristic function at an elementary level for students just beginning to learn about tests, this book is also a handy reference for students who will want to pursue measurement and evaluation at an advanced level.

Finally, the material presented in this book will be helpful or informative to persons who are not specifically included in any of the groups mentioned above but who are interested in sound measurement. These may be parents of students who are tested, program administrators, media persons who write about and report test results, and others. By knowing about the process of constructing test items, they will be better informed, and hence, more likely to make better decisions about tests.

OVERVIEW OF THE REMAINING CHAPTERS

The seven remaining chapters of this book address the topics mentioned in this introduction. Chapter 2 presents a definition of a test item, explains the purpose of test items in measurement, and describes various characteristics of items. Also considered in that chapter are assumptions for test items and an explanation of item formats. Chapter 3 is a discussion of determining the appropriate content for items and other concerns for validity. This chapter includes a thorough treatment of test content specifications, test item specifications, and strategies to increase the congruence of test items to particular specifications.

Chapter 4 describes an array of practical considerations one faces when constructing test items. Some issues discussed in this chapter are gauging an appropriate level of difficulty when writing items, ensuring factual accuracy, determining a correct response, composing items to tap higher-order thinking skills, determining the optimal number of response alternatives for an item, and more. The chapter begins by emphasizing the importance of precision and clarity in writing test items. In many regards, good writing is the heart of constructing good test items, and this discussion should help one garner an appreciation for this important aspect of constructing test items.

Chapter 5 focuses specifically on writing multiple-choice test items. This chapter considers advantages and disadvantages of this format as well as offers style and editorial guides for constructing multiple-choice test items. The chapter includes a description of the evolution of several sample test items from conception to finished product. Chapter 6 parallels the previous chapter by discussing advantages and disadvantages and delineating editorial rules and guidelines for other item formats, such as true-false, matching, short-answer or sentence-completion, and cloze procedure.

Chapter 7 addresses issues of reliability for test items using two categories: random errors and systematic bias. Provided in the discussion of these issues are methods for judging the quality of test items. Chapter 8 discusses ethical concerns for item writers. It also describes pertinent information on obtaining permission to use copyrighted materials and given direction on how to initially obtain a copyright for one's own work. It also discusses special considerations for preparing or modifying items for use with people who have handicapping conditions.

HOW TO APPROACH THE CHAPTERS

The novice reader should read and study the chapters in the sequence in which they are presented. The ideas discussed in each chapter are developed presupposing a knowledge of the information presented in prior chapters. Readers will recognize that the early chapters present more theoretical information than do the later chapters, which are themselves focused on applying the theoretical notions for items. Using the author or subject indexes, advanced readers may refer to discussions of particular points as a reference source.

Chapter 2

Definition, Purpose, and Characteristics of Items

INTRODUCTION

An elementary rule for any writer is to know thoroughly the subject before beginning to write. This is the reason reporters ask questions, researchers investigate hypotheses, and novelists ponder their protagonists, all before they put pencil to paper. So too must writers of effective test items master their subject. Learning about test items means comprehending what test items are, understanding their purpose, and becoming familiar with their characteristics. Knowing the definition of a test item is the first step toward comprehending it. The definition forms the backbone upon which the purposes and characteristics of test items rest.

Learning the purposes for test items is another essential ingredient of comprehension. Test items derive their purpose from psychology; accordingly, a background in behavioral theory is necessary to appreciate their purpose as tools for measurement. And, becoming familiar with their characteristics is also important. Characteristics of test items include the various formats they may take, their essential components, and necessary assumptions underlying their use. Characteristics of a test item define the item by delimiting the type of scores that an item can yield, permitting or disallowing its use in particular situations, and dictating practical considerations, such as the time examinees need to respond.

Some characteristics of items apply generally to all of them, while others pertain only to certain types. For instance, all test items present a stimulus and prescribe a response, but the nature of the stimulus and response of a true-false item is unique to its type. Similarly, the item forms of multiple-choice, matching, sentence-completion, and cloze-procedure each have their unique characteristics.

Another dimension of test items, intertwined with their characteristic features and qualities, is their inherent theoretical basis. It is important for conceptual consistency that test items stem from a theory of measurement and that their particular characteristics complement the theoretical framework. If a test item is to be used properly for psychological measurement, one must understand the relevant theoretical assumptions and give them ample consideration throughout the process of developing the item.

The reason it is important to thoroughly understand the definition, purpose, and characteristics of test items before writing them may seem obvious, but it is so significant that it warrants being stated. By knowing the definition, purpose, and characteristics of test items, one will have at hand a great deal of information about a particular test item, its construction, function, and probable effectiveness. Informed and diligent test-item writers are more likely to produce items of quality—that is, test items that meet criteria for good items—than may be yielded with a haphazard approach to item construction by well-intentioned but uninformed persons. An uninformed approach to constructing test items may lead to a set of questions that can be neatly printed on a page and give the appearance of a test instrument, but will more likely result in gross errors in measurement.

Finally, when discussing the definition, purpose, and characteristics of test items, a standard professional terminology should be used. Currently, a common vocabulary is not followed by most item writers, and there is a need to standardize descriptions of test items, as well as their characteristics and qualities, to provide uniformity of meaning and reduce confusion. This chapter will delineate proper nomenclature for test items, which should be adopted and used when constructing test items.

The following topics are covered in this chapter:

- definition of a test item
- nomenclature for test items
- item formats
- purpose for test items in measurement
- criteria for good test items
- assumptions for test items
- classification of types of test items
- understanding how examinees respond to items

DEFINING A TEST ITEM

In any study, it is important to begin with a definition or scholarly description of terms. Since this book is about constructing test items, it is, therefore, logical to state a precise definition of the term test item. Curiously, however, nowhere in the relevant literature does there appear to be a definitive statement of what a test item is, although there are some rudimentary descriptions (e.g., Gronlund, 1988; Wesman, 1971). The lack of a definition for this important term is surprising since numerous glossaries of the vocabulary of testing define many other terms associated with test items, such as item analysis, item bias, item difficulty index, item discrimination index, item characteristic curve, and more (e.g., APA/AERA/NCME, 1985; Ebel and Frisbie, 1986; Sax, 1980). Even an accurate description for the term test—which is characterized in many glossaries as a collection or set of test items—is not possible until the definition of test item has been established. To address this serious omission in the field, a complete and technically precise definition of a test item is offered here. It is hoped this definition will be adopted for use in the field.

The Definition of an Item

The definition of a test item is the following: A test item in an examination of mental attributes is a unit of measurement with a stimulus and a prescriptive form for answering; and, it is intended to yield a response from an examinee from which performance in some psychological construct (such as an ability, predisposition, or trait) may be inferred.

This definition is comprehensive because it includes all of the requisites for a test item regardless of whether a particular item is used for psychological assessment or educational measurement. Understanding the definition is fundamental to grasping the significance of the purpose for items as well as learning about their characteristics. Accordingly, the constituent parts of the definition merit discussion.

The definition is limited to test items used in tests of achievement, aptitude, or ability. Tests of this sort are used in clinical testing, in educational and psychological testing in schools, in counseling, in employment settings, and in professional and occupational licensing and certification. Other types of tests, such as certain personality inventories, quantifiable data gathered during interviews, and even certain types of essay formats, do not contain the kind of test items covered by the definition.

Still, test items of the type covered by the definition are not limited to strictly paper-and-pencil inventories. For example, they may also be used in tests of physical performance for measuring psychomotor skills, or in measuring oral communication abilities. Additionally, the definition encompasses test items in the kinds of tests mentioned above regardless of whether a particular test is standardized or non-standardized, administered in a group setting or administered individually.

Understanding the Definition

The first aspect of the definition—"A test item . . . is a unit of measurement . . ."—concerns the function of measurement. Measurement means quantification, either objectively or subjectively derived (cf. Lord and Novick, 1968; Stevens, 1946; Torgerson, 1958; Weitzenhoffer, 1951; many others). Hence, a test item by this definition leads to data that is quantifiable in some manner. It is important to grasp the significance of this seemingly obvious point. Test items are intended to yield numerical interpretations. The number associated with a particular examinee's performance is meant to provide a basis for comparison, usually either against a group of peers or against a predetermined standard or criterion.

The numerical interpretation for test items is what differentiates them from instructional activities. Instructional activities are not specifically designed to yield numerical data. The primary purpose for instructional activities is as a heuristic, or helping-to-discover, device. Although test items and instructional activities differ in intention, they often cover identical subject content or psychological processes.

This leads to the next important point in the definition of a test item: "A test item . . . [has] . . . a stimulus and a prescriptive form for answering." Epistemologically speaking, a test item may be considered as etiology because it is a stimulus that causes a response. Further, the response given by an examinee to a test item is prescribed in the sense that the item guides a particular form that the answer should take. For example, in a multiple-choice test item, the test taker is directed to select from among the alternatives offered; or, in a completion or short-answer test item, the examinee must supply a word or phrase as a response and cannot, say, circle one of the words in the item. Even in open-ended test-item formats, the examinee is guided to make a specific response. This is what is meant by saying the response for a test item is "prescribed." It would violate the definition of a test item if the test taker were not directed to make a particular kind of response.

Finally, the definition states that an examinee's response is interpreted in terms of learning something about his or her performance in a particular psychological construct. Psychological constructs are hypothesized concepts for explaining human behaviors and include the kinds of attributes or traits that are the object of assessment by psychological and educational tests, such as reading ability or emotional development. Since a psychological construct is something that is only theoretically conceived and cannot be directly observed, it would be useful to have a way to infer at least the existence of a psychological construct and the relative degree to which it may be exhibited by a particular examinee. Test items perform this function. If a stimulus situation does not provide data that implies a psychological construct, it is not a test item, according to the definition. This issue (which begs a bit of explanation of psychological theory) will be taken up again in a later section of the chapter.

This concludes the discussion of the definition of a test item. The reader is encouraged to review this section thoroughly since much of what follows presumes an awareness and comprehension of the definition of a test item.

TEST ITEM NOMENCLATURE

No Current Uniform Terminology

The lexicon of constructing test items is not well established. There is a need to identify and standardize the stock of terms related to constructing test items. The definition for a test item given above provides a useful start, but many other terms relevant to constructing test items need to be considered. A few of the most important terms are described here. The reader should study them as a specialized, technical vocabulary list.

As one can readily appreciate, a number of terms are important for constructing test items. Table 2.1 lists the terms defined in this book. These definitions should be memorized and applied consistently to promote standardization in the field and to reduce the chance for misunderstanding.

Table 2.1 Key Terms Used in Constructing Test Items	

• constructed-response	• response alternative
• correct response	• response
• dichotomously scored	• selected-response
• distractor	• stem
• examinee	• stimulus
• foil	• test item
• graphic	• test taker
• item format	• text

The Term "Test Item"

A test question or stimulus situation meeting the conditions of the definition discussed in the previous section should be referred to as a *test item*. This term is the most accurate descriptor for this particular kind of technical writing. An item is a single unit in a series or collection and is specified separately. The term *test item* is broad enough to allow for a variety of item formats and item classifying categories, yet sufficiently precise to be useful for technical discussion.

Test items should not be called "questions" since a test item can assume many formats, some of which are not interrogative. For example, most completion or short-answer item formats as well as most matching item formats are not stated as interrogatives. The term *test item*, on the other hand, includes both writings that are stated as interrogatives and those that are not.

Despite its aptness as a descriptor, the term *test item* has not been exclusively employed since the early days of testing. Alfred Binet (in Herrnstein, 1971), one of the first explorers into the world of mental attribute testing, called his tasks "stunts." Examples of Binet's stunts for a six-year-old are to distinguish between morning and afternoon, count thirteen pennies, and copy a diamond shape; and, for a ten-year-old, to arrange five blocks in order of weight and draw two designs from memory (Binet and Simon, 1917). Activities like these have also been referred to as "tasks." Even today, the National Assessment of Educational Progress (NAEP) labels the activities included in the NAEP program "exercises" (Messick, Beaton, and Lord, 1983). NAEP's mislabeling is unfortunate because the NAEP program has wide exposure in the popular media and may inadvertently promulgate idiosyncratic terminology. Regardless, the term *test item* is the most accurate descriptor of writings that meet the conditions for the definition discussed in the previous section, and its use should be adhered to.

The Examinee

The individual who takes the test is referred to as an *examinee*. Examinees are also called *test takers*; however, in most academic contexts, such as during test development or in scholarly research studies of tests or test use, examinee is the preferred term. The examinee takes the test by choice, direction, or necessity and is the most important participant in the testing process.

Regardless of the use intended for the test scores (e.g., assessment of achievement, diagnosis for counseling in clinical settings, licensing and certification, etc.), the welfare of the examinee should be primary in making decisions about tests. The *Standards* (AERA/APA/NCME, 1985), recognizing the paramount role of the examinee in the testing process, devotes an entire section to protecting the rights of examinees.

Specifying Item Formats

As previously mentioned, a variety of *item formats* are available to the writer of test items. (The term *item formats* is sometimes abbreviated to, simply, *item forms*.) The format for a test item is simply its design and layout. Some of the most repeatedly seen item formats are multiple-choice, true-false, matching, sentence-completion, short-answer, and less frequently, cloze-procedure. Illustrative Items 2.1 to 2.6 are examples of each of these item formats, respectively. These item formats are the ones most often employed in many popular tests of mental attributes. Readers should become familiar with each of these formats so that they will be aware of the array of possible formats as well as be able to recognize a particular one when confronted with a specific test item.

Illustrative item 2.1. An example of the multiple-choice format.

There is an 80% chance of snow tonight. Which is the most reasonable interpretation of this forecast?

- A. It will snow tonight.
- B. It will probably snow tonight.
- C. It will probably not snow tonight.
- D. 20% of the area will not receive snow.

Illustrative Item 2.2. An example of the true-false format.

Spanish sympathizers, in an underground movement, provided assistance to the American colonists during the Revolutionary War.

True   False

Illustrative Item 2.3. An example of the matching format.

Match the numbers of the categories on the left with the corresponding letters of the characteristics on the right.

1. SENSATION	a. condolence
2. AFFECTIONS	b. rocks
3. SPACE	c. incombustability
4. PHYSICS	d. hearing
5. MATTER	e. interval

Illustrative Item 2.4. An example of the completion format.

The _____ branch of government is the only
branch empowered to pass spending appropriations.

Illustrative Item 2.5. An example of the short-answer format.

In what city was the Declaration of Independence signed?

_____

Illustrative Item 2.6. An example of cloze-procedure.*

   Bridges are built to allow a continuous flow of highway and traffic
across water lying in their paths. But engineers cannot forget that
river traffic, too, is essential to our economy. The role of 1 is
important. To keep these vessels moving freely, bridges are built
high enough, when possible, to let them pass underneath. Sometimes, however, channels must accommodate very tall ships. It
may be uneconomical to build a tall enough bridge. The 2 would
be too high . . . .

1. a) wind	2. a) levels
b) boats	b) cost
c) weight	c) standards
d) wires	d) waves
e) experience	e) deck

*From *DRP Handbook* (p. 2) Touchstone Applied Science Associates,
1986, New York: The College Board.

Table 2.2 lists several popular tests classified by the type of item format principally used in that test. From the information presented in the table, one can see that although the multiple-choice form is the item format that is most popularly used, others are common. In fact here are still more item formats besides those listed above, including combinations of common item formats. Some of these other item formats are quite complicated and have been invented to serve specialized purposes and are not widely used.

Table 2.2 Tests Classified by Item Format Principally Used

Test	Item Format Principally Used
Analysis of Learning Potential (Harcourt, Brace, & World)	Multiple-choice, completion, and analogy
California Achievement Tests (CTB/McGraw-Hill)	Multiple-choice
Cognitive Abilities Test (The Riverside Publishing Company)	Multiple-choice
College BASE (The Riverside Publishing Company)	Multiple-Choice and writing
Comprehensive Tests of Basic Skills (CTB/McGraw-Hill)	Multiple-choice
Cornell Critical Thinking Test Level X (Illinois Thinking Project, Univ. of Illinois)	Matching
Degrees of Reading Power (College Board, The Psychological Corp.)	Cloze-procedure
Graduate Record Examinations (Educational Testing Service)	Multiple-choice, completion, and analogy
Iowa Tests of Basic Skills (The Riverside Publishing Company)	Multiple-choice

Table 2.2 *(continued)*

Test	Item Format Principally Used
Kuhlmann-Anderson Tests (Scholastic Testing Service)	Multiple-choice
Metropolitan Achievement Tests (The Psychological Corp.)	Multiple-choice and writing
Metropolitan Readiness Test (Harcourt Brace Jovanovich)	Multiple-choice using pictures
Miller Analogies Test (Prentice Hall Press)	Multiple-choice
Minnesota School Attitude Survey (MSAS) (Science Research Associates)	True/false, Important/unimportant
National Registry of Radiation Protection Technologists (NRRPT)	Multiple-choice
Otis-Lennon Mental Ability Tests (Harcourt, Brace, & World)	Multiple-choice
Otis-Lennon School Ability Advanced Form S (The Psychological Corporation)	Multiple-choice with pictures
School and Ability Tests (Addison-Wesley Testing Service)	Multiple-choice and analogy
Secondary Level English Proficiency Test (CTB/McGraw-Hill)	Multiple-choice
SRA Achievement Series (Science Research Associates)	Multiple-choice
Survey of Basic Skills (Science Research Associates)	Multiple-choice
Tests of Achievement and Proficiency (The Riverside Publishing Company)	Multiple-choice

---

Table 2.2 *(continued)*

Test	Item Format Principally Used
Test of Cognitive Skills (CTB/McGraw-Hill)	Multiple-choice
Tests of Adult Basic Education (CTB/McGraw-Hill)	Multiple-choice
The Gifted Evaluation Scale (Hawthorne Educ. Service)	Likert-type rating scale
The Stanford Achievement Test (The Psychological Corp.)	Multiple-choice

---

Still other tests may contain several item formats in the same test instrument. An example of a test with a variety of item formats, as well as other assessment techniques, is the *Alabama English Language Proficiency Test*. The various formats for items used throughout this test are described in Table 2.3. Notice in the test that not only are traditional item formats used, but there is also a portion in which examinees listen to a recorded stimulus and respond by answering a set of multiple-choice test items.

Writing Samples, Exercises, and Essay-Type Questions

Writing samples, writing exercises, and essay-type questions may also be considered item formats because this type of assessment meets all of the conditions for test items described in the definition given earlier. They are a stimulus situation, they have a prescriptive form for response, and they are intended to yield scores that allow for inferences to be made about examinee performance in a psychological construct. However, since they are a specialized format and different from the other item formats discussed in this book, any extended discussion of them is outside the scope of this book. Still, this does not diminish their significance, utility, or appropriateness. In many contexts, they are an extremely important means for assessing certain skills. Readers interested in learning more about writing samples and techniques for scoring them are referred to the excellent book by White (1985).

Table 2.3 Example of a Test in Which a Variety of Formats is Used

---

Alabama English Language Proficiency Test

Content Area	Assessment Method
Reading	A cloze tests of reading comprehension, using multiple-choice items with five choices.
Writing	An essay test, scored by the holistic method.
Language Skills	A multiple-choice test (four choices per item) of basic grammar, mechanics, and reference skills.
Listening	A listening tape of passages read aloud, testing comprehension by multiple-choice items.

Types of Item Formats

Test item formats fall into two broad types: *selected-response* or *constructed-response* (or by some authors, *supply-type*). In a selected-response test item the examinee is given the correct solution to the problem as well as alternative (and usually incorrect) solutions. The examinee is instructed to select the perceived correct answer. Multiple-choice and true-false test items, the most commonly used item formats, are selected-response test items. In these formats, the examinee is instructed to choose one response alternative from among those offered. Illustrative Item 2.7 is an example of a selected-response item type.

Illustrative Item 2.7. An example of the selected-response item type.

Which animal is most likely to have a body covered with fur?

    A. bird
-   B. mammal
    C. amphibian
    D. reptile

By contrast to selected-response test items, in constructed-response test items alternative solutions (correct or incorrect) are not presented to the examinee at all; rather, the examinee must furnish (rather than select) the perceived correct response. Typically, the examinee responds to constructed-response test items by writing down a word or short sentence perceived to be the correct response. The completion or short-answer test item is an example of a constructed-response test item. Illustrative Item 2.8 presents an example of a constructed-response item.

Illustrative Item 2.8. An example of the constructed-response item type.

What common scientific instrument would be most helpful in predicting how the weather will change during the next few hours?

Terms for Parts of the Test Item

The part of the test item which asks the question or sets up the situation for response is referred to as the *item stem*. An item stem is thought of as a *stimulus*, because as etiologies, they cause a response from the examinee. A *correct response* is elicited when an examinee selects, identifies, or provides the answer to the stimulus that is scored positively.

In selected-response test-item formats, the choices provided are labeled *response alternatives*. (Less formally, response alternatives may be called *options*.) The response alternatives offer all of the possible choices that the item writer has provided (correct and incorrect) to the examinee. Response alternatives that are not considered the correct response are labeled *distractors*. The term *distractors* is used because these responses may distract, or daunt, the examinee who is uncertain about the correct response. In England, distractors are often called *foils*, but in the United States the term *distractors* is more accepted.

The multiple-choice test-item format (and to a lesser degree some other test-item formats) is often accompanied by narrative or graphic material. This narrative may be a paragraph or passage from a story (either originally written or excerpted from a longer work), a poem, an article or editorial from a newspaper or magazine, or other such textual material; or, it may be a graphic, such as a cartoon, map, chart, graph, table, or formula. The nomenclature for describing these accompaniments to test items is straightforward. If the type of material is narrative, it is referred to as *text*. If the material is anything other than text, it is called a *graphic*. Mathematical formulas, symbols, geometric shapes, and algebraic expressions are also considered graphics because in many printing operations they are not offset or typeset by the same procedures as is used with text; rather, they are treated as though they are pictures. In some computerized page-layout operations, such figures are contained in a format called PICT.

It is important to realize that when an item contains text or graphic materials, the text or graphic is an integral part of the test item and not a mere addendum. The care spent on preparing the text or graphic should equal the care used in constructing other parts of the item. Chapters 5 and 6 discuss constructing and using these features in detail.

Terms Used in Scoring Test Items

Another important term is regularly used in constructing items, although it does not refer to a specific part of a test item. The term *dichotomously scored test items* is used for identifying and classifying test items. The classification of test items as *dichotomously scored* means that an examinee's response is considered to be in only one of two possible categories, usually either *correct* or *incorrect*. The "correct" response has been predetermined by either the writer of the test item or some clearly established methodology. Obviously, a response other than the correct response is considered "incorrect." Most multiple-choice, true-false, matching, completion or short-answer, and cloze-procedure test items are dichotomously scored.

Although responses to dichotomously scored test items are usually categorized as correct and incorrect, it should be realized that other categories for responses can also be used. For example, sometimes an examinee is directed to respond to a test item with either *agree* or *disagree*, as in the examples given in Illustrative Items 2.9 and 2.10. These test items are dichotomously scored although there is no correct or incorrect response alternative.

Illustrative Items 2.9 & 2.10.

Read each statement below and decide whether it conforms to your personal sentiments. Indicate your opinion by circling one of the choices provided.

2.9. Children should be seen and
   not heard.   AGREE   DISAGREE

2.10. Breaking a mirror will bring
   seven years bad luck.   AGREE   DISAGREE

Test items that are scored dichotomously are sometimes called *zero-one* test items after the representational computer binary logic in which examinees' test scores are sometimes retained in computer records as a "0" to indicate an incorrect response and a "1" to signify a correct response. (In Illustrative Items 2.9 and 2.10 a "1" would indicate "Agree" and a "0" would symbolize "Disagree.")

Not all test items are scored dichotomously. For example, test items that prescribe multiple response options, many (but not all) short-answer test items, and some other test-item formats are not scored as having only two options for response. Often, these test-item formats allow for a variety of responses that could be considered appropriate to the question. Further, there are many models for scaling tests. Some of these scaling models are *polychotomous*, meaning that for an item more than one response alternative is considered in scoring, others are heuristic, and still more may be categorized in the psychologically based scaling methods of item response theory. For practical purposes of learning about constructing test items, however, it will be convenient to consider only items that are dichotomously scored.

Nearly all tests that are electronically scored by an optical scanning device contain only dichotomously scored test items. Some exploratory work is being done to enable optical scanners and their concomitant computers to read multiple response formats, including some kinds of essay examinations. Presently, the application of this work is quite limited, but such work does promise exciting vistas for new testing formats in the future.

Putting Together the Parts of an Item

Thus far, we have discussed several constituent parts of test items, including the stem, response alternatives, text, graphics, and more. Now let us see how they appear in an item. Figure 2.1 notes the constituent parts of a multiple-choice test-item format. Study the placement of the various parts in the item. With few exceptions, the arrangement of parts of a test item will remain fixed. The order is that the directions appear first, followed by a graphic (if any), which is followed by text (if any), which is followed by the stem, and finally the response alternatives.

In this sample test item, the correct response appears in the final, or D, position following all of the distractors. Obviously, in any set of test items the correct response will be positioned variously among the response alternatives. More will be said about determining the correct response among the response alternatives in Chapter 4.

Figure 2.1. Test item nomenclature.

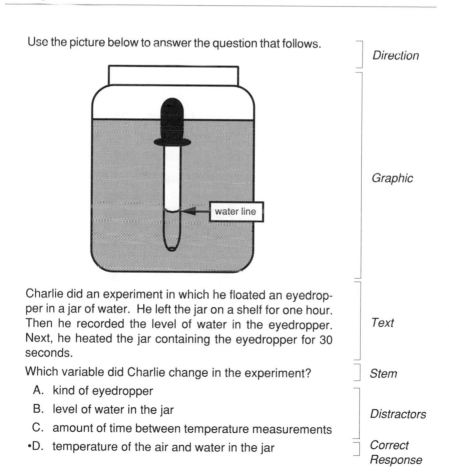

Use the picture below to answer the question that follows. *Direction*

Graphic

Charlie did an experiment in which he floated an eyedrop-per in a jar of water. He left the jar on a shelf for one hour. Then he recorded the level of water in the eyedropper. Next, he heated the jar containing the eyedropper for 30 seconds. *Text*

Which variable did Charlie change in the experiment? *Stem*

  A. kind of eyedropper

  B. level of water in the jar   *Distractors*

  C. amount of time between temperature measurements

•D. temperature of the air and water in the jar   *Correct Response*

In this section all of the constituent parts of a test item have been identified and described. Item writers should refer to these parts by a uniform terminology. Consistent use of terms will foster clearer communication among item writers as well as among test developers, examinees, and other test users.

PURPOSE FOR TEST ITEMS

Psychological Theory as Background to Items

Since the primary purpose for test items is embedded in psychology, a bit of background in behavioral theory is needed before the function of test items in measurement can be explained or appreciated. Psychologists observe human behavior, and when a pattern of behavior is performed consistently over time and in different contexts by many individuals, it is labeled as a *psychological construct* (Cronbach, 1971; Cronbach & Meehl, 1955; Messick, 1975). Accordingly, a construct is a psychological attribute which characterizes individuals' behavior. Since we cannot know exactly what processes are occurring in another's brain, these psychological constructs are only hypothesized, or theoretically imagined. There may be a countless number of them for every individual, explaining the incalculable behaviors people exhibit.

Psychological constructs are such things as verbal or quantitative ability, social or emotional development, reasoning ability, spatial visualization, and the like. Endurance is a frequently used construct in athletics. Such constructs can be hypothesized as explaining broad behaviors, as in the list of constructs just cited, or they may be more narrowly specified, such as vocabulary development.

Psychological constructs are often contrasted with physical attributes such as height, weight, or the color of skin, hair, and eyes. Physical attributes are directly observable, and measuring them is often comparatively easy. Generally speaking, the instruments used to measure physical attributes yield more reliable scores than those employed in assessing psychological constructs. For instance, one does not typically worry about the reliability of a yardstick. And, for most common uses, one yardstick is as good as another.

By contrast to the relative ease of measuring physical features, assessing psychological attributes is challenging at best. There are two important reasons why this kind of measurement is difficult. First, since psychological constructs cannot be observed, they can only be assessed indirectly. The practical consequence of measuring human behavior indirectly is that the instruments used for the assessment are themselves suspect. The reliability of any particular test score of mental attributes can only be *estimated* rather than absolutely known. Further, these tests vary dramatically in quality, and as contrasted to the similarity of most yardsticks, one test cannot be haphazardly replaced by another.

The second reason for difficulty in assessing mental abilities is that a psychological construct is both subject to change and only vaguely understood. It is known, of course, that people can determine and change their behavior volitionally, thereby influencing a construct, positively or negatively. People learn to read, for instance, or juggle balls, or memorize mathematical formulas, or whatever. Thus, a construct itself can change between measurements, complicating reliable measurements. As mentioned, psychological constructs are only theoretically conceived, and little is understood about them.

As a parallel to measurements made in the physical world, imagine trying to use an elastic ruler to determine the diameter of a cloud, whose physical properties are only vaguely understood, and whose dimensions keep changing! Measuring psychological constructs is indeed difficult. Despite the formidable difficulties of measuring psychological constructs, tests of mental attributes are the main means by which one may objectively learn the psychological composition of an examinee.

Items as Measures of Constructs

With this brief background in psychological theory, one is ready to learn the primary purpose for test items, but first a note about terminology, which should make the subsequent discussion a bit easier to follow. In this discussion the terms mental attribute and psychological construct will be used interchangeably. The term ability will be used in descriptions of the degree to which one possesses or exhibits an attribute or construct.

Simply stated, the dominant purpose for test items in the kinds of tests discussed here is to function as a focused stimulus which elicits a response from a particular of a psychological construct. Through test items a psychological construct is operationally set forth as a behavior which an examinee is instructed to exhibit. Such behavior might be to spell a particular word correctly, perform some mathematical operation, or rotate a cube in a specified manner. Of course, the behavior could be any number of things depending upon which construct is being assessed. By responding to the stimulus of a test item, an examinee exhibits behavior from which one may infer the existence of a psychological construct.

So far, this discussion has been relatively straightforward. The situation gains complexity, however, when the dimension of assessing the *degree* to which a psychological construct exists in an examinee is added. E. L. Thorndike (1904), an early proponent of measuring mental attributes, stated that whatever exists at all exists in some amount. Although the existence of psychological constructs is only inferred, it is logical to presume that they must also be present in some amount. Further, since psychological constructs are mental attributes, individuals will possess them in varying amounts, or degrees. Again, test items are the means by which the relative degree of a psychological construct is assessed.

The reader will recall that earlier it was stated that test items are, by definition, a unit of measurement. Therefore, by observing examinee responses to a particular set of test items that exhibit a positive correlational relationship to a specific psychological construct, it is possible to estimate how much of the construct or mental attribute an examinee may possess. It is presumed that for dichotomously scored test items, examinees who respond correctly are exhibiting a greater degree of the particular construct than examinees who do not respond correctly.

Constructs Exist for All Persons

A subtle but important point should be noted in the general case for test items just stated. The inference made is that examinees who respond correctly to items are said to possess *more* of an attribute than those who do not respond correctly. But it is not a correct interpretation to suggest that those who do not respond correctly to items do not possess the construct at all.

A construct, once hypothesized, exists for all persons, regardless of whether they can exhibit behaviors associated with it. Some persons may possess much ability in a construct, while others may have more limited ability. For example, an illiterate person of normal intelligence still possesses the construct "reading ability," since it has been hypothesized to exist in all persons of normal intelligence. However, since the construct has not been developed in the illiterate individual, this person would not be able to perform behaviors (i.e., respond correctly to test items) from which the existence of the construct could be inferred. Presumably, with tutoring assistance and practice, the construct could be developed in the person, after which he or she would likely perform the behaviors requested in test items. By contrast, psychologists have not hypothesized the reading-ability construct to exist in chimpanzees, and no amount of tutoring assistance or practice could cause a chimpanzee to exhibit the behavior of responding correctly (above random marking) to a set of test items designed to assess reading comprehension.

Although the general case for classical test theory was stated above, in many particular instances, an examinee's having additional items correct does not always indicate greater ability in the construct. This is because the complexities of scaling tests, as well as error in measurement and other factors, can make the interpretation of test scores quite complex. For example, tests that are scaled by models of item response theory as well as other polychotomous scaling models use a different set of assumptions than does classical test theory and they may not follow the theory described above. This is why it is important to realize that in interpreting test scores there is not a strictly linear relationship between an examinee responding correctly to test items and the degree to which that individual possesses ability in the construct.

This point may be illustrated with a simple example. Suppose two test items representing a construct were administered to two examinees, one of whom responded correctly to one item and the other responded correctly to both items. It could not be inferred from comparing the performance of the two examinees that the examinee who got both items correct possesses twice the ability in the construct than the examinee who got only one item correct. In fact, all that is known from this simple example is that two examinees exhibited behaviors in the same psychological construct. It is likely that the high-scoring examinee possesses *more* of the ability, but improbable that this person possesses *twice* the ability of the lower-scoring examinee. With only the information given, nothing is known about the *relative degree* to which either examinee may possess the psychological characteristic of interest. A great deal of additional information about the specific measurement instrument used, how it is scored and its scores scaled, the procedures used for selecting the examinee population, and other factors is needed before one may correctly interpret the degree to which examinees possess a particular construct.

In sum, then, test items provide a way for examinees to perform behaviors from which one may infer the degree to which a psychological construct exists in those examinees. This is the function of test items in measurement, and it justifies the earlier claim that test items are the backbone of measuring mental attributes.

CRITERIA FOR GOOD TEST ITEMS

Difficulty of Establishing Criteria

Criteria for good test items are difficult to state in absolute terms. Simple lists of declaratively "good" and "bad" features are inadequate to the task. Constructing good test items involves more than mechanically checking off considerations one by one, and such a simplistic approach will not reflect the complexity of the task. It is difficult to establish strict criteria for good test items for a number of reasons.

One reason for difficulty is that constructing test items demands technical skills. The technical skills required for constructing test items are quite complex and demand sophisticated levels of thinking. Major portions of this book provide a synthesis of the technical skills needed to construct test items.

In addition to technical competence, the skilled item constructor must also possess a penetrating understanding of how examinees respond to test items, including an awareness of how a particular test item may be perceived by different examinees. Internalizing these aspects of examinee performance will assist one in gaining a "sixth sense" about constructing test items. This deeper understanding can foster original and imaginative thinking about test items and will help one become a better writer of test items. Popham (1984) describes writing test items as "art, art, and more art" (p. 40). While this aphorism may be exaggerated, it does point to the element of creativity in constructing test items.

As a simple exercise, after reading this chapter, try to write one or two test items yourself about any subject. You may well realize immediately that in addition to needing a fundamental core of knowledge about test items, you "feel" the need for the creative component. Technical skill, coupled with a creative sense, is necessary if one is to construct good test items.

Another factor that makes it difficult to specify criteria for constructing good test items relates to the specific circumstances in which a test arises or the purposes for the test. Those circumstances or purposes dictate that the test-item writer follow certain guidelines. For example, suppose a test is being constructed as a licensing examination for paramedics who have been instructed in a standardized training curriculum. The items in such a test must assess specific criteria for service in the field by health-care personnel without regard to how a particular individual may have achieved such skills: whether by prior experience, through a required training program, or through self-study. It is the end result that counts in this context.

This is a completely different context from, say, a test that is intended to be used for assessing basic cognitive processes in a group of partially sighted children who have received varying amounts of attention to their individual learning needs. The differing contexts will require different considerations in writing the items.

Accepted Criteria for Good Items

Despite the difficulties mentioned above of specifying criteria for constructing good test items, certain criteria for good test items have been generally accepted. These criteria are standards that should be followed during construction of test items.

The first criterion for constructing good test items, and the most important, is that there must be a high degree of congruence between a particular item and the key objective of the total test. Simply stated, the primary question is, "How well does a particular test item match its intended objective?" (In this discussion, the term *objective* is being used as a synonym for a psychological construct.)

This congruence criterion is the item writer's primary consideration because it is at the heart of validity, the most important consideration in test construction. According to the *Standards* (AERA/APA/NCME, 1985), validity refers to "the appropriateness, meaningfulness, and usefulness of the specific inferences made from test scores" (p. 9). Validity is pervasive throughout the process of constructing test items and is discussed fully in the following chapter. For now, however, keep in mind that congruence between a particular test item and a specific objective (or psychological construct) is the most important criterion for constructing good test items and is related to valid interpretations of a test's scores.

A second criterion for constructing good test items is closely allied with the first criterion. This criterion is that the key objectives must be clearly defined. If a test item is to meet the first criterion, congruence to a key objective, it must be matched to a defined entity. To state loosely that an item will measure some very broad concept, such as critical thinking, without further defining what is meant by critical thinking, diminishes the potential for garnering evidence for validity. The less ambiguously a domain of content or psychological construct is described, the better the chance that the congruence criterion can be met.

The notion of clearly defining the criterion or behavioral domain to be assessed may sound obvious, but it is one of the most difficult of the criteria to satisfy. Perhaps for this reason it is often carelessly ignored or only superficially addressed. Regretfully, many tests, even some published by professional test publishing companies and other professional test developers, do not adhere to this criterion for good test items.

Hambleton and Eignor (1978) proposed a set of guidelines for evaluating criterion-referenced tests. One of the guidelines asks, "Is each objective clearly written so that it is possible to identify an 'item pool'?" The authors report that this guideline was not adequately met in any of eleven popular, commercially produced criterion-referenced tests. Obviously, this is a serious deficit in test construction generally, but one that must be addressed during item construction. How one deals with this criterion in actual test development will be explored in Chapter 3, which discusses thoroughly the issues involved in considering this criterion and offers several strategies for addressing it.

A third criterion of constructing good test items is that each item's contribution to measurement error in a test's scores should be minimized to the extent possible. This means that there should be a systematic consideration of the degree to which test items may contribute to errors of measurement.

These errors may be of two types: random error (which could be caused by a variety of factors, some of which cannot even be identified with precision) and bias (the systematic distortion of measurement). Although the exact source of bias in test items may not be isolated, the fact that it occurs can be discovered. Following the discovery of bias in test items, the sources of bias can usually be reduced or even eliminated by repairing particular items or discarding them from further consideration. Errors of measurement, whether random or systematic, are issues of reliability, itself a special condition of validity. A thorough discussion of random errors of measurement and systematic bias, as well as techniques to detect them, is presented in Chapter 7.

A fourth criterion for good test items is that the format be suitable to the goals of the test. Straightforward, uncomplicated goals generally require simpler item formats than those necessary for assessing complex goals. Further, elaborate item formats usually consume more time during testing than simple item formats. For example, some complex item formats are inappropriate for speeded tests that are intended to cover a broad domain of knowledge under strictly timed conditions. The individual situation will provide the item writer with a context from which a careful consideration of the appropriateness of an item format may be made.

A fifth criterion for constructing good test items is that each item meet specific technical assumptions. These assumptions are psychometric concerns of measurement theory, as, for example, unidimensionality of items or local independence of items. These assumptions are delineated and explained later in this chapter.

A sixth criterion for constructing good test items is that they be well written, following uniform style or editorial standards. These standards cover grammar, diction, usage, spelling, punctuation, and syntax. While there is little disagreement among test specialists about the need for good writing in test items, editorial rules for writing test items are not well established despite some weak claims to the contrary (e.g., Cunningham, 1986). Chapters 5 and 6 articulate clear editorial guidelines and an accompanying rationale for many common item formats.

A seventh and final criterion for constructing good test items is that they satisfy legal and ethical questions. Sometimes, test developers may be tempted to use another's set of well-constructed test items to save time or effort. Often, little or no consideration is given to matching the purposes of their own test. Regretfully, this form of plagiarism happens too often. Not only is this unethical, it can be illegal. When test items are copyrighted—and commercial test publishers and other test specialists frequently take pains and expense to ensure that they are—using the test items without permission infringes on federal copyright statutes.

This does not mean that all test items on every new test must be originally constructed. Frequently, the original author or copyright holder of particular test items will grant use to someone else, especially when the items are intended to be used for research purposes. Of course, test items may also be exchanged, sold, or loaned. Such use of another's work is ethical and legal if done with permission and a legal contract when appropriate.

These seven criteria for constructing good test items are summarized in Table 2.4. The careful writer of test items will become informed about these criteria and make a diligent effort to ensure that they are adhered to for each test item written. In doing so, the writer will increase the probability of writing test items that have technical merit.

ASSUMPTIONS FOR TEST ITEMS

Assumptions as Theoretical Background to Constructing Items

Descriptions of modern test theories, especially those which emphasize the psychologically based nature of constructs and particu-

---

Table 2.4 Criteria for Constructing Test Items

- must be congruent with key objective (or psychological construct)
- must have clearly defined key objective (or psychological construct)
- writer shoud consider the degree to which test items may contribute to errors in measurement
- the test items format should be appropriate to the goals of the test
- must meet technical assumptions for test items
- should follow prescribed editorial standards and style guidelines
- writer should review ethical and legal concerns

---

larly item response theory, often emphasize relevant assumptions of mathematical models (see Allen & Yen, 1979; Birnbaum, 1968; Crocker & Algina, 1986; Hambleton & Swaminathan, 1985; Lord & Novick, 1968; Thorndike, 1982; Wright & Stone, 1979; many others). But, items used in tests constructed by traditional, or classical, test theory should also be consistent with assumptions of mathematical models. The assumptions described below apply to all test items, regardless of whether they are included in tests developed according to classical or modern test theories. A basic awareness of these assumptions is necessary if one is to fully understand test-item construction. Furthermore, heeding them while writing items is necessary to producing good items. The three fundamental assumptions for test items are: unidimensionality, local independence, and item characteristic curves. Each of these assumptions is explained in this section.

Because this section describes items in the context of measurement theory, it may appear more difficult than some other portions of this book. Regardless, the reader is encouraged to study this section slowly and carefully. Each issue is explained thoroughly, although, as theory, some of the points made are conceptually difficult. In fact, this may be the hardest section of the entire book to read and understand. But, an understanding of the assumptions for test items, as well as an intuitive grasp of their significance, is important for the skilled item writer.

The Assumption of Unidimensionality for Items

The first assumption underlying a mathematical model for test items is that the items are *unidimensional*. Unidimensionality of a test item means that an examinee's response to a test item can be (by inference) attributed to a single trait or ability. In other words, a test item is designed to measure one, and not more than one, psychological construct. For example, a test item that is designed to assess the trait quantitative ability measures only that trait and does not also assess other traits or abilities, such as verbal ability. Additionally, in theory, if it were possible to identify all of the possible test items for a particular construct (this would undoubtedly be an infinite number), they would define fully every aspect of the construct or latent ability.

In practice, the assumption of unidimensionality can never be fully met because there are simply too many unknown or uncontrollable factors which affect an examinee's response, making it impossible to state with absolute certainty that a particular response was because of a specific psychological construct. Such unknown or uncontrolled factors might include the degree of motivation for the examinee, practice in responding to multiple-choice test items, familiarity with marking answers on an answer sheet, test anxiety, weariness, and many more.

Despite the difficulties in meeting fully the assumption of unidimensionality, it is applicable to test-item construction for two important reasons. First, without the assumption of unidimensionality, the interpretation of test items would be profoundly complex. This may be readily seen by considering the following circumstance. If an item is thought to assess two abilities, there is no reliable method to infer from an examinee's response the degree to which either of the two abilities contributed to a correct response. Was the correct response due completely to the examinee's ability in just one of the two traits? And, if so, which one would it be? Or, did the examinee correctly respond to the item by drawing upon abilities in both areas? If so, to what degree did each ability contribute? By current methods of scaling, it is hopelessly complicated to attempt reliable interpretations for test items that are other than unidimensional.

Theoretical work has explored the possibility of interpreting test items in multidimensional tests; however, this work is preliminary, limited in scope, and of no practical application at this time (see Muliak, 1972; Samejima, 1974). Nevertheless, the future for work in this area seems bright. Reckase (1979; 1985; 1986) and Reckase, Ackerman, and Carlson (1988) have investigated multidimensional scaling models with item response theory and their work appears to offer enormous potential for new test scaling models and untapped test score interpretations.

A second reason for the importance of the unidimensionality assumption is that it is widely accepted by test constructors as a conceptual notion. Osterlind (1983) noted:

> *The practicalities of score interpretation make the assumption of unidimensionality almost universally accepted by test constructors. Items from a unidimensional test may not correlate highly with each other, but only a single ability accounts for an examinee correctly responding to an item or set of test items. (p. 57)*

Two further considerations about the assumption of unidimensionality are 1) understanding that it is contextually related and not an absolute within a particular test item, and 2) understanding there are some, albeit rare, instances where it does not apply, such as in some timed tests. Regarding the first consideration, while it is convenient to think that in most circumstances all well-constructed test items are unidimensional, a given test item does not possess the characteristic of unidimensionality once and forevermore. A single test item resides in the context of a set of test items, which are governed by the purposes for the whole test. A test item may be unidimensional for one test but not for another. The veracity of the unidimensionality assumption will depend upon the purposes of the test as well as the particular set of test items used.

This concern becomes particularly acute when tests are translated from one language to another or are used with examinees whose cultural background is different from the cultural background of the group for whom it was originally written. When test items are translated literally into a foreign language, whole new dimensions of meaning arise which can distort the original intention. The assumption of unidimensionality of any particular test item may be violated by literal translation of test items from one language to another. Further, the denotations, connotations, and various nuances of language can vary markedly between different cultures who may share a common spoken and written language.

This phenomenon may make a very good test item in one setting inappropriate in a new situation. For example, in New Guinea, English is the language of government, education, and business, just as it is, of course, in the United States. In New Guinea, however, there is a different concept of time from that held by most Americans. Therefore, to ask a Papuan child to order the months of the year would be nonsensical, although it may be a very good exercise for an American youngster.

One further feature of the assumption of unidimensionality needs mention. Embedded in the assumption is the notion that test items are not administered under speeded conditions (Hambleton & Swaminathan, 1985). Speeded conditions are employed in tests that have instructions for administration requiring examinees to complete as many test items as possible under rigorous time limits. The speed at which examinees respond to items is itself a variable for measurement in such tests. Under speeded conditions examinees are not expected to complete all of the test items, especially those test items that are more difficult or are located at the end of the test; hence, not all of the test items adhere to the assumption of unidimensionality.

The importance of the assumption of unidimensionality should be apparent from this discussion. Traub (1983) has investigated the veracity of the assumption of unidimensionality of test items relative to the training examinees receive; and Hattie (1981) has compiled an extensive review of the literature on definitions of unidimensionality and methods by which it may be assessed. Readers are referred to these sources for more detailed discussion. Still, it is not the only important assumption in understanding characteristics of test items. There are at least two more, which will be considered below.

The Assumption of Local Independence for Items

The second assumption for test items is *local independence*. This assumption is distinct from the unidimensionality assumption, although it sometimes takes a bit of study to realize the distinction. McDonald (1980a, 1980b, 1982) has investigated the equivalence of the assumptions of unidimensionality and local independence for test items.

The discussion which follows is organized into two distinct parts: a theoretical description of local independence and the practical consequences of the assumption. If the theoretical description is difficult to follow, go on to read the practical discussion. Then, return to study carefully the theoretical discussion. It will probably become clearer after this review.

Unidimensionality, it was pointed out, exists in the sense that a single psychological construct explains for each homogeneous subpopulation the assessment garnered by the test item, or set of test items. This assessment is valid only for the subpopulation who may be located at a single point along a continuum of ability, from low to high. The continuum is labeled "low" to "high" because the behavior or trait is extant in all persons, although in varying degrees. The point along the ability continuum at which the veracity, or truthfulness, of the assumption may be checked is called "local independence" since what has been said about the examinees at this point on the continuum is unaffected by other subpopulations at any other point on the continuum.

Hambleton & Swaminathan (1985) provide a mathematical definition of this assumption for tests guided by item response theory: ". . . the assumption of local independence applies when the probability of the response pattern for each examinee is equal to the product of the probability associated with the examinee response to each item" (p. 23). Osterlind (1983) demonstrated this point mathematically by considering the probability of occurrence of a given five-item pattern of responses on a test. A statistical test to check the independence of item responses for examinees is provided by Lord (1952).

The practical consequence of the assumption of local independence is more straightforward than this theoretical description. In practice, local independence means that an examinee's response on any particular test item is unaffected and statistically independent from a response to any other test item. In other words, local independence presumes that an examinee approaches each test item as a fresh, new problem without hints or added knowledge garnered from responding to any other test item.

We can see the effect of violating this assumption by examining two test items in sequence, Illustrative Items 2.11 and 2.12. The point to notice when considering the two items is that the information provided in 2.11 provides clues which can be used to answer the next item, 2.12. By correctly recognizing that one characteristic of a herbivore is worn, flat teeth in the back of the mouth (cf. 2.11), the astute examinee could immediately use this knowledge to study the graphic for 2.12 and match it to response alternative C. This makes an examinee's response to 2.12 dependent upon his or her response to the preceding item. The response to 2.11 is not similarly advantaged. The items are linked in an undesirable (and unintended) way. With the local independence assumption violated, a proper interpretation is not possible.

One should not confuse local independence with the idea that test items cannot share a text or graphic. Having several items refer to a common text or graphic is unrelated to local independence for items. In fact, sharing a textual passage or a graphic among several items is a useful economy in item construction. It can reduce the amount of reading required and allow for more items in a test.

Illustrative Item 2.11.

Which physical characteristics is a herbivore most likely to have?
-   A. long, grasping tail
- • B. worn, flat teeth in the back of the mouth
-   C. short legs with long claws
-   D. sharp, pointed teeth in front of the mouth

Illustrative Item 2.12.

Use the sketches below to answer the question that follows.

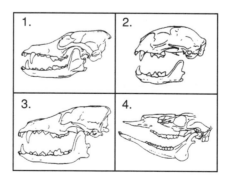

Skull 4 probably came from which type of animal?
-   A. parasite
-   B. carnivore
- • C. herbivore
-   D. saprophyte

The Assumption of Item Characteristic Curves

A third assumption important for constructing test items concerns the item characteristic curve (ICC). The ICC is a feature of methodologies for scaling people according to their responses to the stimulus of test items. It is particularly useful for analyzing test items. In a later chapter which discusses analyzing items for quality, the practical applications of ICCs are featured prominently. Here, however, they are described in more theoretical terms, as an assumption for constructing test items. As with the two previous assumptions, the use of ICCs applies to all test items regardless of whether a particular test item is included on a test that follows classical or modern theories for developing and scaling tests.

In the language of psychometricians, ICCs represent the regression of item scores on an ability variable. Nunnally (1978) had a simpler description of ICCs that may help explain them here: "Nearly all models for scaling people can be depicted by different types of curves relating an attribute to the probability of responding in one way to items versus another" (p. 68). These descriptions for ICCs may become clearer to the reader when they are graphed and the graph studied directly. Four different types of ICCs are displayed in Figures 2.2 to 2.5.

Study Figures 2.2 to 2.5 and notice in the figures that the attribute described in the ICC may be considered equivalent to a independent variable in that it is the thing being measured. It may be an observable behavior, a learned or applied skill, or an inferred trait. The ICC records this "independent variable" along an ability continuum, from low to high, on the abscissa, or X axis. This is the same ability continuum described earlier for the local independence assumption, but here it is graphically portrayed rather than only theoretically conceived.

Next, observe in the figures that the ordinate, or Y axis, of ICCs is a measure of probability of a correct response to an item, ranging from 0, no probability, to +1, perfect (or 100%) probability. Persons possessing or exhibiting a low degree of the attribute will tend to

Figure 2.2. An ascending linear trace line for a test item.

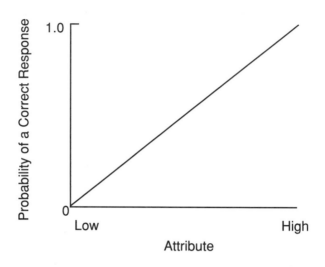

have a small probability of responding correctly to a test item that is a valid measure of the attribute. Conversely, someone who possesses or exhibits a high degree of the attribute will tend to have a high probability of responding correctly to the same test item. Figure 2.2 displays this relationship between ability in a construct and probability of a correct response to an item.

A correct response to a test item is expressed as a "probability" because test items are fallible, that is, they are unreliable. As is emphasized in this book as well as throughout all measurement theory, test items do not measure psychological constructs with unfailing accuracy; rather, test items permit inferences to be made about psychological constructs with a specified degree of confidence. If a test item were a perfectly reliable measure of an attribute, persons at any given ability level would have either a zero chance or a 100% chance of responding correctly to the test item. The ICCs in the figures reflect this probability.

Figure 2.2 is described as ascending, meaning that this particular ICC always increases, and linear, noting that it is a straight line

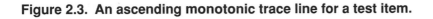

Figure 2.3. An ascending monotonic trace line for a test item.

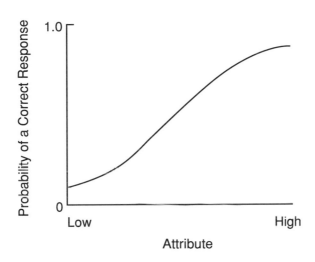

because one unit of increase in the attribute means a corresponding one unit increase in the probability of responding correctly. However, in practice the relationship between ability and probability of a correct response to an item is more complex. Figures 2.3 to 2.5 each present different aspects of this complex relationship.

Figure 2.3 is described as monotonic because the item trace line does not begin at zero probability and, on the upper end, approaches, but never reaches, one, or perfect probability. This means that low-ability examinees still have some (albeit very low) probability of a correct response and very-high-ability examinees never achieve a perfect chance of a correct response. Figure 2.3 may be contrasted with Figure 2.4, which displays a nonmonotonic trace line.

Figure 2.5 displays an ICC for a poor item because low-ability examinees have a greater probability of a correct response to the item than do highly able examinees. Such a circumstance can occur when a badly worded item is taken at face value by less-able examinees but found confusing by more-able persons. This phenomenon will be examined in greater detail in Chapter 4.

Figure 2.4. A nonmonotonic trace line for a test item.

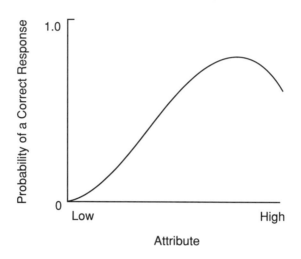

Figure 2.5. A descending monotonic trace line for a test item.

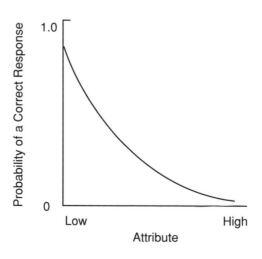

As can be seen from this brief discussion, ICCs are extremely important in constructing test items. We shall return to them again at several points throughout this book. For now, however, it is important to appreciate the role they may serve in mathematically describing characteristics for assumptions of test items.

The Importance of the Assumptions

This section—certainly the most theoretical discussion of the entire book—examined three important assumptions for test items. These are the assumptions of unidimensionality, local independence, and the item characteristic curve. While understanding these concepts may require study and review, such in-depth consideration will be worth the effort. With a thorough understanding of the assumptions for test items, one realizes why particular practical steps in item construction are needed to produce good items. Additionally, the theoretical underpinnings provide a strong rationale for a consistent and uniform theory of test item construction.

CLASSIFICATION OF ITEMS

Test items can be organized in a variety of ways. One classification scheme that is especially useful organizes them according to the function they may serve in a final test instrument. By one scheme there are four functions for items, or four item types: 1) mastery-type test items, 2) power-type test items, 3) speed-type test items, and 4) independent variable-type test items. Each of the item types has a special purpose which will be described momentarily.

Some readers knowledgeable about tests may recognize that similar terminology is also used to classify types of tests. However, it should be realized that the terminology used for classifying test items does not imply that each particular item type must or will appear in a test that is similarly termed. In other words, tests that are classified as mastery, power, or speeded tests may or may not contain mastery-type, power-type, or speed-type test items, respectively. For example, a power test may contain any one type or all four types of test items. The specifications for any given test can require that one, two, three, or all four types of test items be included. The distinction between types of tests and test-item types will become clearer with a description of the test-item types.

Mastery-type test items are intended to measure essential minimums that all examinees must know. These items are typically low-level test items requiring simple memorization of facts or computation. This type of test item is commonly used in licensing and certification tests. Several airlines pilot tests contain virtually all mastery-type test items, wherein examinees are required to respond correctly to every test item. Examples of typical mastery-type test items from these tests may be to ask examinees to supply or select the correct radio frequency for control tower operations at the Los Angeles International Airport, or to determine the length of runway required for sufficient speed to achieve the necessary lift for take-off given an airplane's thrust, total weight, and other pertinent information.

Power-type test items are designed to measure what typical or most examinees may be expected to know. These test items may range in difficulty from very easy to very hard, depending upon the subject matter and the context for the test. An example of power-type test items may be seen in a spelling test in which vocabulary words are selected for inclusion from an appropriate word list. Some words may be easy and others difficult for a given examinee or group of examinees, but most of the examinees should recognize or supply the correct spelling for most of the words. A spelling test for average-achieving fifth-graders may include words from a word list appropriate for, say, fourth- to sixth-graders. Achievement tests typically contain many power-type test items.

Speed-type test items should tap the more difficult concepts and skills that typically only the most able examinees may know. Speed-type test items should not be confused with speeded tests, in which the administration of a set of items under strictly observed time limits is itself a variable for measurement. In this context, speed relates the act of responding to test items to a theory of intelligence which postulates that intellectual ability is positively correlated with the speed with which people mentally process information (Jensen, 1980; 1982a; 1982b). This proposition, while still a theory, has strong supportive evidence and underlies most tests of mental abilities.

Independent variable-type test items have a special purpose of their own. They are designed to measure achievement in subject matter areas in which the content is evolving. For example, in the medical field new drugs typically emerge and gradually replace older ones. Often there is divided opinion and debate about which of two or more drugs (singly or in combination) may be indicated (or contraindicated) for a particular set of symptoms. Consensus among physicians, chemists, or others is slow to emerge because side-effects and consequences of drugs sometimes take years to develop. Examinees' familiarity with new drugs may be tested with independent variable-type test items.

In some circumstances independent variable-type test items are incorporated into a test instrument but not included in an examinee's score. Also, on occasions in which parallel test forms are being developed concurrent with a test's administration, it may be convenient or necessary to include test items for trial purposes as independent variable-type test items. This practice is relatively common, particularly in large-scale assessment programs in which there are parallel forms required from one test administration to the next. Again, such test items usually do not contribute to an examinee's total test score.

As may be guessed, the name independent variable-type test item is derived from research methodology wherein an independent variable is considered to be the presumed cause and the dependent variable the presumed effect. While independent variable-type test items are not in themselves the independent variable of a research methodology, conceptually they serve a loosely parallel purpose, hence, the same term is used.

Understanding How Examinees Respond to Items

Although it is superficially appealing to imagine that examinees respond to test items on the basis of either complete knowledge of the information requested or lack of complete knowledge, in fact the situation is more complicated. It has long been recognized by test developers and psychometricians that examinees respond successfully or incorrectly to items for many reasons, including complete information, partial information (of the stem or one or more of the response alternatives), misinformation, blind guessing, as well as a variety of other reasons.

Hughes and Trimble (1965) identified six combinations of information which might influence an examinee's response to an item. These are

- positive correct information which leads to a successful response,
- partial information which leads to a successful response,
- complete lack of information wherein an examinee's response is a blind guess,
- partial information which leads to an incorrect response,
- positive incorrect information which leads to an incorrect response, and
- an examinee's belief that the item is trivial, inane, or factually incorrect, and although the "correct response" is surmised, the examinee opts not to select or supply it.

This information is important for item writers to consider when preparing items for two reasons. First, by being aware of how examinees respond to test items, the writer can more suitably tailor an item to achieve a desired end. Using the same thinking strategies adopted by most examinees, the writer can read a freshly-prepared item and imagine each of these six combinations of information brought to the item by an examinee for insights into the wording proposed for the item. Second, in a general sense, the more knowledgeable the writer is about examinees as an audience for this particular kind of technical writing, the better chance he or she has of reaching it. As Wainer, Wadkins, and Rogers (1983) point out, producing high-quality test items "involves the consideration of every possible interpretation of the item" (p. 3). Good item writers must certainly put forth an extra measure of effort to ensure that the items they produce are of high quality.

CONCLUSION

In this chapter a number of concepts important to constructing test items have been introduced, including the definition of a test item and associated terminology, an explanation of the purpose for test items in measurement, a description of item formats and some examples, an exposition of criteria for good test items, a discussion of relevant assumptions, and a listing of types of test items. Finally, a brief discussion was offered of the combinations of information an examinee may bring to an item. The reader should master these concepts because the following chapters build upon the information that has been presented here. In the next chapter we will explore the idea of validity in test items by focusing on issues and strategies for determining the content of test items.

Chapter 3

Determining the Content for Items: Validity

INTRODUCTION

Determining the content for test items can be a perplexing experience. The item writer may search through textbooks or encyclopedias for grist to put into his or her item-writing mill, only to find that the result is an item whose content is trivial, pedantic, or arcane. Further, the item writer must not only find subject matter that is above the inconsequential, but in order to write items that tap complex cognitive processes, he or she must also judge the level of mental processing required of examinees to respond to a particular item. It is important to appreciate this point because determining appropriate content for items requires a complex view of items as measures not just of subject content but of psychological processes as well.

Without proper guidance, the intricate considerations of subject content and psychological processes for items are likely to result in a haphazard guess at what content is appropriate and which cognitive skills a particular item may tap. Untutored item writers may discover that what superficially appears to be a simple process of finding content often turns into a frustrating search for something usable.

Selecting appropriate content to use in constructing a test item requires more than a review of curriculum sources and certainly more than blind hope that an item taps a specified level of cognitive processing. It requires an understanding of what an item is, as well as a working familiarity with criteria for good items (these were discussed in the preceding chapter). Further, it necessitates a consideration of how the item may contribute to evidence of validity for an entire test. In fact, determining appropriate content for items is, in a very real sense, a consideration of validity. Because of the importance of validity to tests generally, this chapter focuses upon issues of validity as they relate to determining the content for individual test items.

Although validity refers to supportable interpretations of scores yielded by a whole test and not to single items, inferential interpretations for tests are possible only because the stuff of validity is imbued in the individual items. Single test items contain the "genetic material" which can bring to life supportable interpretations of measurement, and hence, test validity. Ebel (1983) even goes so far as to state that careful item construction is de facto evidence for validity.

Before one can appreciate the relationship between constructing an item and validity, one should have an unambiguous understanding of the concept of validity. To this end, this chapter begins with an explanation of basic concepts of validity. A discussion of the relationship between constructing test items and validity follows. This information provides the necessary background material from which careful item writers can make informed choices about the content of test items.

When determining whether the content for a particular test item may contribute to eventual evidence for validity, the skilled item constructor must consider several factors. First, the item writer must have a clear conception of the test's purpose, and must work from an exactly defined domain of content or psychological construct. Second, in order to determine appropriate content for items, the item writer frequently needs to have at hand carefully crafted test specifications and item specifications. It is appropriate for the item writer to work with the test developer (if not already the same person) in developing test and item specifications.

Finally, skilled item writers also need to be mindful of systematic methods for reviewing the congruence between an item and the skills or cognitive processes that are intended to be assessed. By attending to these considerations, the knowledgeable item writer can assure that the content of particular items both matches the curricular goals of the test and assesses the intended psychological processes. This chapter describes these considerations and explains strategies for dealing with them during the item-construction process.

The following topics are covered in this chapter:

- basic concepts of validity
- relationship between constructing test items and validity
- conditions for items to contribute to validity
- initial considerations when selecting content for items
- achieving clarity in a test's content
- developing test content specifications
- melding cognitive processing levels with item content
- item specifications
- consistency of an item with its specification

BASIC CONCEPTS OF VALIDITY

Understanding Validity

The concept of validity is the paramount concern in test item construction, and understanding it is an important prerequisite to writing good items. One can begin to understand validity by careful scrutiny of a definition. A commonly cited definition of validity was set forth in 1971 by Cronbach in a classic article titled "Test Validation." Cronbach described test validation as a process in which evidence is collected by the developer of a test to support the types of inferences that may be appropriately drawn from test scores. One immediately notices in Cronbach's definition that the emphasis of validity is not on the instrument itself; rather, the emphasis is upon the interpretation of the scores yielded by a test.

This definition of validity is in contrast to Garrett's (1937) traditional wording, in which he described validity simply as "... the fidelity with which [a test] measures what it purports to measure" (p. 324). Although Garrett's definition is cited by some persons as the definition of validity, it is clearly much more limited than Cronbach's and reflects a difference in emphasis. Item writers should adopt Cronbach's more sophisticated view of validity.

Recently, Cronbach (1988) addressed the changing nature of validity by describing it as a concept to be viewed from varying perspectives. One may look at validity from varying perspectives by examining the following definitions by other researchers.

Ebel and Frisbie (1986): "The term *validity*, when applied to a test, refers to the precision with which the test measures some cognitive ability" (p. 89).

Anastasi (1988): "The validity of a test concerns *what* the test measures and how well it does so" (p. 139).

Messick (1988): "Validity is an overall evaluative judgment, founded on empirical evidence and theoretical rationales, of the *adequacy* and *appropriateness* of *inferences* and *actions* based on test scores. As such, validity is an inductive summary of both the adequacy of existing evidence for and the appropriateness of potential consequences of test interpretation and use" (pp. 33-34).

Sax (1980): "Validity is defined as the extent to which measurements are useful in making decisions relevant to a given purpose" (p. 289).

Mehrens and Lehmann (1987): "Validity can be best defined as the extent to which certain inferences can be made from test scores or other measurement" (p. 74).

A Complete Definition of Validity

From these citations, the reader can easily recognize the significance of validity to the process of measurement in general and to constructing test items in particular. Let us consider, however, a fuller description of validity. Citing the AERA/APA/NCME *Standards* (1985):

> *Validity is the most important consideration in test develop-ment. The concept refers to the appropriateness, meaningful-ness, and usefulness of the specific inferences made from test scores. Test validation is a process of accumulating evidence to support such inferences. A variety of inferences may be made from scores produced by a given test, and there are many ways of accumulating evidence to support any particu-lar inference. Validity, however, is a unitary concept. Al-though evidence may be accumulated in many ways, validity always refers to the degree to which that evidence supports the inferences that are made from the scores. The inferences regarding specific uses of a test are validated, not the test itself. (p. 9)*

Given the importance of the concept of validity to constructing good test items, it is worthwhile to closely examine the points made in this description. The first point to notice is that this description refers to *inferences* that are made rather than to direct measurements. This point should be unmistakably clear since it is consistent with the definition of a test item presented earlier and was discussed thoroughly in the section explaining the purposes for test items in Chapter 2.

Note especially in the description of validity that a given instru-ment is not itself validated; rather, it is the interpretation of the test scores that has meaning. Evidence for a particular interpretation of scores is evidence for validity. Thus, test validation is the process of gathering evidence for a specific interpretation of the scores yielded by a given test.

This important aspect of validity is not widely appreciated. It is a common misconception that validity is a particular phenomenon whose presence in a test may be concretely evaluated. One often hears exclamations that a given test is "valid" or "not valid." Such pronouncements are not credible; they reflect neither the focus nor the complexity of validity.

Further, test validation is a *process* of gathering evidence. As is noted in the description, there are many different methods for gauging and documenting evidence that justify particular inferences. Some methods for gathering evidence may corroborate data gathered by other methods. Conversely, some evidence may dilute the effect of or negate other types of support for specific inferences. And, some evidence may be appropriate for certain kinds of inferences but not for other inferences.

Actually, the evidence gathered establishes the kinds of inferences that may be appropriately made. For example, suppose a given set of test items is designed to assess verbal reasoning. If sufficient evidence supports the interpretation that a low score on the set of items means an examinee is low in the construct of verbal reasoning, then such an inference may be quite proper. However, it would not be correct to infer from the same low score that the examinee is also low in the construct of emotional maturity (or, for that matter, any other construct or ability). The evidence gathered only substantiates one type of inference, in this case the inference for an examinee's verbal reasoning ability.

Of course, it may be entirely possible to gather many types of evidence for valid interpretations of test scores, each directed at substantiating a different inference. Each inference, however, that leads to a conclusion about an examinee's performance must have its own supporting evidence.

Additionally, it is important to realize that validity is not like an on-or-off switch, but is expressed in degrees. A large amount of evidence may support a high degree of validity for certain inferences, a moderate amount of evidence supports inferences only moderately, and little evidence supports inferences only weakly.

Finally, the description of validity specifies that it is a *unitary concept*. Considering validity as a unitary concept means that there are not different "types" of validity. What had formerly been thought of as *construct validity, content validity*, and *criterion-related validity*, each with independent criteria (cf. AERA, 1955; APA, 1966; APA/AERA/NCME, 1954), are now considered to be merely convenient categories of evidence for a single notion of validity. As is noted in the most recent edition of the AERA/APA/NCME *Standards* (1985), "The use of category labels does not imply that there are distinct types of validity . . ." (p. 9). Validity is a single notion.

As a unitary concept, validity may include several different types of evidence. The current conception refers to *construct-related evidence, content-related evidence*, and *criterion-related evidence*. These categories may be further delineated for convenience, but they are not in themselves different kinds of validity. In optimal circumstances, evidentiary support for validity is gathered from all three categories.

Construct-Related Evidence for Validity

From the item writer's point of view, evidence that validity is related to psychological constructs is especially important. The reader will recall from Chapter 2 that a psychological construct is a pattern of behavior consistently observed over a period of time (as, for example, reading ability), and that it is assumed that such traits can be indirectly assessed by test items. Many theoreticians believe that the notion of construct-related evidence is so intrinsic to making mental measurements by test items that all forms of evidence for validity actually fall under the generalized rubric of construct validation (Angoff, 1988; Guion, 1977; Messick, 1975, 1980, 1988; Tenopyr, 1977).

Other theoreticians, however, argue that actually establishing construct-related evidence for validity is difficult, if not impossible. For example, Ebel (1983) asserts that while "the process of construct validation is intriguing . . . the product is seldom decisive . . . . This is a neat conception in the abstract, but it has turned out not to be very practical" (p. 10). Further, Ebel claims that most measures of school achievement and employee or professional competence assess skills that can be operationally defined and that these are not the kind of latent traits that Cronbach and Meehl (1955) had in mind when they defined construct validation originally. Therefore, Ebel and Frisbie (1986) argue, such tests

> *. . . should not require any special construct evidence of validity for the test user to make appropriate or meaningful inferences on the basis of the scores derived from them. Validity evidence is incorporated in the test-development process by rational statements about what abilities are measured and why the tasks are appropriate for measuring those abilities. (pp. 96-97)*

As one can see, considerable diversity of opinion exists about the practicality of establishing construct-related evidence for validity. Wainer and Braun (1988) and Mitchell (1986) document many important aspects of this controversy, and the interested reader is referred to these authors for a more complete analysis. Regardless, the importance of construct-related evidence for validity, even if only theoretically conceived, is not disputed.

THE RELATIONSHIP BETWEEN CONSTRUCTING TEST ITEMS AND VALIDITY

Abetting Validity in the Item Construction Process

It is important to note that even a careful, well-planned item-construction process does not constitute evidence for validity per se. Describing the steps taken to ensure that standards of quality are present in the items is important for producing good items and tests, but such a description is not direct evidence for validity. The procedures used during item construction do not authenticate a particular inference, nor do they offer direct proof that evidence for validity may eventually be garnered. Validity is concerned with the veracity of interpretations for test scores, not with how tests are constructed.

A rough analogy may be made to judging a musical recital. Imagine that a fine violinist is playing for a panel of expert judges. The judges attend to the sounds produced by the violinist, not to the steps taken by the violin maker to manufacture a quality instrument. If the judges feel moved by the music, this is akin to evidence for validity. The judges are more likely to be so moved if the violinist plays on a well-constructed instrument, but the construction process is not in itself grounds for the judges to be stirred to emotion. To be sure, the violinist will more likely produce music with the desired effect if he or she plays on a well-crafted violin rather than on an instrument whose characteristics are poor or unknown. So, too, constructing test items according to accepted standards of quality will enhance the likelihood that substantive evidence for valid test interpretations may be eventually gathered.

From this discussion one can garner a sense that the relationship between constructing test items and validity is both complex and important. Clearly, good items make valid interpretations for a test's scores possible, even though the procedure used to imbue quality into the items is not itself direct evidence for inferential interpretations. Concomitantly, recording the method employed for constructing the items is important, for it establishes the framework within which specific, valid interpretations may be supported.

Documenting the Item-Construction Steps

Documenting the steps taken to produce test items is necessary for two reasons. First, as with any endeavor in either the social sciences or the physical sciences, the work should be documented so that a knowledgeable person can replicate the task. One should anticipate that if the documented procedures are followed by another scientist, results similar (within chance fluctuations) to the original would be obtained. Within the context of constructing test items, this means that if an informed writer of test items followed accepted criteria for constructing good items and carefully documented the procedures he or she used, another informed item writer could replicate the procedures and expect items of about equal merit.

A second reason it is necessary to write down the steps used in the item-construction process is that the description itself will likely be of enormous assistance in determining whether a specific interpretation for a test's scores is valid. This fact is immediately apparent when one realizes that items for a given test are constructed with a specific purpose in mind and that this same test's scores have a particular interpretation. The more clearly articulated and understood are the purposes for the test items, the better one is able to gauge whether a specific interpretation for the scores is warranted. For these reasons it is essential to document the procedures used to construct the items.

CONDITIONS FOR ITEMS TO CONTRIBUTE TO VALIDITY

In addition to ensuring that a well-considered process is employed in constructing test items, certain conditions should be met for there to be eventual evidence for validity. These conditions are: 1) a well-defined purpose for the test, including precise delineation of the test's content, 2) a set of specifications for items consistent with the test's purpose and content, and 3) a defensible methodology for reviewing the congruence between the test items and their specifications. Each of these conditions should be carefully considered when seeking evidence for validity, especially when such evidence is content-related. They are conditions for constructing test items which set the stage for producing items that will meet the criteria for merit described in Chapter 2.

Defining a Test's Purpose

The first condition, clearly defining a purpose for the test and identifying the content, is extremely important. Obviously, one should eschew constructing items for tests for which no purpose has been established or content identified. Although such a comment may appear so evident that it should scarcely warrant stating, Haertel and Calfee (1983) report that even this basic condition is routinely overlooked in test construction.

In addition to the obvious need for an articulated purpose for every test, the AERA/APA/NCME *Standards* (1985) dictate that test developers should compile evidence for the need for distinct information *prior to* publishing a particular test as well as specify the content intended to be sampled by the items. Without such clarity of content, the interpretation of a test's scores is necessarily restricted only to the performance on the specific items and cannot be generalized. Since most tests seek interpretations beyond just the performance on the specific items to larger content domains and to psychological constructs, a restricted interpretation would clearly be a disadvantage for a given test.

The consequences of constructing tests for which there is no clearly defined purpose or domain of content have become increasingly serious in recent years. Litigation involving the denial of a property right, such as a high school diploma, on the basis of a low test score frequently includes discussions of ill-conceived purposes and inadequately specified content (Yalow and Popham, 1983).

A clearly defined purpose and domain of content are important for all tests, whether criterion-referenced, norm-referenced, or some other type. A common misconception is that since norm-referenced tests are typically geared to assess an examinee's relative performance on open-ended achievement, a precise definition of the intended content is unnecessary. Nothing could be further from the truth. Clearly defining the content to be tested is important in any kind of measurement, and is not a distinction between criterion-referenced measurement and norm-referenced measurement. In fact, recognizing the significance of elucidating the content antedates even the introduction of the term *criterion-referenced testing* (Ebel, 1962a; Flanagan, 1962; Nitko, 1984b).

Devising Specifications for Tests and Items

The second condition of item preparation for there to be eventual evidence for test validity is devising specifications for tests and items consistent with the test's purpose. This condition is important yet deceptively difficult to accomplish.

Regrettably, preparing specifications for tests or items is all too often ignored in test-item construction. One carefully done study of eleven widely used, criterion-referenced tests—all produced by commercial test publishers—revealed than none of the tests' developers used domain specifications when preparing the tests' items (Hambleton & Eignor, 1978). This is a sad commentary on the lack of care taken by many test developers. One hopes that with proper information, this omission will decrease for future test-production efforts. Two later sections of this chapter describe strategies for writing test specifications and item specifications.

Content-Related Evidence for Validity

The third condition for constructing test items is mainly relevant to amassing evidence for validity that is content-related. Throughout this chapter it has been emphasized that following the seven criteria for good items explained in Chapter 2 and the conditions just described does not in itself provide evidence for validity. Such evidence must be garnered through a validation study. A validation study, like all research efforts, should be conducted according to a rigorous methodology so that other researchers can reproduce the methodology and approximate the same results. Later, in Chapter 7, information is given on how to conduct a content-validation study as well as suggestions for gathering other types of validity evidence. If one follows the seven criteria for good items and the first two conditions for validity, there is a high likelihood that this third condition—a validation study—will yield a high degree of the desired evidence.

INITIAL CONSIDERATIONS WHEN SELECTING
CONTENT FOR ITEMS

The Relationship Between Tests and Curriculum

Although it is emphasized throughout this book that test items are measures that reflect psychological constructs, it is tempting to unthinkingly adopt the proposition that tests automatically reflect curriculum. Accordingly, this faulty logic may continue, the subject content for a given test's items will always directly emanate from the same primary sources as the curriculum, as for example, textbooks and other program materials. This simplistic postulate can lead one to imagine that merely opening a textbook or other curriculum material will be sufficient when considering subject matter for test items. However, the relation between tests and curriculum materials or programs is not so simple.

Merely opening a textbook and writing items is an uninformed approach to determining the content of test items that can lead to a gross mismatch between what is measured and what is intended for measurement. Further, when this mismatch is not recognized, the errors in score interpretation can be chronic. It is necessary, then, to take a more informed approach to determining the content for test items, an approach that considers not only the precise subject matter, but the goals for the curriculum as well as the purposes for measurement. In this section we will examine the complex relationship between curriculum and assessment, and in several subsequent sections we will develop strategies to use this informed background to advantage in constructing good test items.

The reader will recall from earlier discussions in this book that tests are indirect measures of psychological constructs. Accordingly, test items do not simply restate curriculum facts. To produce good tests and good test items, one must be aware of how learning experiences impact psychological processes in students. The place to start such an inquiry is knowledge of the curriculum's basis and not merely its content. A few leading questions may direct one to the appropriate focus: Is the purpose of an instructional experience to communicate particular facts, or to imbue an appreciation for the significance of the facts? Or, is it to stimulate in the student a willing desire to learn? Or, is it for some other purpose?

Obviously, the same curriculum as well as a nearly identical lesson plan could serve any, or even all, of the purposes for a curriculum mentioned above. But identical test items would not ordinarily be used for assessing such diverse goals. More usually, different test items—with different content—would be used to assess the various curricular goals. Without identifying the purpose, or the basis, for the curriculum, it would not be possible to ascertain the appropriate content for items. It is apparent, then, that the item writer must begin the search for appropriate content for test items, not from the textbook that may have been used to teach the curriculum, but from an awareness of the goals of the curriculum.

Modern Goal Conception

Tyler (1949), in his imaginative and seminal work on establishing behavioral objectives, advocated that "Tests must actually be based upon the objectives of instruction rather than simply sampling the content of instruction . . ." (p. 402). While many psychologists and others have advanced Tyler's work to more sophisticated levels, his essential point—that the adequacy of measurement by test items rests squarely upon those items reflecting clearly formulated instructional objectives—remains relevant to determining the content for test items.

Today, psychological understanding of cognitive learning has advanced to the point where it is possible to devise instructional goals in the language of cognition. These new interpretations seek to delineate educational goals in a way that permits subject content to fit in the context of an examinee's mental processes. A leading educational psychologist, R. E. Snow (1980), describes this enlightened view as follows.

> *Modern cognitive psychology now forces upon us a much richer conception of achievement than educational psychology heretofore embraced. The view of complex learning now extant emphasizes the organization, representation, and use of knowledge over the long haul, not just its short-term accumulation . . . . School achievement is no longer to be understood as simply the accretion of facts and content-*

specific skills; but, rather, a significant part of the learner's task is to continually assemble, reassemble, structure, and tune the cumulating body of knowledge into functional systems for use in thought, and in further learning. Thus, achievement is as much an organization function as it is an acquisition function. (pp. 42-43)

Such complex considerations make the task of ascertaining the content for test items more challenging, but also more worthwhile. The task is more difficult because the item writer must adopt a wider perspective than merely considering subject content. The item writer must also contemplate how well a particular test item represents a specific psychological construct and how an examinee's response to the item may provide inferential clues to his or her ability level in that construct. With this enlightened view, the task of selecting appropriate content for test items is more meaningful because well-constructed test items can significantly contribute to eventual evidence for valid interpretations of a test's scores.

ACHIEVING CLARITY IN A TEST'S CONTENT

Importance of Specificity in Content

As has been emphasized throughout this book, a clear understanding of the content intended for a test is central to constructing good test items. Unfortunately, achieving clarity in articulating content is difficult and is often only superficially attempted. To merely report that a test is measuring language arts or quantitative skills or some other loosely defined content is to misunderstand the importance of specifying the test's content.

To illustrate the point, consider the following example. Suppose a test developer wishes to construct a test designed to assess social studies. He or she communicates this to the item writer. While this is necessary to the item writer's work, it is insufficient information for the test item writer to do a good job. Too much is unstated. The number of items that could legitimately fall under the category *social studies* is limitless. The item writer could just as easily select the content from among myriad historical facts, or from the fields of geography, economics, political science, or even the social sciences. The measurement of a construct so inexactly defined can provide only cursory assessment at best. Regretfully, this scenario is all too common.

Now, suppose the test developer specified to the item writer that only history can be included in the content of this social studies test. This limitation greatly enhances the specificity of content. The item writer's task is now more manageable but still not sufficiently clear to provide real focus to the items.

If the test developer further delimited history to include one specific objective—for example, to recognize the chronology and significance of major events and movements in United States history—the clarity of content would be advanced. The test developer has articulated a clearly defined domain of content within which the item writer can focus his or her efforts. The probability of overall evidence for valid content-related interpretations of the test scores is similarly increased.

Examples of Clearly Defined Content

It is possible to describe the content with even more specificity than is provided by the objective cited above. The utility of further clarity will depend upon the purpose for the test. If the test is designed to be a criterion-referenced measure of particular subject content, then even further limitation of content is desirable. Table 3.1 provides an example of a more specific social studies content. Notice the precision of language, defining the content in terms of subject area, cluster, skill, and enabling subskill, including the annotations. This content description prescribes the item writer's task beneficially and is an excellent example of clearly stated test content.

Table 3.1 Content Description for a Social Studies Skill

Subject Area: Social Studies
  Cluster: History
    Skill: Recognize the chronology and significance of major events and movements in United States history.

Enabling Subskills:

A. Identify and compare key institutions and participants[1] in major events and movements of United States history.

B. Identify the sequence of major events and movements[2] in United States history.

C. Describe the significance of major events and movements in United States history, including their causes and effects as well as their relationships to broader historical trends.

D. Identify technological developments and environmental changes[3] in United States history and relate them to historical events and movements.

E. Describe the principles and development of American Constitutional democracy and the significance of major Supreme Court decisions.

F. Describe the interaction among peoples of different national origins, races, and cultures and how such interaction has shaped American history.

[1] For example, public schools, daycare industry, New York Stock Exchange, Chicago Commodities Exchange, Congress; Thomas Jefferson, Susan B. Anthony, Carrie Nation, Franklin Roosevelt, Martin Luther King, Jr.

[2] For example, Revolutionary War, Louisiana Purchase, Lincoln-Douglas debates, Civil War, populist movement, woman suffrage, Prohibition, Great Depression, civil rights movement, first moon landing.

[3] For example, telephone, automobile, airplane, satellite communications, genetic engineering, acid rain, depletion of the ozone layer, deforestation of rain forests.

From *College BASE Guide to Test Content* (p. 16) by S. J. Osterlind, et al., 1989, Chicago, IL: Riverside. Reprinted by permission.

Table 3.2 presents another good example of clarity of description for a test's content. This example is from a test of reading comprehension, a commonly tested area that is often only vaguely articulated. Here, real clarity is achieved and the item writer's task is evident.

Table 3.2 Content Description for a Reading Comprehension Skill

---

Subject Area: English
Cluster: Reading and Literature
Skill: Read a literary text analytically, seeing relationships between form and content.

Enabling Subskills:

A. Identify and analyze common semantic features such as connotation and figures of speech.

B. Identify conventional literary genres, elements, and devices[1] and relate such formal elements to the content of the passage in which they are found.

C. Identify the tone, mood, and voice of a literary text through an analysis of its linguistic features and literary devices.

D. Identify the theme of a literary text and the ways it is embodied by formal elements.

[1] For example, sonnet, epic, lyric, conflict, setting, exposition, blank verse, couplet, point of view.

From *College BASE Guide to Test Content* (p. 3) by S. J. Osterlind, et al., 1989, Chicago, IL: Riverside. Reprinted by permission.

The scenario described above, and augmented by the examples of good content descriptions in Tables 3.1 and 3.2, suggests that carefully crafted wording is worth the effort. The skilled item writer should work with the test developer in achieving this degree of understanding of a test's content.

DEVELOPING TEST CONTENT SPECIFICATIONS

Planning for Test Content Specifications

Attending both to the criteria for good items articulated in Chapter 2 and the conditions under which items can contribute to validity discussed in the preceding sections requires careful planning. One operational step that will facilitate planning is to develop a blueprint for the test instrument itself. Such a test plan is referred to as the test content specifications and will typically have three elements: 1) a description of the content areas that are to be tested, 2) a statement of the objectives or mental processes to be assessed, and 3) a description of the relative importance of #1 and #2 to the overall test. Before describing a method for constructing a table of test content specifications, however, it may be instructive to examine the context for their development by looking briefly at the work of several researchers in this field.

Researchers' Work in Promoting Clarity of Content

Prescribing test content specifications is a widely accepted idea in test development. Baker (1974), Millman (1974b), and Popham (1975; 1984) all advocate specificity in description of content as a way to improve understanding between a test's developer and the item writer. These researchers describe their work variously as *amplified objectives, domain specifications*, or *test content specifications*. Precise distinctions among these terms are not of substantive importance when planning for item construction since they all focus on precision in language to aid understanding so that test items may optimally reflect their objective. All of these efforts fall under the general rubric of test content specifications.

Other researchers have also contributed significantly to this area. Ebel (1962b) devised examples of domain specifications as a way of clarifying vaguely worded objectives. And, Hivley, Patterson, and Page (1968) offered two requirements for their specifications:

1. All of the items which could be written from the content domain to be tested must be written (or known) in advance of the final item-selection process.

2. A random or stratified random sampling procedure must be used in the item selection process.

While these conditions are conceptually appealing, they are unworkable in practice for several reasons. First, it is naive to presume that enough is known about learning theory to be able to describe completely any domain of content or intellectual process; and, second, to prepare enough good test items to cover an entire domain (regardless of how tightly described) would be an undertaking of enormous proportions. Nevertheless, they are important guiding principles when thinking about test content specifications.

Establishing a Table of Test Content Specifications

One convenient way to establish a set of test content specifications is in terms of a table. The table should show the three basic elements of test content specifications: content, processes, and the importance of each. Such a table may be organized with processes across the top and content topics in the left column. Table 3.3 presents an example of using a two-way grid as a table of test content specifications.

Note in this table, which gives test content specifications for a test of reading comprehension, that the left side depicts the content areas to be included on this test of critical reading skills. Across the top of the table, the intellectual processes are listed: Interpretive Reasoning, Strategic Reasoning, and Adaptive Reasoning. Also notice in the table that the relationship between the two dimensions is expressed as the number of items to be assigned to each category. Thus it can be seen that all of the elements of test content specifications are given in this table. Note also that not every cell is filled, indicating that no items are required for some areas.

Table 3.3 Sample Table of Test Content Specifications

Skill: Read critically by asking questions about a text, by recognizing assumptions, and by evaluating ideas.

Major Content Areas   **Intellectual Process**

	Interpretive Reasoning	Strategic Reasoning	Adaptive Reasoning
Identify the literal meaning of a text and recall its details.	4 *	3	
Identify the main idea of a text and differentiate it from subordinate ideas.	2	4	
Summarize the rhetorical development or narrative sequence within a text.	4	4	1
Recognize the implicit assumptions and values that inform a text.	3		2
Assess the logical validity of the rhetorical development within a text.	3		1
Evaluate ideas in a text by their implications and relation- ships to ideas outside the text.	1	2	

   * number of items

Table 3.4 Sample of Test Content Specifications for a Biology Test.

CONTENT AREAS	Process Objectives		Recognizes Terms and Vocabulary 30%
	Identifies Specific Facts 20%		
A. Nutrition, 40%	Nutrients Vitamins Enzymes Metabolism Oxidation	Incomplete Protein Complete Protein Amino Acids Glycogen Carbohydrate	Nutrients Essential to Health Good Sources of Food Nutrients Parts of Digestive System Process of Digestion of Each Nutrient Sources of Information About Foods and Nutrition
	4 or 5 items		7 or 8 items
B. Communicable Disease, 40%	Immunity Virus Carrier Antibodies Incubation Period	Epidemic Pathogenic Endemic Protozoa	Common Communicable Diseases Incidence of Various Diseases Methods of Spreading Disease Types of Immunization Symptoms of Common Communicable Diseases
	4 or 5 items		7 or 8 items
C. Noncommunicable Diseases, 20%	Goiter Deficiency Diseases Diabetes Cardiovascular Diseases Caries		Specific Diseases Caused by Lack of Vitamins Specific Disorders Resulting from Imbalance in Hormones Incidence of Noncommunicable Diseases Common Noncommunicable Diseases of Adolescents and Young Adults
	3 or 4 items		2 or 3 items
Number of Items	18		12

From *Measurement and Evaluation in Psychology and Education*, 4th ed. (pp. 18-21) by R. L. Thorndike, 1977, New York: Wiley. Adapted by permission.

Table 3.4 *(continued)*

| Identifies Principles, Concepts, and Generalizations 30% | Process Objectives | | Number of Items |
	Evaluates Health Information and Advertisements 10%	Applies Principles and Generalizations to Novel Situations 10%	
Bases of Well Balanced Diet Enzyme Reactions Transfer of Materials Between Cells Cell Metabolism Functions of Nutrients in Body	Analyzes Food and Diet Advertisements Interprets Labels on Foods Identifies Good Sources of Information About Foods and Diets	Identifies Well Balanced Diet Computes Calories Needed for Weight-Gaining or Weight-Losing Diet Predicts Consequences of Changes in Enzymes on Digestive System Identifies Services and Protection Provided by the Federal Food and Drug Act	24
7 or 8 items	2 or 3 items	2 or 3 items	
Basic Principles Underlying Control of Disease Actions of Antibiotics Body Defenses Against Disease Immune Reactions in Body	Distinguishes Between Adequate and Inadequate Evidence for Medicines Identifies Misleading Advertisements for Medications	Recognizes Conditions Likely to Result in Increase of Communicable Disease Identifies Appropriate Methods for Sterilizing Objects Gives Appropriate Reasons for Regulations, Processes, or Treatments	24
7 or 8 items	2 or 3 items	2 or 3 items	
Pressure Within Cardiovascular System Control of Diabetes Inheritance of Abnormal Conditions Abnormal Growth of Cells	Identifies Errors or Misleading Information in Health Material Identifies Appropriate Source of Information for Health Problems	Predicts Consequences of Changes in Secretion of Certain Hormones Predicts Probability of Inheriting Abnormal Conditions	12
3 or 4 items	1 or 2 items	1 or 2 items	
18	6	6	Total number of items 60

Table 3.5 Sample Table of Test Content Specifications that Includes Information on Item Formats

Recall (Knowledge and Comprehension)

Major Skill Group	Subordinate Skills	Behavioral Objectives	Item Format[a]	Number of Items
Capitalize words (prerequisite skill)	1. State the rule for capitalizing words	1.1 From memory state the rule for capitalizing words.	W	1
		1.2 Select the rule for capitalizing words from a set of alternative rules.	S	1
Common nouns (prerequisite skill)	3. Define terms *person, place, thing,* and *idea*	3.1 From memory, define the terms *person, place, thing,* and *idea*.	W	4
		3.2 Match the terms *person, place, thing,* and *idea* with their definitions.	S	4
	5. Define the term *noun*	5.1 From memory, define the term *noun*.	W	1
		5.2 Given the definition for term *noun*, identify it as such.	W/S	1

From *Measuring and Evaluating School Learning* (pp 84-85) by Carey, L. M., 1988, Boston: Allyn and Bacon. Adapted by permission.

Table 3.5 *(continued)*

Subordinate Skills	Application Behavioral Objectives	Item Format[a]	Number of Items
2. Capitalize any word	2.1 Given a list of several words, select the letter in the words that should be capitalized.	S	5
	2.2 Given some words that are properly capitalized and some that are improperly capitalized, select those that are properly capitalized.	S	5
4. Discriminate words that represent persons, places, things, and ideas from lists of words containing these and other concepts	4.1 Given a list of words that contains persons, places, things, and ideas, classify each word into the appropriate category	S	12
6. Classify words that are common nouns	6.1 Given a list of words containing common nouns and other parts of speech, select the common nouns.	S	15
7. Give several examples of common nouns	7.1 List several words that refer to persons.	W	2
	7.2 List several words that refer to places.	W	2
	7.3 List several words that refer to things.	W	2
	7.4 List several words that refer to ideas.	W	2

[a] Item format codes: W = Write response from memory; S = Select response from alternatives; W/S = Either write or select response.

Table 3.4 presents another example of a table of test content specifications. In this table, the content areas are listed along the top and the intellectual processes (here they are called "process objectives") are cited in the left column. And, the table indicates the relation between the two as the approximate number of items that are to be included in the final test assigned to each content area and process objective. The percentage of total items intended for each category is also given for each column and row. Also, note that this table includes in every cell very specific information about the content for the items. This narrowly focused content is common in tests that are criterion-referenced, and typical in many tests used for licensing and certification.

While it is often useful to organize test content specifications into a two-way table, there is a tendency to believe that every cell must be filled or a deficiency exists. This is not accurate. For some tests, classifications along a single dimension may be more appropriate. Alternatively, complex tests may require more dimensions and fuller descriptions of its characteristics. For example, various formats for the items can also be specified in a table of test content specifications. Table 3.5 displays a table of test content specifications that includes directions for item formats in addition to identifying the content and processes.

As can be seen in Table 3.5, the left side of the table consists of the major skill groups (e.g., "Capitalize Words," "Common Nouns"). Across the top of the table are the major cognitive levels of recall and application. Below these levels are the subordinate skills and the behavioral objectives that provide the criteria for the attainment of the subordinate skills.

As mentioned, the content specifications displayed in Table 3.5 also dictate the item format that is to be used for each skill and objective. For example, for Behavioral Objective 1.1, the recommendation is for the "write response from memory" format, or typically, sentence-completion or short-answer, the constructed-response format. Behavioral Objective 1.2 specifies that the selected-response format, such as multiple-choice or true-false, should be used.

Sometimes the instructions for item format are displayed in item specifications, rather than in test specifications. There is no particular advantage to displaying item formats in test specifications unless there are no item specifications offered for a particular test. In these cases, the prescription of an item format is desirable.

Alternative Ways to Present Test Content Specifications

While tables of specifications such as those displayed in Tables 3.3, 3.4, and 3.5 are commonly used for presenting test specifications and may be adequate for a particular instrument, they are not the only possible manner of organizing test content specifications. Complex sets of specifications are not uncommon. In fact, Ebel and Frisbie (1986) stipulate that the firmest basis for a good set of test content specifications should include fully seven elements, indicating the following:

- formats of test items to be used,
- number of items of each format,
- kinds of tasks the items will present,
- number of tasks of each kind,
- areas of content to be sampled,
- number of items in each area, and
- level and distribution of item difficulty.

Systematic attention to all seven of these elements will facilitate the development of comprehensive test content specifications. Clearly, such thorough test content specifications will give a tight focus to the item writer's task. But regardless of whether the test content specifications are complex or comparatively simple, they should address at least the three basic elements (viz., content, processes, and importance of each).

The Test Developer's Responsibility
for Preparing Test Content Specifications

Preparing test content specifications is the responsibility of the test developer. Such preliminary organization precedes the work of actually writing test items. The item writer will use this information to carry out the intentions of the test developer. Frequently, however, the work of the test developer and the item writer is carried out by the same person or group of persons. This dual role can be an asset to good test development because the goals of the test may be more precisely understood by the item writer if he or she is the same person who developed the goals originally. One caution to be heeded with this two-in-one role, however, is that it can be tempting to cut corners in the test development process by only visualizing the test content specifications rather than actually writing them out. This is a poor substitute for writing clear, well-thought-out test content specifications.

Although developing test content specifications may appear to the untutored item writer to be a laborious step that is tempting to skip, they are crucial to a skillful determination of the content for test items. They are simply too important to ignore.

MELDING COGNITIVE PROCESSING LEVELS
WITH ITEM CONTENT

Identifying Levels of Cognitive Processing

Bloom's taxonomy is probably the most widely employed scheme for labeling and articulating levels of cognitive processes in test construction today, as it has been for the past two decades. It is used in variously modified versions by the developers of many popular tests. Bloom's original work in describing mental processing in the cognitive domain was seminal, bringing widespread attention to the notion of classifying psychological processes into categories that could be exploited for measurement. The taxonomy has been elaborated upon and fitted with numerous examples of test items for each category in a later publication by Bloom, Hastings, and Madaus (1971). The taxonomy includes these primary categories, described in Bloom's original wording:

1.00 KNOWLEDGE

Knowledge, as defined here, involves the recall of specifics and universals, the recall of methods and processes, or the recall of a pattern, structure, or setting. For measurement purposes, the recall situation involves little more than bringing to mind the appropriate material. Although some alteration of the material may be required, this is a relatively minor part of the task. The knowledge objectives emphasize most the psychological processes of remembering. The process of relating is also involved in that a knowledge test situation requires the organization and reorganization of a problem such that it will furnish the appropriate signals and cues for the information and knowledge of the individual possesses. To use an analogy, if one thinks of the mind as a file, the problem in a knowledge test situation is that of finding in the problem or task the appropriate signals, cues, and clues which will most effectively bring out whatever knowledge is filed or stored.

2.00 COMPREHENSION

This represents the lowest level of understanding. It refers to a type of understanding or apprehension such that the individual knows what is being communicated and can make use of the material or idea being communicated without necessarily relating it to other material or seeing its fullest implications.

3.00 APPLICATION

The use of abstractions in particular and concrete situations. The abstractions may be in the form of general ideas, rules of procedures, or generalized methods. The abstractions may also be technical principles, ideas, and theories which must be remembered and applied.

- Application to the phenomena discussed in one paper of the scientific terms or concepts used in other papers.
- The ability to predict the probable effect of a change in a factor on a biological situation previously at equilibrium.

4.00 ANALYSIS

The breakdown of a communication into its constituent elements or parts such that relative hierarchy of ideas is made clear and/or the relations between the ideas expressed are made explicit. Such analyses are intended to clarify the communication, to indicate how the communication is organized, and the way in which it manages to convey its effects, as well as its basis and arrangement.

5.00 SYNTHESIS

The putting together of elements and parts so as to form a whole. This involves the process of working with pieces, parts, elements, etc., and arranging and combining them in such a way as to constitute a pattern or structure not clearly there before.

6.00 EVALUATION

Judgments about the value of material and methods for given purposes. Quantitative and qualitative judgements about the extent to which material and methods satisfy criteria. Use of a standard of appraisal. The criteria may be those determined by the student or those which are given to him.

Difficulty of Using Bloom's Taxonomy to Write Items

Regardless of its widespread use, Bloom's taxonomy of educational objectives is often constrictive to test developers. This is so because developing test items which conform to the language of the taxonomy results in too many items being labeled in the knowledge dimension, the lowest-level category. With care, some items may be written to the comprehension or even the application category, but by Bloom's descriptions few items can be constructed to assess processes at the high-end taxonomy levels of analysis, synthesis, or evaluation.

This deficit has become increasingly apparent in recent years with the closer scrutiny by modern measurement experts of items that tap complex cognitive processing. Concomitantly, as test developers and item writers place more importance on the language of cognition, there is a growing sensitivity to the importance of defining the levels of cognitive processing and identifying how particular test items assess mental processing. No longer is it adequate to assign items cursorily to process categories and pay little heed to the consequences. Today, the careful item writer must be precise in the definitions of cognitive levels adopted for use, and must consider carefully the precision with which particular test items may tap specific levels of mental processing.

Yet another problem arises with Bloom's taxonomic scheme: there is an inherent difficulty in validating the properties of the levels within the taxonomy. Madaus, Woods, and Nuttall (1973) claim that Bloom's scheme has no structural hierarchy beyond what can be explained by a general intelligence, or "g" factor. And, Seddon (1978), after reviewing the relevant literature, maintains that no one has been able to demonstrate the veracity of Bloom's levels. An extreme position is advocated by Blumberg, Alschuler, and Rezmovic (1982), who state that Bloom's scheme should not be used for test development at all until the "significance of taxonomic levels has been established . . ." (p. 6). While we should discount neither the importance nor the utility of Bloom's work, it is wise to take council from these researchers and proceed with a clearer understanding of the merits and limitations of using Bloom's taxonomy of the cognitive domain for developing test items.

Over the years, theoreticians and researchers have sought to develop Bloom's idea of making a taxonomy of educational objectives and have had new and important perspectives. For example, Ebel (1972), Thorndike and Hagen (1977), Hannah and Michaelis (1977), and others have contributed their own taxonomies of mental processing for the cognitive domain. Most of these taxonomies have attempted to provide test developers and item writers with more felicitous descriptions of the cognitive domain than Bloom's.

The Framework for Instructional Objectives Taxonomy

Of the theoreticians mentioned above, the taxonomy developed by Hannah and Michaelis (1977) has the most potential for aiding construction of test items. The Hannah and Michaelis system, called the Framework for Instructional Objectives (FIO), was developed to give educators the generic vocabulary and common perspective needed to integrate instruction with evaluation by stressing the interrelated nature of these activities. By providing a detailed framework for writing instructional objectives, FIO aids the design of objectives-based assessment. The primary function of FIO is utilitarian. It does not break any new theoretical ground.

FIO is divided into four domains, with each domain separated into levels. These are illustrated in Table 3.6. Understood as a hierarchy, the levels—called behaviors—define the domains. The first and primary domain, data gathering, consists of observing and remembering. These are prerequisite to the more complex learning processes. This domain underpins the other three domains so that observing and remembering act as the understood first and second levels of the behaviors in each domain. Roughly speaking, FIO uses the designations *Intellectual Processes* for cognitive behavior, *Skills* for psychomotor behavior, and *Values and Attitudes* for affective behavior. Of course, there is overlap, and some of the intellectual processes of the cognitive domain would be requisite to the values and skills domains. The levels of each domain are arranged in a hierarchical order according to the criteria which defined the domain's behavior: complexity (Intellectual Processes), independence (Skills),

Table 3.6 Framework for Instructional Objectives Schema

Intellectual Processes		Skills	Attitudes & Values
Inferring	Evaluating	Improvising	Integrating
Generalizing	Predicting	Applying	Preferring
Classifying	Hypothesizing	Mastering	Accepting
Comparing	Synthesizing	Patterning	Complying
Interpreting	Analyzing	Imitating	Responding

Data Gathering
Observing   Remembering

From *A Comprehensive Framework for Instructional Objectives* (p. 16) by L.S. Hannah, and J. U. Michaelis, 1977, Reading, MA: Addison-Wesley. Reprinted by permission.

and integration (Attitudes and Values). Table 3.6 illustrates the relationship of the levels of behavior inside the domains.

Of FIO's three major domains, only Intellectual Processes clearly lends itself to evaluation through the kinds of test-item formats discussed in this book (viz., selected-response and constructed-response). Further, Intellectual Processes is also the domain which relates directly to the traditional school curriculum: English, mathematics, science, social studies, and the like. Therefore, this domain may be the most widely applied in the process of constructing test items.

FIO is useful in constructing test items because it provides an internally consistent framework from which one can discuss content-related evidence and construct-related evidence for validity. To appreciate this aspect of FIO, recall that it was mentioned earlier that it is difficult to prepare test items consistent with Bloom's taxonomy in any category beyond the lowest one or two (viz., knowledge and comprehension). The FIO classification scheme is more flexible because it does not contain a formal definition of the domain of knowledge as such; rather, each level contains lists of suitable objects and conditions for the desired behaviors, and these lists provide the information usually contained in classifications of the domain of knowledge. For instance, an overt behavior for the level of Interpreting is "restates," and a suitable object for this behavior is "main ideas."

Similarly, an overt behavior for the level of Classifying is "names," and a fitting object for this behavior is "objects." This level of detail is more appropriate to actual construction of items than to planning for test specifications. Applying these behavioral descriptions to item construction is discussed fully in Chapter 4, with a complete listing of the categories and their concomitant behavior provided. Now, however, the point to notice is how the FIO may be used when preparing test content specifications.

TEST ITEM SPECIFICATIONS

Test item specifications are a specialized kind of technical writing used in developing a set of items. Just as test content specifications describe the content and intellectual processes for an entire test, item specifications give directions for preparing particular items. However, the similarity between test content specifications and item specifications is only general. Test item specifications are not merely a more specific version of test content specifications. They differ in purpose, scope, and function. Test item specifications are formal, systematized directions from a test developer to the item writer that seek to put the test content specifications into action. They may include such information as eligible item formats, kinds of directions, limits for the stem, characteristics of the response alternatives, as well as features for the correct response and distractors.

Test item specifications can be brief, or they may need to be lengthy if the test developer wishes to convey a lot of information to the item writer. The purposes of the test will, in great measure, dictate the amount of information needed to describe item specifications.

An example of an item specification is given in Table 3.7 below. Obviously, when preparing item specifications, stating the goal, objective, skill, or standard for assessment is necessary, and it is usually given first. In the sample item specification, the subject for assessment is science, and it is further limited to laboratory and field work. The objective to be assessed by items in Table 3.7 is as follows: Recognize the role of observation and experimentation in the development of scientific theories.

Note in the sample item specifications, that the content for potential items has been broken into three types, Item Types A, B, and C. Collectively, the descriptions for the three item types define the entire skill. By comparing the wording of the skill to that of each item type, one will recognize that each of these types contains information specific to a particular portion of the skill. Additionally, notice that the sample item specification contains stimulus characteristics and response characteristics for each content type. Study the detail in this table of item specifications, attending especially to the differences between it and the examples of test content specifications presented earlier in Tables 3.3, 3.4, and 3.5.

The first detail to notice when comparing test content specifications with item specifications is that the item specifications are typically much more detailed and prescriptive. While it was noted earlier that sometimes test content specifications identify the format to be used for an item, they do not prescribe characteristics beyond this. In contrast, item specifications are extensively prescriptive, including dictating characteristics of the stem and features for the response alternatives. Notice in the item specification presented in Table 3.7, for example, that the items are constrained by the specification to have exactly four response alternatives, and stimulus characteristics and response options are described. Further, each item type is accompanied by a sample item.

Another example of test item specifications is displayed in Table 3.8. There are obvious similarities and differences between the sample item specifications given in Tables 3.7 and 3.8. One similarity of special importance is the degree to which the content of the test is specified and the stimulus and response attributes are described. One difference between the item specifications is the format, content, and directions statements. Of course, each test development situation will need slightly different item specifications.

The Role Of Test Item Specifications

Test item specifications are usually intended as a working document internal to a test's development. They are not designed for examinees or test users as a guide to a test's content, nor are they pertinent to instruction. Lest there be confusion on this point, it is important to state that providing information to examinees and others about the particular content and features of a specific test is appropriate. In fact, such information may be necessary to fulfill the

(continued on page 104)

Table 3.7 Sample of Test Item Specifications for a Science Test

---

Subject Area: Science

Cluster: Laboratory and Field Work

Skill: Recognize the role of observation and experimentation in the development of scientific theories.

Item Format: Multiple Choice, four responses.

Item Type A: Isolate and define a scientific problem or area for scientific study.

   1) Stimulus Characteristics:
      a. The stimulus will direct the student to identify a statement that best defines a scientific problem or topic for investigation.
      b. The stimulus will provide a thorough description of observational data from which the student will discern the area to be investigated.
      c. The material should neither be so well known that the student is likely to be familiar with actual scientific work in the area nor so technical that specialized knowledge is required.

   2) Response Options:
      a. The correct answer will be a sentence or brief paragraph that presents an accurate and clearly defined statement of the scientific problem or area of study.
      b. Distractors will be sentences or brief paragraphs that fail to define the scientific problem or area of study accurately, and which may be incorrectly or too broadly stated or may describe material that is irrelevant or outside the scope of the observation.

Table 3.7 *(continued)*

Sample Item: A researcher studying the use of radiation to slow the spoilage of vegetables harvested four dozen tomatoes of a variety that had been grown under identical conditions and were approximately the same size and weight. After randomly selecting them for placement in sterile racks containing a dozen each, she subjected two racks to a fixed amount of radiation. Then she placed one irradiated rack and one that had not been irradiated in refrigerators which maintained the same temperature. She stored the other two racks, one of which had been irradiated, at room temperature. She checked all four racks every six hours for signs of spoilage. When she found signs of spoilage in at least three of the tomatoes in a rack, she recorded the elapsed time and disposed of the tomatoes in that rack. The researcher found that the irradiated tomatoes spoiled at the same rate as those that were not irradiated. Repetition of the experiment gave the same results.

Which variable would it be best for the researcher to alter in her follow-up experiment?

    A. amount of radiation

    B. ctorage temperature

•   C. number of tomatoes

    D. size of tomatoes

Item Type B: Recognize the principal elements in an experimental design, including the hypothesis, independent and dependent variables, and controls.

    1) Stimulus Characteristics:

      a. The stimulus will direct the student to identify a hypothesis control, dependent variable, independent variable, result, or conclusion in a specified experiment design.

      b. The material should neither be so well known that the student is likely to be familiar with actual

Table 3.7 *(continued)*

scientific work in the area nor so technical that specialized knowledge is required.

c. Although the research may be fictitious, the situation will be realistic and the goal practical.

2) Response Options:

a. The correct answer will be a word, phrase, sentence, or brief paragraph describing the experimental element called for in the stimulus.

b. Distractors will be words, phrases, sentences, or brief paragraphs describing other aspects of the experiment or, in the case of a hypothesis, stating overly general, overly specific, or simply erroneous summaries of what is being investigated in the experiment.

Sample Item:

Science

In the nineteenth century, Louis Pasteur performed an experiment in which he bent the necks of flasks into "S" shapes, leaving their ends opened. Then he boiled broth in the flasks to force air out and kill any microbes inside. After the flasks cooled, he left some of them upright for observation. Before setting aside others to observe, he tilted them so that the broth moved up into the bent necks and then back into the flasks. After the flasks had been prepared, he watched them for signs of microbial growth.

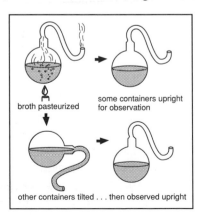

Table 3.7 *(continued)*

Which hypothesis was Pasteur testing in this experiment?

    A. Flasks with bent necks would cause microbes to grow in the broth.

    B. Cooling broth in the flasks would cause microbes to grow in the broth.

•   C. Heating broth in the flasks and then cooling it would cause microbes to grow in the broth.

    D. Contact of the broth with something in the necks of the flasks would cause microbes to grow in the broth.

Item Type C: Evaluate an experimental design by analyzing its ability to test the hypothesis, identifying weaknesses and improvements, and discerning inherent limitations and assumptions.

    1) Stimulus Characteristics:

      a. The stimulus will direct the student to identify a flaw, improvement, limitation, or assumptions in a specified experimental design.

      b. The material should neither be so well known that the student is likely to be familiar with actual scientific work in the area nor so technical that specialized knowledge is required.

      c. Although the research may be fictitious, the situation will be realistic and the goal practical.

    2) Response Options:

      a. The correct answer will be a word, phrase, sentence, or brief paragraph describing the flaw, improvement, limitation, or assumption called for in the stimulus.

Table 3.7 *(continued)*

---

b. Distractors will be words, phrases, sentences, or brief paragraphs describing flaws not present in the experiment, aspects of the experiment that are **not** flaws, changes that do **not** improve the experiment, assumptions that do **not** apply to the experiment or its conclusions.

Sample Item: **Read the passage below and answer the question that follows.**

A researcher studying a species of hawk noticed that an increasing number of their eggs were not hatching. He suspected that the problem was related to heavy use of a new pesticide in the area. To investigate the matter further, he acquired three hawk eggs immediately after they had been laid and placed them in an incubator. Next, he diluted a sample of the pesticide, which was not water soluble, in alcohol. He then injected one egg with the solution of pesticide and alcohol and a second egg only with alcohol. He sealed the injection sites in both eggs with wax. The third egg received no injection. He placed all three eggs back in the incubator for observation.

109. Which would most clearly improve the experiment?

   A. sealing the injection sites with tape rather than wax
 • B. using more eggs for each of the three conditions
   C. soaking the eggs in pesticide rather than injecting it
   D. experimenting with newborn hawks rather than eggs

Table 3.8 Sample Test Item Specifications for Minimum Student Performance Standards in Computer Literacy

---

GRADE: 5   SUBJECT: Computer Literacy

GRADE:	5	SUBJECT: Computer Literacy
STANDARD:	D	The student will recognize the impact of computer technology in society and the need for its ethical use.
SKILL:	22	Identify an example of a computer application in each of the following areas: home, school, and business.

CLARIFICATION OF SKILL: The student will identify ways a computer is used in the home, at school, and in business.

STIMULUS ATTRIBUTES

A. Format: An incomplete statement or a question.

B. Content   Requires student to identify a computer application at home, school, or business.

C. Directions:
1. Select a way the computer is used (at home, school, or business); or
2. Computers can be used at (home, school, business) to . . . ; or
3. In (homes, schools, business) computers can be used to . . .; or
4. Which does NOT need a computer? or
5. A computer is NOT needed to . . . .

RESPONSE ATTRIBUTES

A. Format: Short phrases.

B. Options:
1. Correct Response: Applications that can (or cannot) be done by a computer at (home, school, business).

From *Test Item Specifications for Minimum Student Performance Standards in Computer Literacy: Grades 3, 5, 8, and 11.* Tallahassee: Florida Department of Education, 1987.

Table 3.8 *(continued)*

---

	2. Other Options: If question asks for an application that can be done by a computer, other options will be applications that cannot be done by a computer; and vice versa.
SAMPLE ITEM	Computers can be used at school to

- A. help students practice math. (1)
  B. erase the blackboard.   (2)
  C. sharpen pencils.   (2)
  D. clean the windows.   (2)

(continued from page 97)

purpose of some domain-referenced and criterion-referenced tests; however, such a guide to the content and features of a specific test is not the same as a statement of test item specifications. Item specifications are intended primarily for the item writers so that their work will be focused in a way that reflects the test developer's intentions.

Item specifications are especially useful in tests that require a large number of items which are constructed by several item writers. In these instances, they add a consistency of approach to the task, ensuring that no one writer will prepare items that are incompatible with those prepared by the others.

A final point needs to be made about item specifications: One test item specification describes just one item. Test item specifications are not usually meant to describe the features of several items varying in format, content, process category, and other features.

Happily, it is not necessary to write as many item specifications as there are items planned for a test. The same item specification may be used several times in a test. In fact, test developers commonly prepare only the number of item specifications equal to the number of cells on a two-way grid of test content specifications. This is all that is usually needed because in each cell for a table of test content specifications, the test developer stipulates that a certain content aimed at a specified level of cognitive processing may be assessed by several items. This makes it necessary to prepare only one item specification which can apply to all items within that cell. The idea of reusing an item specification several times in the same test should markedly reduce the number of separate item specifications needed.

Caution Against Making Test Item Specifications Too Prescriptive

In recent years, specifications for writing test items (especially items intended for use in domain-referenced tests) have sometimes been prepared in too much detail. Some item specifications have attempted to describe nearly every conceivable delimitation to an item. Enormous amounts of time and energy are spent in preparing elaborately detailed item specifications. Even W. J. Popham (personal communication, April 1987), an early and vigorous advocate of thorough test content and item specifications, has retreated from using laboriously detailed specifications. Test item specifications are helpful only to the extent that they convey useful information to item writers. Beyond conveying needed information, they become hindrances rather than helpful aids.

Very narrow or laboriously defined specifications can lead to trivial items. In fact, an item writer's creativity may be inhibited if the limits imposed by the item specifications are too constraining. Frequently, brief item specifications are all that is necessary. A delicate balance needs to be struck between providing item writers with explicit, carefully considered ingredients and limits in writing test items and overly restricting a writer's ingenuity and creativity. A simple analogy may be made to using a road map to guide one in driving to a given destination as contrasted to a route ticket on a bus which dictates the exact roads and time of departure and arrival, leaving no room for deviation. Test item specifications should be more like a road map that can lead one toward a given goal without dictating every aspect of the course to be taken. When test item specifications are carefully prepared and skillfully used, they should aid the writer's task of making an item consistent with its intended objective.

MAKING AN ITEM CONSISTENT WITH ITS SPECIFICATION

The Importance of Item-Objective Congruence

Achieving the maximum degree of congruence between the knowledge, skill, or ability actually assessed by an item and the intention for that item (as articulated by its specification) is of paramount concern to the item writer. It directly affects the interpretation of an item for content-related evidence of validity, and it influences the error of measurement, or reliability. Hence, the item-objective match is highly important. Unfortunately, determining the strength of that match is difficult. It involves an awareness of the full implications of the objective or skill to be assessed as well as a nearly complete command of the subtleties of the language selected for the item. Several examples will illustrate this point. The first example will be obvious; subsequent examples will convey various subtleties of the item-objective congruence problem.

To begin, suppose that Illustrative Item 3.1 is designed to gauge a student's skill is solving simple problems that involve proportions. As can be seen from a casual inspection, this problem involves recognizing units of measure and is unrelated to proportions. Hence, the item-objective congruence is lacking. This item is inappropriate for assessing this objective because of this mismatch.

Illustrative Item 3.1.

Which is equal to 5 pounds?
- A. 80 grams
- B. 16 ounces
- • C. 80 ounces
- D. 7,000 grains

In contrast, consider Illustrative Item 3.2, which is meant to assess the same skill of using proportions. This item does require the examinee to use proportions, and thus exhibits a high degree of congruence to the objective. Of course, in this simple comparison of Illustrative Item 3.1 to 3.2, we are not concerned with whether the level of item difficulty is appropriate to the examinees, as well as other considerations for good items; rather, it is used only to make the point of item-objective congruence.

Illustrative Item 3.2.

Bill spends 45 minutes each day exercising, Karen exercises for 15 minutes a day, and Jack exercises 60 minutes daily. What is the ratio of how long Bill exercises to how long Jack exercises?

A. $\dfrac{45}{120}$

B. $\dfrac{45}{60}$

C. $\dfrac{60}{45}$

• D. $\dfrac{45}{15}$

Another point warrants attention when looking at Illustrative Items 3.1 and 3.2: Although Illustrative Item 3.1 cannot be used for the specified purpose of assessing this objective because of its lack of congruence to the objective, the item may not need to be discarded out-of-hand. It may be matched to another more appropriate objective. In that new context, the item could suit its purpose.

Next, consider another example by again looking at two items designed to assess the same skill. One item is poorly matched to the skill while the other is well suited to its intended purpose. The objective is to classify the type of lenses used to produce particular images depicted in ray diagrams. In this example, difficulties with subject content cause a mismatch.

Illustrative Item 3.3.

Use the diagram below to answer the question that follows.

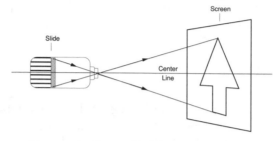

What type of image is shown in the diagram?

- • A. virtual
    B. fragmented
    C. real
    D. negative

Illustrative Item 3.4.

Use the diagram below to answer the question that follows.

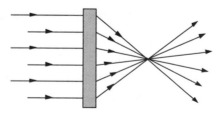

Which lens would produce this light pattern?

  A. convex
- • B. concave
  C. colored
  D. polarized

First, examine the item that is poorly matched to the objective, Illustrative Item 3.3. Despite the seemingly impressive graphic, this item does not assess the skill because it gives a ray diagram and asks about the image. The graphic is therefore inappropriate to the question asked in the item's stem. If the stem had asked about what lens was used, the item probably would be fine.

It should be obvious to the reader from these examples, especially the preceding two illustrative items, that it takes a thorough knowledge of the subject matter to determine whether congruence exists. Often it is necessary to seek the advice of subject specialists to verify the content.

In addition to problems with content difficulty, the degree of congruence between a particular item and an objective is sometimes not obvious for reasons of language. Subtleties of language, such as shifts in word meaning, can be difficult to detect. For example, consider Illustrative Item 3.5.

Illustrative Item 3.5.

Read the passage below and answer the question that follows.

The soft, confident, quiet way in which Sam Carr spoke made Alfred start to button his coat nervously. He felt sure his face was white. Sam Carr usually said, "Good night," brusquely, without looking up. In this six months he had been working in the drugstore Alfred had never heard his employer speak softly like that. His heart began to beat so loud it was hard for him to get his breath.

What does **brusquely** mean in this paragraph?

- A. abruptly
  - B. quietly
  - C. nervously
  - D. shyly

The objective intended for the item is a commonly used one: Determine a particular word's meaning from the context of a given paragraph. Here, however, the word *brusquely*, which usually has one meaning (i.e., "abruptly"), by the context has another (i.e., "quietly"), thereby causing it to be incongruent with its intended skill. If, as intended, *brusquely* is an unfamiliar word at this level, the examinee will have trouble. The meaning is not evident from the context as the skill stipulates. In fact, the context would suggest response alternative B as the answer rather than A.

Practice in Determining Congruence

As can be seen, examining items for congruence often requires intense scrutiny of the item and its objective. By now, the reader probably realizes that judging a mismatch is not always obvious. Practice will help attune one to the complexities and nuances of language that affect an item's degree of congruence to an objective. To assist the reader, a few more examples are offered to help one recognize the subtleties involved in gauging item-objective congruence, as well as to garner an appreciation for this important ingredient of item validity.

Consider an objective that is typical of many in achievement tests: Solve problems requiring estimation in consumer, geometric, and physical situations. Illustrative Item 3.6 is meant to assess this objective. But does it really? Study this item and determine whether you think it does.

Illustrative Item 3.6.

Which is the best estimate in feet of the circumference of a circular pool with a radius of 2.2 feet?

    A. 5

  • B. 15

    C. 25

    D. 50

At first glance, one may be tempted to believe that this item is a good match to the objective. After all (one may reason), the match exists because both the objective and the item contain the word *estimation*. However, upon close inspection of the item, one realizes that in order to arrive at a correct answer, examinees would not estimate. In fact, examinees are required to calculate. Further, the item assumes that examinees know the formula for circumference and the approximate value for *pi*, knowledge not specified in the objective. Rounding off *pi* to 3 and using 2.2 for radius gives an answer of 12, which is not an option. Using 3.14 for *pi* and 2.2 for the radius gives an answer of 13.816, which is much closer to 15. It becomes clear upon scrutiny that this item is indeed confusing. The complexity of thinking and subtleties of language explained in these sample items are common.

Now, examine the problem of item-objective congruence by looking at three similar items, all intended to assess the same objective. We will see which item is best suited to this objective: Study the causes of soil erosion in an area, analyze the problems, and choose the appropriate action to prevent further erosion. Read Illustrative Item 3.7 and decide whether you believe it provides a good measure of the objective.

Illustrative Item 3.7.

The Dust Bowl in the Great Plains region was the most dramatic example of wind erosion in the United States. How have people in that area prevented this from happening again?

    A. planting trees to form windbreaks
    B. plowing regularly with tractors
-   C. irrigating the region
    D. building many houses

Close comparison of the item with the objective shows that the item is a poor measure of the objective. The objective asks for an analysis of methods, but Illustrative Item 3.7 is a historical question rather than an analysis. The stem might just as well ask which action would best prevent wind erosion—the response alternative with "wind" (option A) being correct.

Now, consider the same objective but addressed by another item, Illustrative Item 3.8. This item has greater congruence to the skill than did Illustrative Item 3.7, but it still does not achieve very strong congruence. In this item the actual skill required to answer the item is more general than the one the item is supposed to assess. The stem might just as well have asked which action would increase erosion and left out the notion of its frequency (viz., "usually").

Illustrative Item 3.8.

How do human activities usually increase soil erosion?
- A. prevent natural erosion
- B. increase the sediment in streams
- • C. deplete soil fertility
- D. remove the vegetative cover

Finally, consider Illustrative Item 3.9. This item is a good measure of the objective because it is well-matched. It presents a situation particular to an area (as is stipulated in the objective), it requires an analysis (another stipulation), and it presents response alternatives which are plausible solutions to preventing further erosion. It is a good test item.

Illustrative Item 3.9.

In a generally flat, sandy area, which is the best method of conserving soil?
- A. clearing forests
- • B. planting shelter belts
- C. plowing grasslands
- D. controlling weeds

From these examples, one can see that determining the degree of congruence between a particular test item and a given objective or skill is neither obvious nor easy. It requires careful attention to the objective and to the item. A practiced eye will help. Such attention and practice are important requisites to becoming a writer of good test items.

CONCLUSION

This chapter presented information necessary for determining the content for test items as well as discussion of why this information is important. It described the basic tenets of validity and explained the relationship of these concepts to writing test items. As discussed, understanding these issues is an integral part of determining the content for test items.

Also, determining the content for items implies a scheme for organizing the content. To that end, this chapter offered a thorough description of test content specifications and item specifications. Finally, and importantly, there was a rigorous discussion of the importance of congruence between an item and the objective which it is intended to assess. Several examples elucidating various aspects of this consideration were offered.

This chapter and the preceding one described characteristics of items with special attention to their theoretical underpinnings. Such a complete understanding of items sets the stage for the following chapters, which focus upon several important practical considerations for writing items and editorial rules for formatting items. When set in a theoretical context, practical steps have meaning and can be undertaken with confidence that they will yield items of merit. We are now ready to turn to such practical considerations.

Chapter 4

Starting to Write Items: Practical Considerations

INTRODUCTION

The preceding chapters described features of test items from a theoretical perspective. These discussions included a variety of topics, from a comprehensive description of a test item to various analyses involving requisite characteristics and conditions for good test items. The information in these chapters provides a foundation of knowledge necessary if one is to construct items that will contribute to sound measurement.

This chapter brings a change in focus. The concern here is with practical matters the item writer faces when actually preparing items. The chapter identifies and discusses several of the most common practical considerations faced by item writers as they approach their task. It begins with a discussion of the importance of precise wording in test items and suggests sources to which one may turn for assistance in improving one's writing. It continues by addressing several pertinent topics, including using taxonomies in writing test items, deciding upon the optimal number of response alternatives, choosing whether to use "all of the above" or "none of the above," knowing when to construct complex response alternatives, determining the appropriate verb and direct object for an item's stem, and more. Throughout the chapter, examples of test items are used to illustrate particular points.

The discussions in this chapter will typically focus on items in the multiple-choice format; however, nearly all of the issues addressed in this chapter apply to a variety of item formats.

Of course, there are scores of practical considerations for the conscientious item writer to bear in mind when preparing test items, so the specific concerns addressed in this chapter are only a few of the possible considerations that could be addressed. As such, they are suggestive of a larger list of issues. But, they are the most commonly faced practical issues.

Further, the considerations addressed in this chapter will be augmented by the information presented in Chapters 5 and 6. In those chapters, the focus will be on many formatting and stylistic considerations, most of which are particular to a specific item format. Although the issues addressed in the later chapters are different, they interact with the practical concerns addressed in this chapter.

By a superficial glance at the title of this chapter, one may be tempted to imagine that this is the "important stuff" that the item writer really needs to know and that by a quick check of the contents of this chapter one could sit down and actually start to write test items. Although knowing how to handle these practical concerns when writing items will assist one beginning the task, the reader is cautioned from being too eager to start writing items before a requisite background has been acquired.

The following topics are covered in this chapter:

- clarity of expression in test items
- sources for the elements of style
- taxonomies of cognitive processing levels
- distinctness between an item's stem and the response alternatives
- importance of an interrogative stem
- the correct response in absolutely correct and best-answer types of items

- the optimal number of response alternatives
- plausibility in response alternatives
- using "all of the above" or "none of the above" as response alternatives
- specific determiners
- complex response alternatives
- time examinees need to respond to items

THE IMPORTANCE OF GOOD WRITING IN TEST ITEMS

All wordsmiths—novelists, essayists, students, teachers, researchers, journalists, and others—know first-hand that writing is difficult. It requires a thorough familiarity with the subject, proficiency in language mechanics (e.g., grammar, spelling, and punctuation), and careful contemplation of the words used. Review and rewriting is usually needed, sometimes even three, four, or five times, before clarity of expression is achieved. Further, technical writing—such as preparing test items—is especially difficult because it demands an extraordinarily high degree of precision in language use.

In a test item, every word counts. The item writer, unlike the novelist or essayist, cannot rely upon a larger context to assist in conveying the meaning of a word, sentence, or passage. Subtleties of expression are rarely possible in the brief wording of most test items. The examinee must derive from the sentence stem the exact meaning intended by the item writer, and in the response alternatives the examinee should be able to realize distinct and reasonable solutions. Communication between the item writer and the examinee is crucial if a measure of the particular construct is to yield valid score interpretations.

The stem for most items consists only of a single sentence, which must present examinees with a specific problem or situation that demands a particular response. By its very brevity, there is little room for ambiguity in wording. It should not include superfluous or irrelevant words. Tautologies, repetitious phrasing, and words with plural meanings should be avoided. And, of course, the punctuation must be technically correct.

Writers refer to these elements of writing, and the myriad other ingredients of style, as language mechanics, syntax, and diction. Language mechanics refers to uniform use of punctuation, citations, and other editorial rules, whereas syntax is the arrangement of the words in a sentence, paragraph, or passage to achieve clarity of expression. Diction is the choice of the precise word that most clearly communicates an intended meaning. When preparing an item, writers should scrupulously follow the rules of writing included in good mechanics, syntax, and diction. Some sources for standard elements of style are cited in a later section of this chapter.

One overarching rule for good writing in a test item's stem is the simple old dictum, repeatedly told to many of us by a caring teacher in our early days of learning how to write effectively: "Specific is terrific!" Its meaning is self-evident, but implementing it is another, and very difficult, thing. Regardless of the difficulty of achieving specificity in writing an item's stem, this rule should always be the guide.

In addition to precision, other aspects of language must be considered when preparing test items. Item writers, like all human beings, can inadvertently contaminate their writing with stereotypical, prejudicial, or biased language. Although usually unintended, such offensive language can distract examinees from the problem presented in the item. While it is appropriate to express one's opinions and feelings in some types of writing (editorial writing, for example), there is no place for opinion or evocative language in a test item. The vigilant item writer will carefully avoid all offensive words and phrases.

Correct use of language in an item's response alternatives is just as important as in the stem. While some specialized rules of editorial style are prescribed for an item's response alternatives—for example, when to use incomplete sentences (these rules are described in Chapter 5 for items in the multiple-choice format and in Chapter 6 for items in other formats)—the language mechanics, syntax, and diction should always promote clarity of expression. And, of course, the grammatical construction of the response alternative should be consistent with the leading stem.

Some examples will help to reinforce the importance of good writing in test items. First, consider an item that is not well written, Illustrative Item 4.1. This item contains wording that is ambiguous, making it difficult for examinees to respond. The phrase (used as a verbal) in the stem is to proceed, but given the context, it is imprecise as to whether it refers to Ted's dilemma about his broken-down car, or his problem in getting to work. If one surmises that the intention of the item is to address Ted's automobile dilemma, then response B could be selected because it is the only response alternative that offers Ted a solution to his car problems. If, however, one construes the stem's question as referring to Ted's alternatives for getting to work, then any of the response alternatives could be selected with equal justification. This ambiguity is the result of imprecise wording.

Illustrative Item 4.1.

Ted Sullivan's old car just broke down, and it will cost a great deal to repair. He must have a car to get to work each day. Which would be the best way for Ted to proceed?

    A. finding a cheap used car quickly
    B. fixing the old car because new cars cost a lot of money
    C. thinking carefully about his transportation needs
    D. using public transportation because it is cheaper

Further, Illustrative Item 4.1 contains unacceptable wording beyond the imprecision already described in the stem. Several of the response alternatives also contain imprecise wording. For example, alternative C is grossly inadequate as a plausible distractor because the wording is too vague for an examinee to deduce anything from it. And, response alternative D needs a referent for the comparative form: e.g., "using public transportation because it is cheaper than fixing-up Ted's old car." Without doubt, Illustrative Item 4.1 is poorly worded, and it does demonstrate the importance of precise-wording to test items by showing the confusion and errors that can result when items are not well written.

There are any number of ways to improve the wording for Illustrative Item 4.1. One improved version is given in Illustrative Item 4.2. Juxtapose this wording with the earlier version. Immediately one senses that with the improved wording, the accuracy of measurement is improved.

Illustrative Item 4.2.

Ted Sullivan's old car just broke down, and he has discovered that it will cost more money to repair than he has available for that purpose. He must have a car to get to work each day. Which would be the best way for Ted to get to work tomorrow?

   A. buy a new car
   B. fix the old car regardless of how much it costs
 • C. arrange to get a ride with a co-worker
   D. walk to work

Illustrative Item 4.3 is another example of imprecise wording in test items, but in this example the faulty wording creates a different situation than was presented in Illustrative Item 4.1. In 4.3, the problem is that the response alternatives do not directly address the item's question in a significant way. Study the ambiguities in this item.

Illustrative Item 4.3 can be repaired in a number of ways. First, the information presented in the stem's initial sentence should be directly tied to the question. One fix for this could be to combine sentences one and two as follows: "Mr. Ray is considering using his

$30,000 in savings to buy the grocery store where he works. What is Mr. Ray's most likely result if he purchases the store?"

The problem with the response alternatives is, of course, that there is insufficient information to select one among them as "most likely." Alternatives A, B, and D could each result.

Illustrative Item 4.3.

Mr. Ray has $30,000 in savings. He wants to buy the grocery store where he works. If he buys the store, which result is most likely?

    A. He will make more money than he does by working there for someone else.

    B. He will probably loose money and go out of business.

    C. He could either make money or loose money.

    D. I le will probably double his investment within a year.

Response alternative C is so imprecise as to provide no useful information for either selecting or rejecting it. The item is poorly constructed and should be discarded or rewritten entirely.

These examples illustrate the importance of unambiguous, well-considered wording for test items. The careful item writer should use full diligence to ensure clarity of expression in test items. Strategies to improve writing in particular item formats will be addressed in the following section, as well as elsewhere in this chapter and in Chapters 5 and 6.

SOURCES FOR INFORMATION ON WRITING STYLE

Although writing with precision and clarity of expression is difficult, item writers need not feel alone when pondering how to achieve good writing. Many excellent references are available from which one can seek guidance. Below is a list of some popular sources of information on writing style and usage. The list is annotated to assist the reader in selecting the source that may be most helpful.

- Bates, J. D. (1980). *Writing with precision: How to write so that you cannot possibly be misunderstood* (3rd ed.). Washington, D.C.: Acropolis Books.

  Describes fundamentals of writing, offering practical advice on preparing specific kinds of materials.

- Copperud, R. H. (1980). *American usage and style: The consensus*. New York: Van Nostrand Reinhold.

  Cites language experts and rhetoricians to describe common usage problems from various points of view.

- Fowler, H. F. (1965). *A dictionary of modern English usage* (2nd ed.). New York: Oxford University Press.

  The classic dictionary of usage and punctuation.

- Hodges, J. C., & Whitten, M. E. (1986). *Harbrace college handbook* (10th ed.). New York: Harcourt Brace Jovanovich.

  Popular reference on many college campuses to style and punctuation.

- Scott, Foresman and Company. (1977). *Reference handbook of grammar and usage*. New York: Author.

  Complete reference on punctuation, citations, and general usage.

- Strunk, W. Jr., & White, E. B. (1982). *The elements of style* (3rd ed.). New York: Macmillan.

  Small but classic book which discusses many practical features for producing clear, focused writing.

- Tarabian, K. L. (1973). *A manual for writers* (4th ed.). Chicago: U. of Chicago Press.

  Popular, handy reference on style and usage; condensed from University of Chicago's Manual of Style.

- *Webster's standard American style manual.* (1985). Springfield: Merriam-Webster.

  Complete reference on style with emphasis upon American English.

Many experienced technical writers routinely depend upon sourcebooks for information on usage. It is common to find two, three, or even more of the books from the above list (or books like them) on the experienced writer's desk, with many of the pages dog-eared from frequent use. Further, some individuals find one or two particular books especially helpful to them in their work, and they develop favorites. This is an excellent attitude to adopt. Explore these titles, as well as other ones, with the intention of adopting one or two to become "old friends."

Of course, standard equipment for every writer is a good dictionary and a good thesaurus. Many excellent ones are readily available. Some especially good ones are:

- *Webster's third new international dictionary.* (1981). Springfield: Merriam-Webster.

- *Webster's ninth new collegiate dictionary.* (1984). Springfield: Merriam-Webster.

- Chapman, R. L. (Ed.). (1977). *Roget's international thesaurus* (4th ed.). New York: Harper & Row.

Computer Dictionaries and Thesauruses

A further note about dictionaries and computers is needed. It is, of course, common today for writers to work directly on a computer, using a word-processor to record their writing in a convenient way. And, most current word-processors have a built-in dictionary or spelling checker. Some even have a thesaurus. While it is expedient to use these electronic programs, one is cautioned from over-dependence on computer-based spelling-checkers and thesaurus programs. Currently, most of these programs are incomplete and inadequate, and some even have numerous errors. (The errors frequently occur because some of these programs rely upon algorithms of logic to check the spelling of words rather than word lists; and, some others that do use word lists have misspelled words in their lists!) An additional shortcoming of electronic spelling-checkers is that they do not catch misspellings like "that" for "than" or "examine" for "examinee." Despite the convenience of word-processors, the skilled item writer will always have a good, book-copy dictionary and a thesaurus handy.

USING TAXONOMIES IN WRITING ITEMS

It was explained in Chapter 3 that despite the popularity of using Bloom's taxonomy of educational objectives to categorize test items into levels of increasingly complex cognitive processing, the actual practice of writing items that tap the higher cognitive functioning levels is very difficult. To facilitate the instrumentation of the taxonomy at the more advanced levels of Bloom's taxonomy, several writers offer lists of verbs and direct objects useful for writing sentence stems which could be used to elicit examinee responses at particular levels. One such list, by Metfessel, Michael, and Kirsner (1969), is presented in Table 4.1. Of course, to comprehend the information presented in the table one must understand the cognitive levels cited along the left column. This information is provided in Chapter 3 in the section titled "Identifying Levels of Cognitive Processing." The numbering system used in Table 4.1 parallels Bloom's numbers.

This table can be extremely helpful to item writers by prodding their thinking and illustrating relationships. For example, notice in Table 4.1 the examples of verb infinitives and direct objects for sentence stems. The examples offered at the lowest level, Knowledge, are self-evident. For verbs, some offerings are to define, to distinguish, to recall, and to identify; and, for direct objects, some examples are terms, facts, and properties.

Table 4.1 Instrumentation of the Taxonomy of Educational Objectives: Cognitive Domain

		Key Words	
Taxonomy Classification		**Examples of Infinitives**	**Examples of Direct Objects**
1.00	Knowledge		
1.10	Knowledge of Specifics		
1.11	Knowledge of Terminology	to define, to distinguish to acquire, to identify, to recall, to recognize	vocabulary, terms, terminology, meaning(s), definitions, referents, elements
1.12	Knowledge of Specific Facts	to recall, to recognize, to acquire, to identify	facts, factual information, (sources), (names), (dates), (events), (persons), (places), (time periods), properties, examples, phenomena
1.20	Knowledge of Ways and Means of Dealing with Specifics		
1.21	Knowledge of Conventions	to recall, to identify to recognize, to acquire	form(s), conventions, uses, usage, rules, ways, devices, symbols, representations, styles(s), format(s)
1.22	Knowledge of Trends, Sequences	to recall, to recognize, to acquire, to identify	action(s), processes, movement(s), continuity, development(s), trend(s) sequence(s), causes, relationship(s), forces, influences
1.23	Knowledge of Classifications and Categories	to recall, to recognize, to acquire, to identify	area(s), type(s), feature(s), class(es), set(s), division(s), arrangement(s), classification(s), category/ categories
1.24	Knowledge of Criteria	to recall, to recognize, to acquire, to identify	criteria, basics, elements
1.25	Knowledge of Methodology	to recall, to recognize, to acquire, to identify	methods, techniques, approaches, uses, procedures, treatments
1.30	Knowledge of the Universals and Abstractions in a Field		
1.31	Knowledge of Principles, Generalizations	to recall, to recognize, to acquire, to identify	principle(s), generalization(s) proposition(s), fundamentals, laws, principal elements, implication(s)

From Instrumentation of Bloom's Taxonomies for the Writing of Educational Objectives by N.S. Metfessel, W.B. Michael, and D.A. Kirsner, 1969, *Psychology in the Schools, 6*, (pp. 227-231).

Table 4.1 *(continued)*

	Key Words	
Taxonomy Classification	**Examples of Infinitives**	**Examples of Direct Objects**
1.32 Knowledge of Theories and Structures	to recall, to recognize, to acquire, to identify	theories, bases, inter-relations, structure(s), organization(s), formulation(s)
2.00 Comprehension		
2.10 Translation	to translate, to transform, to give in own words, to illustrate, to prepare, to read, to represent, to change, to rephrase, to restate	meaning(s), sample(s), definitions, abstractions, representations, words, phrases
2.20 Interpretation	to interpret, to reorder, to rearrange, to differ-entiate, to distinguish, to make, to draw to explain, to demonstrate	relevancies, relationships, essentials, aspects, new view(s), qualifications, conclusions, methods, theories, abstractions
2.30 Extrapolation	to estimate, to infer, to conclude, to predict, to differentiate, to determine, to extend, to interpolate, to extrap-olate, to fill in, to draw	consequences, implications, conclusions, factors, ramifications, meanings, corollaries, effects, probabilities
3.00 Application	to apply, to generalize, to relate, to chose, to develop, to organize, to use, to employ, to transfer, to restructure, to classify	principles, laws, conclusions, effects, methods, theories, abstractions, situations, generalizations, processes, phenomena, procedures
4.00 Analysis		
4.10 Analysis fo Elements	to distinguish, to detect, to identify, to classify, to discriminate, to recognize, to categorize, to deduce	elements, hypothesis/hypotheses, conclusions, assumptions, statements (of fact), statements (of intent), arguments, particulars
4.20 Analysis of Relationships	to analyze, to contrast, to compare, to distinguish, to deduce	relationships, interrelations, relevance, relevancies, themes, evidence, fallacies, arguments, cause-effect(s), consistency/consistencies, parts, ideas, assumptions

Table 4.1 *(continued)*

Key Words

Taxonomy Classification	Examples of Infinitives	Examples of Direct Objects
4.30 Analysis of Organizational Principles	to analyze, to distinguish, to detect, to deduce	form(s), pattern(s), purpose(s point(s) of view(s), techniques, bias(es), structure(s) theme(s), arrangement(s), organization(s)
5.00 Synthesis		
5.10 Production of a Unique Communication	to write, to tell, to relate, to produce, to constitute, to transmit, to originate, to modify, to docum~nt	structure(s), pattern(s) product(s), performance(s), design(s), work(s), communications, effort(s), specifics, composition(s)
5.20 production of a Plan, or Proposed Set of Operations	to propose, to plan, to produce, to design, to modify, to specify	plan(s), objectives, specifiction(s), schematic(s), operations way(s), solution(s), means
5.30 Derivation of a Set of Abstract Relations	to produce, to derive, to develop, to combine, to organize, to synthesize, to classify, deduce, to develop, to formulate, to modify	phenomena, taxonomies, concept(s), scheme(s), theories, relationships, abstractions, generalizations, hypothesis/hypotheses, perceptions, ways, discoveries
6.00 Evaluation		
6.10 Judgments in Terms of Internal Evidence	to judge, to argue, to validate, to assess, to decide	accuracy/accuracies, consistency/consistencies, fallacies, reliability, flaws, errors, precision, exactness
6.20 Judgments in Terms of External Criteria	to judge, to argue, to consider, to compare, to contrast, to standardize, to appraise	ends, means, efficiency, economy/economies, utility, alternatives, courses of action, standards, theories, generalizations

Item writers need not necessarily employ the specific words from the list; rather, they will find the actions required by the suggested verbs and direct objects as appropriate to assessing a particular level of cognitive function. This point can be seen by studying several items. For example, writing test items at the lowest level, Knowledge, could be a classifying activity, such as placing events in chronological order. Illustrative Item 4.4 exhibits an item at this very low level of cognitive functioning.

Illustrative Item 4.4.

Which event occurred first?

    A. Civil War
-   B. American Revolution
    C. abolishing of slavery
    D. writing of the constitution

Most items at the Knowledge level require only rote memory and seldom present novel ideas to examinees. Still, such items can be extremely useful for measuring particular facts. This kind of item is very common on tests of academic achievement as well as on licensing and certification examinations. It also represents the kind of low-level cognitive tasks requested of examinees by many novice item writers.

While such low-level items are popular and useful, they are also limiting. The inferences yielded about examinee performance are typically restricted to a given set of factual information. These items reveal almost nothing about an examinee's level of cognitive functioning. To garner evidence for this sort of information, the item writer must move into the higher levels of the taxonomy.

Writing Items at the Higher Taxonomic Levels

Continuing with the examples of verbs and direct objects for sentence stems presented in Table 4.1, examine another test item, this time at the level of Analysis. According to Bloom's taxonomy of cognitive processing levels, Analysis is the fourth highest of six processing-level categories. Illustrative Item 4.5 displays an item which may elicit this level of cognitive functioning from examinees.

In this item, the examinee is required to classify the elements of the paragraph and deduce the missing organizational characteristic. As one can readily realize, comparing elements of correct English composition and discovering interrelationships are necessary to

---

Illustrative Item 4.5.

It was my first camping experience and I wanted to prove that I could do my share. The leader assigned each of us to a group. My group first unpacked the tents and camping equipment. Next, we put up the tents and set out the necessary equipment for preparing dinner.

What characteristic is **not** evident in this paragraph?

    A. effective sentence
- B. concluding sentence

    C. logical sequence
    D. related supporting details

arrive at a correct response to the item. The examples of verb infinitives and direct objects presented in Table 4.1 suggest these activities for this level of cognitive skill.

Next, examine Illustrative Item 4.6, which draws upon a still higher taxonomic level, Evaluation. This item is from a test used to license paramedics for practice in the field in emergency situations where evaluation and judgment are needed. The item requires one to analyze the internal evidence of a given medical situation, synthesize the information structures, and form an evaluative judgment. In sum, one is required to use all of the cognitive processes, including

---

Illustrative Item 4.6.

A 45-year-old male, weighing 220 pounds, complains of severe substernal chest pain. Oxygen has been started and an IV line established. The patient suddenly becomes unresponsive and the monitor shows ventricular tachycardia. There is no carotid pulse palpable. What treatment is indicated at this time?

- A. Defibrillate at 300 joules.

    B. Administer lidocaine (Xylocaine).
    C. Administer sodium bicarbonate.
    D. Perform synchronized cardioversion.

the highest taxonomic level delineated by Bloom, Evaluation, to solve this rather complex problem. Again, notice that Table 4.1 can offer the expert item writer suggestions for preparing items that tap this taxonomic level.

Independence of Subject Matter from Cognitive Processing Level

Another important consideration if one wishes to use Table 4.1 for constructing test items is that the subject content for items will vary in sophistication independent of the level of cognitive processing required of examinees to elicit a correct response. In other words, the two considerations for determining the content for a test item—subject matter and level of cognitive processing—are independent. Low cognitive-processing-level items may include very simple content or they may include rather sophisticated content. Conversely, an item designed to assess complex processing skills may be contextually set in either simple or complicated subject matter.

It is a common mistake to presume that every low-level cognitive skill yields a very simple-minded item. To illustrate the point, consider Illustrative Item 4.7 which contains rather sophisticated subject content but requires only a low level of cognitive processing.

Illustrative Item 4.7.

What does it mean for an individual to apply for a *writ of habeas corpus*?

    A. A person who has been arrested may refuse to submit to a body search.
- B. A person in jail may ask to be taken before a judge, who will decide if he is being held lawfully.

    C. A person has the right to say what he believes without any penalty.

    D. A person may worship with others without interference by the state.

Or, examine two more items, one designed for third graders and another designed for tenth grade students, Illustrative Items 4.8 and 4.9. Note particularly that while the content of the items is very different—each appropriate to the intended audience—they both require from their respective examinees a similar level of cognitive processing, in this case, Evaluation, or level 6, the highest level in Bloom's system of classifying cognitive skills.

Illustrative Item 4.8.

A newly built bridge connects the cities of Greenwood and Saxton. What change is likely to happen in Saxton because of the new bridge?

- A. More people from Greenwood may shop in Saxton.
  B. All the people of Saxton will move to Greenwood.
  C. The gas stations in Saxton will close.
  D. Mail service will stop between Saxton and Greenwood.

Illustrative Item 4.9.

Read the paragraph below (from the Mayflower Compact) to answer the question below.

"We combine ourselves together into a civil body politick for our better ordering and preservation . . . and do enact . . . such just and equal laws . . . as shall be thought most convenient for the general good of the colony, unto which we promise all due submission and obedience."

Which principle of government is described in this quotation?

   A. equal opportunity for all
   B. submission and loyalty to the king
   C. importance of religious freedom
- D. obedience of the community's laws

The item intended for third graders, Illustrative Item 4.8, requires evaluation from children of normal development who are about eight or nine years old. It may not require such complex cognitive processing for an adult to arrive at a correct solution, but that is irrelevant to its cognitive processing level for third graders because the item is not intended to assess adult cognitive processing.

Similarly, the other item, Illustrative Item 4.9, written for tenth grade students, also requires evaluation, but this time evaluation from students of normal development who are in the tenth grade. Obviously, almost no third grader could respond correctly to Illustrative Item 4.9 (except by chance), but that is, again, irrelevant.

To further illustrate the point that the level of cognitive processing required of examinees to respond to a particular test item is independent of the item's content, consider two more items, Illustrative Items 4.10 and 4.11. One item is of comparatively simple subject content but which requires examinees to exhibit Bloom's highest cognitive taxonomic level and another item is of relatively

---

Illustrative Item 4.10.

Use the picture to answer the question below.

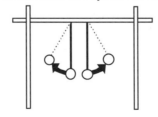

Which fact would account for these pith balls moving away from each other?

    A. They are uncharged.
-    B. They have the same charge.
    C. They have different charges.
    D. One is charged and one uncharged.

sophisticated content but which requires a lower level of cognitive functioning.

Illustrative Item 4.10 is comparatively simple in content—merely two balls swinging in opposite directions—but requires examinees to perform a very high level of cognitive processing. The examinee must appraise the internal evidence, consider alternatives based upon prior knowledge external to the item (viz., the polarity of electrical charges), and arrive at a conclusion. This is, indeed, an item that requires sophisticated thinking.

Contrast 4.10 with the subject content and requisite cognitive skill of Illustrative Item 4.11. In this item the content is more

---

Illustrative Item 4.11.

The graph below shows the relationship of temperature and time as constant heat is applied to an ice cube.

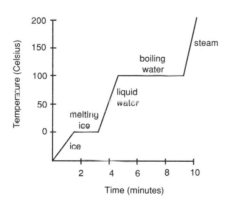

Which statement is consistent with the graph?

- A. The temperature of melting ice remains constant until all of the ice is melted.
- B. The rate of boiling equals the rate of ice melting.
- C. The same amount of heat is required to melt ice as to boil water.
- D. More heat is required to melt ice than is required to boil water.

difficult because one must analyze the elements of the graph to deduce a correct relationship between the effect of the variables time and temperature on physical states of water. But the level of cognitive processing is less difficult since only an analysis is needed to arrive at the correct response.

As can be seen in these examples, the subject matter used with items can vary in difficulty just as the level of cognitive processing required by examinees to respond to that item can differ. But, they are independent considerations when constructing test items.

Suggestions for Writing Items with Other Cognitive Processing Taxonomies

The Framework for Instructional Objectives of Hannah and Michaelis (1977) is another schema for organizing intellectual processes. This plan's theoretical basis was discussed in Chapter 3. And, just as Table 4.1 suggested verbs and direct objects for item stems to tap specified taxonomic levels for Bloom's scheme, Table 4.2 offers an instrumentation for the Hannah and Michaelis' framework. However, Table 4.2 is not merely a Hannah and Michaelis restatement of Table 4.1; instead, Hannah and Michaelis describe a slightly more sophisticated method of instrumentation, which will be presented in two tables, Tables 4.2 and 4.3. It may be worthwhile to fully explain these tables so that their utility to item writers can be more easily grasped.

First, notice in Table 4.2 a list of illustrative assessment devices of key abilities is presented. The list is organized around the ten Intellectual Processes of the FIO taxonomy: Interpreting, Comparing, Classifying, Generalizing, Inferring, Analyzing, Synthesizing, Hypothesizing, Predicting, and Evaluating (cf. Table 3.6). Illustrative assessment devices focus on "key abilities" for each level of the taxonomy; and, these are paralleled by "questions to appraise" each level.

Table 4.2 Illustrative Assessment Devices for Key Abilities

Interpreting

1. Key abilities in interpreting

Defines terms or symbols
States the main idea and related details
States or illustrates relationships (e.g., growing season and
    climate)
Translates into another form
Makes a summary or states a conclusion
Describes feelings that are aroused

2. Questions to appraise interpreting

Is the meaning of terms and symbols clear?
Has a way of stating or illustrating the main idea been identi-
    fied?
Have details that support the main idea been identified?
Have alternative ways of expressing the main idea been
    identified?
Has attention been given to making a conclusion or summary?
Has consideration been given to feelings?

Comparing

1. Key abilities in comparing

Identifies bases for making a comparison
Identifies specific features of items being compared
Describes similarities and differences
Summarizes similarities and differences

2. Questions to appraise comparing

Have reasonable points of comparison been identified?
Have the main features of each item been identified?
Are likenesses and differences clear?
Have features to be included in a summary been identified?

From *A Comprehensive Framework for Instructional Objectives* (p. 81ff) by L.S.
Hannah and J. U. Michaelis, 1977, Reading, Mass: Addison-Wesley. Adapted by
permission.

Table 4.2 *(continued)*

Classifying

1. *Key abilities in classifying*

    Stating a clear purpose for grouping
    Describing likenesses and differences
    Stating a basis for grouping
    Arranging groups which do not overlap
    Naming each group

2. *Questions to appraise classifying*

    Is there s clear purpose for grouping?
    Have likenesses and differences among items been identified?
    Have characteristics for grouping been defined?
    Have mutually exclusive groups been identified?
    Has a name been stated for each group?

Generalizing

1. *Key abilities in generalizing*

    Identifies evidence and key concepts
    Identifies and states the common or general idea
    Bases the stated idea on the data but does not go beyond
        them
    States facts or instances that can support the general idea
    Tells how the stated general idea checks with previously
        studied situations

2. *Questions to appraise generalizing*

    Have essential facts been gathered?
    Have common or general elements been identified?
    Have relationships been identified?
    Have facts been identified that support the generalization?
    Has consideration been given to checking the generalization?

Inferring

1. *Key abilities in inferring*

    Describes the facts and situation
    States a pertinent generalization
    States a reasonable extension of what is given
    Bases the extension on a sound generalization that fits the
        situation

Table 4.2 *(continued)*

States how the inference is related to what is given

2. Questions to appraise inferring

Have the facts and the situation been clarified?
Has a pertinent generalization been identified?
Is the extension of what is given reasonable? Does it make
sense?
Can the generalization or premises used to go beyond the data
be stated?
Has the inference been double-checked against what is given?
Can reasons be stated in support of the inference?

Analyzing

1. Key abilities in analyzing

Describes and defines main parts
Describes cause-effect or other relationships
Describes structure or organization
States how parts are related to each other and to the whole
Groups data under each part, relationship, or structural
component

2. Questions to appraise analyzing

Have main parts or elements been identified?
Have relationships among parts been identified?
Is the structure or organization clear?
Can the way the parts fit together be described?
Can data be placed under each part, relationship, or structural
feature?

Synthesizing

1. Key abilities in synthesizing

States the purpose for the activity
Selects and states the main parts to be included
Describes relationships among the parts
Selects and describes a verbal, pictorial, or other appropriate
means of presentation
Plans an exhibit, report, model, or other effective form of
presentation

Table 4.2 *(continued)*

---

2. *Questions to appraise synthesizing*

How well has the purpose been achieved?
Have the essential parts been included?
Are the relationships among the parts clear?
How effective is the means of presentation?
How effective is the form of presentation?

Hypothesizing

1. *Key abilities in hypothesizing*

States a proposition that is testable and guides the search for
   data
States a proposition that is highly probable in light of estab-
   lished facts, a principle or a theory
States the hypothesis so that it may be tested using available
   procedures and data
States the proposition so that it applies to most or all cases
Collects data in a systematic manner
Presents an analysis of the data to confirm (or not confirm) the
   hypothesis

2. *Questions to appraise hypothesizing*

How well does the hypothesis serve as a guide to collection of
   data?
What data, principle, or theory serves as the basis for the
   hypothesis?
Can the hypothesis be tested by means of available procedures and data?
Does it apply to most or all cases rather that to a particular
   instance?
Has adequate information been collected in a systematic
   manner?
Has an analysis been made of the data to confirm or not
   confirm the hypothesis?

Predicting

1. *Key abilities in predicting*

Identifies and weights main conditions or factors
Collects and analyzes related evidence
Describes trends and new developments

Table 4.2 *(continued)*

Identifies cause-effect relationships
Selects or states a theory, rule, or principle to explain
  phenomena studied
Identifies possible outcomes or consequences
States level of probability of occurrence of the prediction

2. *Questions to appraise predicting*

Have conditions or factors been stated and weighted?
Is the evidence adequate? What additional evidence is
  needed?
Have trends and new developments been considered?
Are relationships between causes and possible effects clear?
Have possible consequences of the predicted change been
  stated?
Have strong and weak aspects of the prediction been consid-
  ered?

Evaluating

1. *Key abilities in evaluating*

Defines the item to be appraised
States a purpose or reason for evaluation
Defines standards or criteria
Applies standards consistently
Gathers and records evidence for each standard
Supports judgement by citing evidence or reasons

2. *Question to appraise evaluating*

Has the object or activity to be appraised been defined?
Has the purpose of the appraisal been clarified?
Have evaluation standards been applied?
Are reasons or data given to support the judgement?

Examination of one portion of the table will help one to understand its complete organization. For example, under the seventh intellectual process, Synthesizing, a key ability is, "Selects and states the main parts to be included." This could be the ability desired for assessment of the synthesizing cognitive function. And, under the questions to appraise is, "Are the relationships among the parts clear."

Recognizing these components in items can be enormously help-ful to item writers. Suppose, for example, the writer wishes to tap the synthesizing intellectual process. The writer could initially prepare an item which requires examinees to select or state the main parts of an entity, as suggested by the key ability. The writer could then examine the item to ensure that the relationship among the parts of the entity are demonstrably clear, as suggested by the appraising questions. When used in this way, the framework can provide the writer assistance in aiming an item at a given cognitive function.

Hannah and Michaelis' framework provides writers additional assistance in finding the precise words needed to fit an intellectual process. According to the framework, the key abilities for each level of intellectual functioning are manifest by an individual's behavior, both overtly and covertly. Table 4.3 presents terms suggestive of the overt and covert behaviors for each of the ten intellectual processes. The table also includes the two processes of the precursory function Data Gathering: Observing and Remembering. These two processes will be appropriate for very low-level items. This table is parallel in function to Table 4.1 explained earlier.

From this discussion one can see how test items can be written with the use of a taxonomy. There should not be slavish adherence to a particular level or words, which may inhibit creativity, while conversely there is much to be gained by following the suggestions for tapping specified levels of cognitive processing. The two ap-proaches described here (Bloom and the FIO) can be of enormous values to item writers because they present ideas which the item writer can craft into items with specific characteristics.

Table 4.3 Covert and Overt Behaviors

	Behaviors				
(covert)			*(overt)*		
Observing					
detects	observes		cites	records	
distinguishes	perceives		describes	relates	
finds	picks	a	expresses	reports	
identifies	selects	n	indicates	shares	
isolates	separates	d	lists	states	
locates	-------------		names	-------------	
notes	-------------		points out	-------------	
notices	-------------		points to	-------------	
Remembering					
associates	remembers		chooses	reports	
distinguishes	selects		cites	reproduces	
identifies	-------------	a	describes	restates	
recalls	-------------	n	lists	states	
recognizes	-------------	d	matches	tells	
reconstructs	-------------		names	writes	
			points out	-------------	
			relates	-------------	
			repeats	-------------	
Interpreting					
composes	transforms		demonstrates	renders	
concocts	translates		depicts	rephrases	
converts	-------------		dramatizes	restates	
defines	-------------	a	draws	retells	
estimates	-------------	n	enacts	role plays	
interprets	-------------	d	explains	simulates	
summarizes	-------------		expresses	sketches	
			graphs	states in own words	
			illustrates	tells	
			pantomimes	writes	
			paraphrases	-------------	
			presents	-------------	

From *A Comprehensive Framework for Instructional Objectives* (pp. A-08 to A-20) by L.S. Hannah and J. U. Michaelis, 1977, Reading, Mass: Addison-Wesley. Adapted by permission.

Table 4.3 *(continued)*

	Behaviors		
(covert)		*(overt)*	
Comparing			
detects	locates	cites	points out
differentiates	notes	describes	reports
discriminates	------------	explains	states
distinguishes	------------	expresses	writes
identifies	------------	lists	-----------
		names	-----------
		outlines	-----------
Classifying			
associates	reorders	arranges	places
distiguishes	restructures	catalogs	rearranges
identifies	structures	labels	sorts
orders	------------	names	------------
organizes	------------	outlines	------------
Generalizing			
composes	generates	expresses	states
constructs	makes	identifies	writes
derives	produces	presents	----------
develops	----------	proposes	----------
forms	----------	relates	----------
formulates	----------		
Inferring			
deduces fills in		expresses	states
develops	formulates	identifies	writes
derives	generates	presents	----------
draws	-----------	proposes	----------
extends	-----------	relates	----------
extrapolates	-----------		
Analyzing			
analyzes	examines	cites	relates
breaks down	extracts	describes	states
deduces	identifies	expresses	writes
detects	points out	illustrates	----------
differentiates	separates	lists	----------
discriminates	-------------	outlines	----------
distinguishes	-------------	points out	----------
divides	-------------		

Between the covert and overt columns, vertically: a n d

Table 4.3 *(continued)*

	Behaviors			
(covert)			*(overt)*	
Synthesizing				
composes	integrates		assembles	proposes
creates	organizes		constructs	puts together
derives	originates	a	depicts	relates
designs	plans	n	explains	reports
develops	synthesizes	d	expresses	tells
devises	-------------		illustrates	writes
formulates	-------------		makes	------------
			presents	------------
			produces	------------
Hypothesizing				
composes	formulates		expresses	states
designs	originates	a	identifies writes	
develops	produces	n	presents	---------
devises	-------------	d	proposes	---------
forms	-------------		relates	---------
Predicting				
anticipates	predicts		expresses	states
forecasts	projects	a	identifies	writes
foresees	----------	n	presents	----------
foretells	----------	d	proposes	----------
			relates	----------
Evaluating				
appraises	ranks		argues	relates
assesses	rates	a	criticizes	reports
decides	rejects	n	describes	supports
evaluates	validates	d	explains	-----------
grades	weighs		justifies	-----------
judges	-----------			

DISTINCTNESS BETWEEN STEM
AND RESPONSE ALTERNATIVES

Although a particular test item may have a well-worded stem and carefully crafted response alternatives, one circumstance that is peculiar to the technical writing task of preparing test items demands another look at the language used. This situation occurs when the wording in an item's stem actually conveys hints that steer examinees to select a particular response alternative. The examinee selects the correct response, not on the basis of knowledge or ability, but because he or she may find an unintended association between the words in the stem and in one response alternative. Sometimes the associations between an item's stem and the options are obvious, as in Illustrative Item 4.12, where only one response alternative meets the condition described in the stem that it is a drug.

Illustrative Item 4.12.

Which drug is involved in about half of deaths due to car accidents?

- • A. alcohol
-    B. water
-    C. orange juice
-    D. milk

More often, however, the clues of association are more subtle, as in Illustrative Item 4.13. In this item the stem specifies the litigants in the famous case of *Brown v. Board of Education of Topeka*. The astute examinee will recognize that only one response alternative deals with education, as does one of the litigants. He or she would

---

Illustrative Item 4.13.

What was a result of the supreme court decision in *Brown v. Board of Education of Topeka*?

-    A. initiation of a draft lottery
-    B. establishment of legal abortion clinics
-    C. reading of suspect's rights upon arrest
- • D. desegration of public schools

likely select the correct option on this basis alone, regardless of whether he or she recognizes the case.

Many more examples of this circumstance could be given because it occurs frequently in poorly constructed test items. In fact, a small body of nontechnical literature suggests that every multiple-choice test item can be guessed correctly without any content knowledge by using either associations between the stem and a single response alternative or by looking for common characteristics among several response alternatives and then selecting the option that does not possess that communality. Such "tricks" that attempt to guess by converging upon a correct answer speak more to the volume of badly worded items than to any real thinking strategy.

As an item constructor, however, one can guard against an unintended association between a stem and the correct response alternative by being aware of this circumstance, and then, when writing or reviewing an item, by looking specifically for it. Eliminating this association is fairly easy when one is looking for it.

IMPORTANCE OF AN INTERROGATIVE STEM

One frequently encounters multiple-choice items in which an incomplete statement is presented in the item's stem and the sentence is completed in the response alternatives. Illustrative Item 4.14 presents an example of this type of multiple-choice item.

Illustrative Item 4.14.

The native tribe that occupies the Kalahari desert in southern Africa is the

    A. Mongol.
    B. Kaffir.
•   C. Bushman.
    D. none of these.

This incomplete-sentence type of multiple-choice item should be discontinued. The format should be replaced by multiple-choice items whose stems are worded as a complete sentence, whether interrogative or declarative. The reasons for recommending that item writers discontinue the incomplete-sentence format are easily recognized and significant. First, with this format, one or more of the response alternatives often do not make grammatical sense. Consequently, in items of this type one routinely discovers poor or awkward wording for at least one of the response alternatives. In Illustrative Item 4.14, alternative D does not make grammatical sense. Although such items can be worded to establish subject-verb consistency between the stem and the response alternatives, they typically are not. In virtually every circumstance, these incomplete-sentence type items could be rewritten in the interrogative, and would then be good multiple-choice items.

Putting the stem in the interrogative is superior to the incomplete statement since the language could be improved by this rewriting. For example, Illustrative Item 4.14 is rewritten with the stem as an interrogative in Illustrative Item 4.15. As can be seen, 4.15 is worded with more grammatical rigor than was 4.14; hence, it communicates with greater clarity.

Illustrative Item 4.15.

Which native tribe occupies the Kalahari desert in southern Africa?

    A. Mongol
    B. Kaffir
•   C. Bushman
    D. None of these

A second reason that the incomplete statement for the multiple-choice format should be avoided is that this format often reduces items to a fill-in-the-blank style, thereby arbitrarily constraining them to questions requiring rote memory, a very low level of cognitive processing. While the more desirable item form (i.e., stem as an interrogative) still assesses the same very low level of cognitive processing in this example, the interrogative allows items to be at higher cognitive levels as well.

The recommendation that the item stem always be worded as an interrogative (and that the incomplete stem not be used) is so often violated that it is worthwhile to examine it through a few more examples. To start, consider Illustrative Item 4.16, an item derived from a licensing examination used to access the qualification of police officers for promotion to the ranks of lieutenant and captain.

Illustrative Item 4.16.

The pyromaniac is most difficult to detect because

- A. He may assist in rescue work and help firemen in extinguishing the fire.
- B. He starts a series of fires under similar circumstances in a particular district.
- • C. Of the lack of motive and the peculiarity of working alone.
- D. He is a victim of a special psychopathological condition.

Illustrative Item 4.16 demonstrates contrived wording common in multiple-choice items having an incomplete stem. In order to fit the stem to a number of response alternatives, the word *because* is used. There are two faults with this use of *because*. First, it reads awkwardly, making the examinee's task more difficult than necessary. Second, it begs the pronoun *he* repeatedly. To suggest that the masculine pronoun simply be replaced with *he or she* is not a good solution since this reads even more clumsily. Happily, there is a simple solution out of this muddle of words: to rewrite the item so that the stem is an interrogative and the response alternatives naturally follow. Illustrative Item 4.17 displays this rewritten item.

Illustrative Item 4.17.

Which single reason makes it difficult to detect many pyromaniacs?

    A. It is common for pyromaniacs to assist in rescue work and help firemen in extinguishing the fire.

    B. Pyromaniacs often start a series of fires under similar circumstances in a particular district.

•   C. There is no known motive for this behavior.

    D. Pyromaniacs are the victim of a special psychopathological condition.

By examining Illustrative Item 4.17, one discovers that not only is the wording more grammatically consistent throughout the item, but the response alternatives are slightly reworded to improve clarity of thought as well. In this way, 4.17 is superior to 4.16.

Summarily, then, the well-tutored item writer should word the stem for all items in the multiple-choice format as an interrogative. This strategy not only improves grammatical consistency for the item and thus clarity of expression, but also allows for increased rigor of scientific thought.

DETERMINING THE CORRECT RESPONSE FOR TEST ITEMS

Correct responses for test items in the selected-response format generally fall into one of two types: *absolutely correct* and *best answer*. For test items that are absolutely correct there is little or no disagreement about which response alternative should be considered the correct one. For best-answer type test items, on the other hand, determining the correct response alternative can be more difficult. Both types of test items need explanation for complete understanding.

Absolutely-Correct Type Test Items

Absolutely-correct type items tend to ask for literal recall of facts or information. For example, knowing that James Monroe was the fifth president of the United States, indicating that 865 minus 323 equals 542, or recognizing the parabola shape are subjects for test items for which there would likely be universal agreement about a correct response. Such test items have an absolutely correct response alternative. Illustrative Items 4.18 and 4.19 are examples of items with an absolutely correct response alternative.

Illustrative Item 4.18.

At $0.10 per kilowatt-hour, how much would it cost to use a 60-watt light bulb for 2 hours?

- ● A. $0.012
    B. $0.024
    C. $0.120
    D. $0.240

Illustrative Item 4.19.

Use the diagram below to answer the question that follows

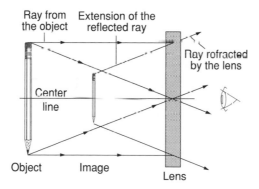

Which lens would produce an image like this?
    A. chromatic
    B. convex
    C. planar
- ● D. concave

Occasionally, debate may rage about what appears to be a test item with an absolutely-correct response alternative. In one highly publicized case, a mathematical item from the Scholastic Aptitude Test (SAT) of the Educational Testing Service (ETS) that superficially seemed correct was found to be faulty (Wainer, Wadkins, & Rogers, 1983). At the time of the controversy (about 1981), there was extensive television reporting of the incident, and articles about it appeared in more than 600 newspapers. The test item, a geometry question that is reproduced in Figure 4.1, has come to be known as "the Rolling Circle Problem." The principal fault with the test item was that a correct response did not appear among the response alternatives, although this fact was not discovered until the item had

---

Figure 4.1. The "Rolling Circle Problem"

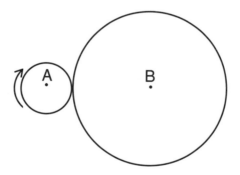

In the figure above, the radius of circle A is 1/3 the radius of circle B. Starting from position shown in the figure, circle A rolls along the circumference of circle B. After how many revolutions will the center of circle A first reach its starting point?

A. 3/4
B. 3
C. 6
D. 9/2
E. 9

been administered over a period of several years to more than 100,000 examinees. An important lesson can be learned from ETS's experience with the Rolling Circle Problem: meticulous care for factual accuracy is required in writing test items for sometimes even the correct response for absolutely-correct test items can be illusive.

Best-Answer Items

The second variety of correct response, and the one that carries some increased risk for confusion and controversy, is the *best-answer* test item. In this type of correct response, more than one of the response alternatives may have some germane or factually relevant information, but only one choice is allowed. The examinee is instructed to select the "best" or "most appropriate" or "most complete" of the response alternatives offered relative to the information presented in the item's stem. Two examples of test items of this type are given in Illustrative Items 4.20 and 4.21.

Illustrative Item 4.20.

Which best describes the environmental effects of increasing industrialization In northeastern areas of the United States?

- A. Canada is experiencing increasing amounts of acid rain.
- B. Deep-sea burial of nuclear waste is altering production of oceanic crust.
- C. Radioactivity around nuclear power plants has increased at an alarming rate.
- D. The cost of supplying fossil fuels has made the use of alternative energy sources very common.

Illustrative Item 4.21.

Which sentence uses specific nouns and vivid verbs?

    A. There were many pools of rain left by the storm in all sorts of places.

 • B. The thunderstorm left puddles of water in the street, across sidewalks, in the front seats of cars, and on counter tops near open kitchen windows.

    C. Big pools of water left by the large, violent storm were seen everywhere, even in streets, cars, and houses.

    D. Many pool of water had been left everywhere in the big storm, including pools in the street, across sidewalks, in front seats of cars, and on counter tops near open kitchen windows.

Since these test items require discrimination and judgment by examinees, they tend to be more difficult than test items that have an absolutely correct response alternative. Another example of a best-answer type item is given in Illustrative Item 4.22. Notice that in 4.22 all four response alternatives contain some truth, especially response alternative B. But, a consensus of knowledgeable persons judged response alternative D as containing the most factually germane information; hence, it is the correct response as the best answer.

Illustrative Item 4.22.

What was the basic purpose of the Marshall Plan?

    A. military defense of Western Europe

    B. reestablishment of business and industry in Western Europe

    C. settlement of differences with Russia

 • D. direct help to the hungry and homeless in Europe

Determining Which Response Is Best

One obvious problem when creating best-answer type items is the very practical consideration of deciding which response alternative is considered the correct one. Fortunately, there is a criterion to guide item writers in judging the relative value of response alternatives in best-answer type test items: A response alternative may be considered the correct response when there is consensus of opinion among knowledgeable persons that it represents the most complete or most appropriate information considering the facts or circumstance presented in the test item's stem.

Two conditions must be met to satisfy this criterion for any particular test item. First, more than one person must be involved in evaluating the response alternatives; and second, the persons involved must be sufficiently familiar with the relevant subject matter to have an informed opinion.

There is no set number of persons who should be involved in determining a correct response for best-answer type test items. For some test items only two or three persons may be sufficient to determine the correct response, while in other contexts, or for some other test items, more persons should be included in the consensus. It is recommended that for large-scale assessment programs a minimum of three persons, and desirably four or even five, should be included in the consensus. Under no circumstance should just one person judge a best-answer test item. It would obviously be faulty to have only the item writer judge it.

Of course, all of the individuals who are involved in the consensus should be knowledgeable about the content considered in the test item. It would be of little value to ask someone to contribute an uninformed opinion.

A Technique for Judging Items

One strategy to build consensus for judging response alternatives to test items is to use a modified Delphi technique (Udinsky,

Osterlind, & Lynch, 1981). In this consensus-building process, rounds of ranking a single test item's response alternatives are used.

In the first round, each panelist is instructed to rank the response alternatives hierarchically, with their first choice for the correct response labeled number one, their second choice labeled number two, and so forth. They may also be instructed to justify their ranking with a sentence or two of explanation. A matrix aggregating the panelist's rankings is prepared by the coordinator. Table 4.4 presents an example of a first-round response alternative ranking matrix using five experts. It can be seen from Table 4.4 that four of the five panelists (panelists #1, #2, #4, and #5) agree that response alternative C should be considered the correct response. Panelist #3 ranked response alternative B as the correct response.

Table 4.4 Example of a Response Alternative Ranking Matrix

Raters Ranking of Response Alternatives

	A	B	C	D	E
#1	3	2	1	4	5
#2	2	3	1	5	4
#3	3	1	2	4	5
#4	3	2	1	4	5
#5	3	2	1	4	5

Next, a second round of consensus building by the panelists is begun. In this round, using the scenario presented in Table 4.4, the brief justifications given by panelists #1, #2, #4, and #5 are sent by a coordinator to panelist #3, the lone dissenter. Panelist #3 is instructed to review the four justifications for selecting response alternative C and comment whether this information will change his or her initial ranking. Concurrently, the justification for the first choice offered by panelist #3 in the first round is sent to the other panelists for their consideration and reaction.

If it is suspected that the handwriting of a particular panelist or the stationery on which comments are written could be recognized by other panelists, the coordinator can enhance anonymity by typing these comments on plain paper before distributing them to the panelists. Consensus on a correct response for the test item is usually reached after this round. If consensus is still not reached, the item should probably be rewritten or discarded.

Although this procedure may seem involved, typically only a few test items need to be scrutinized by this method. The rigor of the procedure suggests that the effort is worthwhile.

Difficulty in Writing Best-Answer Items

Writing test items that have a best-answer response alternative is usually more difficult than writing those that offer a single absolutely correct response alternative and clearly incorrect distractors. For best-answer test items, an evaluative judgment must be made by the writer to determine the worth of each response alternative in relation to the information given in the item's stem. More than one response alternative will contain information that is relevant or correct; however, one of these should be more complete or more relevant to the specific information given in the item's stem.

Obviously, special care is needed when writing the response alternative that will be the correct one. Often novice item writers provide too much specific detail in the correct response alternative, making it simple for examinees to arrive at the correct response by merely eliminating the less specifically worded distractors.

On the other hand, one should eschew overly vague wording in the correct response alternative since this may make it susceptible to multiple interpretations. A middle ground is best. In addition, extra attention should be given to constructing the item's stem, since it provides the context from which judgments about all of the response alternatives are made.

DETERMINING THE OPTIMAL NUMBER
OF RESPONSE ALTERNATIVES

Test items in the multiple-choice format will typically contain three, four, or five response alternatives. Items with fewer or more options are uncommon. Determining the optimal number of options among three, four, or five is important because, all other things about a test being equal, the number of response alternatives will affect the reliability of a test. Generally, the more response alternatives to an item, the higher the reliability. Lord (1977a) demonstrated that this is particularly true when reliability is estimated by the Spearman-Brown prophecy formula or another formula which relies on internal consistency of items, the common case.

Early research into the question of determining the optimal number of response alternatives focused on the relative time required of examinees to respond to test items with varying numbers of options (e.g., Ruch and Stoddard, 1927; Ruch and Charles, 1928; Ruch, Degraff, and Gordon, 1926; Toops, 1921). This early work tended to reach conclusions favoring a greater number of response alternatives (i.e., four or five). The most commonly cited reason was the increase in reliability.

More recent research (e.g., Ebel, 1969) suggests that test reliability may be optimized by considering the point at which more items on a test, each with fewer response alternatives, is traded-off against fewer items, each composed with more response alternatives. For example, the reliability of a one-hour test may be increased by presenting to examinees 70 items with three response alternatives rather than 50 four-response-alternative items. This concept is called *proportionality*. The idea is to determine the point at which proportionality is maximized. In this context, maximized means that a test's reliability is greatest. The idea of proportionality was originally developed by Tversky (1964) and later extended with modification by Grier (1975, 1976) and Costin (1970).

Most proponents of proportionality support the idea of fewer response alternatives (typically, three) coupled with an increase in the number of items. However, Lord (1977b) makes the point that while this practice may improve a test's efficiency for highly able examinees, it will decrease its efficiency for low-level examinees who may guess at a response alternative on a considerable number of items. Offering an even stronger criticism, Budescu and Nevo (1985) argue that the assumption of proportionality is itself flawed. Given these mixed findings by researchers, the careful item writer should use cautiously the concept of proportionality for determining the number of response alternatives.

The structure of the item's stem will also play a role in deciding upon an appropriate number of response alternatives. For example, consider Illustrative Item 4.23, in which only three response alternatives are naturally needed. As can be seen from a casual inspection of the item, adding any other distractors would make little sense.

Illustrative Item 4.23.

In relative size, how does a hectare compare to an acre?

- A. It is larger than an acre.
  B. It is smaller than an acre.
  C. It Is the same size as an acre.

It is not a good item-writing tactic to merely fill in with another distractor to force an item to contain four or five response alternatives. It would be far better to suggest only three well-thought-out, plausible response alternatives than to write more options for their own sake, or to make every item on a test have an equal number of alternatives.

The response alternatives *all of the above* and *none of the above* may sometimes seem ready grist for the item-writer's mill when an additional response alternative is wanted. But these options carry with them a number of subtleties that can be easily overlooked, and they should be used only after considerable forethought. The issues related to using *all of the above* and *none of the above* as response alternatives are described in depth later in this chapter.

Finally, there is the very down-to-earth fact that it is easier for an item writer to create fewer alternative responses. After having written three, a lazy item writer may be tempted to say, "That's enough!" And occasionally, even conscientious item writers may suffer from writer's block when attempting to find novel ideas for plausible response alternatives, especially after having prepared several items in a long sitting. Perhaps the best suggestion would be to take a break until the creative powers return.

One can clearly see from this discussion that determining the optimal number of response alternatives for a test item should not be done without considerable forethought. A test's reliability will be affected by the number of response alternatives for the individual items, as will the amount of time consumed by examinees responding to those items. Also, the nature and structure of a particular item will naturally draw an experienced item writer away from artificially contriving pointless distractors or from precluding good, discriminating response alternatives. Attention to these considerations will set the appropriate context for determining the optimal number of response alternatives.

MAKING RESPONSE ALTERNATIVES PLAUSIBLE

When preparing a multiple-choice test item, making distractors plausible is an important consideration. If distractors are implausible, they will not serve a useful function in measurement, but will usually be easily avoided by examinees. Most often, implausible distractors are arcane or trivial, as in option D in Illustrative Item 4.24.

On the other hand, if several of the distractors are overly plausible (particularly in best-answer type test items), it may be difficult to obtain a consensus of opinion from knowledgeable persons about which response alternative is the correct one. This results in a poorly constructed item, as in Illustrative Item 4.25.

Illustrative Item 4.24.

Which wood is used most often for drawer interiors?

- • A. maple
    - B. pine
    - C. oak
    - D. doesn't matter because it's on the inside

Illustrative Item 4.25.

Which reason best describes America's motive to enter W.W. II?

- A. containment of expansion by the Soviet Union
- B. containment of Hitler and his annexation of neighboring countries
- C. aid sagging domestic economy
- D. Japanese invasion of Pearl Harbor

This item is poorly constructed because historians disagree about the most important reason for American's entry into W.W. II. The four response alternatives present no best answer that would be agreed upon by a consensus among knowledgeable persons. Careful item writers should avoid the ambiguity displayed in Illustrative Item 4.25.

Number of Distractors and Highly Able Examinees

Further, it has long been realized among test constructors that making distractors overly plausible disadvantages the more-able examinee (e.g., Lindquist, 1936). This is so because a highly able examinee may know more about the subject than is conveyed in a single test item, and that examinee's additional knowledge interferes with a response based solely on the information presented. The examinee can only guess about the degree of additional knowledge that the item writer has presumed for him or her. In another, and possibly more realistic, context than a test item, the examinee would recognize the correct information immediately. An example of this phenomenon can be seen in Illustrative Item 4.26.

Illustrative Item 4.26.

What is an example of a chemical change?

    A. lightning
    B. burning tree
    C. melting snow
    D. rainbow

Notice in the item that an examinee with only superficial knowledge of the subject (in this case, chemical and physical properties of certain natural phenomena) will reasonably choose alternative B as the correct response. However, a very able examinee will recognize that A, B, and D are all examples of changes that are both electrical and chemical and that only C is clearly not a chemical change (viz., melting snow is only a change in physical state). Hence, the able examinee would be confused by the limited information presented in the item.

Psychologists sometimes use the term proactive inhibition to describe the phenomenon in which more-able examinees bring knowledge to an item beyond what the item writer intended (Lefrancois, 1988; Schwartz, 1977). Test items in which *proactive inhibition* impairs an examinee's response discriminate against high-ability examinees. Consequently, they exhibit an unwanted systematic bias and thus are poor items. This subtle but important fact makes the work of the item constructor even more significant in producing tests that will measure validly examinees' true ability.

Humorous Distractors

Novice item writers sometimes attempt to be humorous by offering a ludicrous distractor. This practice should be avoided. It does not serve the purpose of sound measurement by test items, and the consequences of most tests are too serious to be trivialized by deliberately preparing poor items. Unfortunately, the use of ludicrous distractors is widespread among fledgling item writers, especially when the item writer knows the examinees, as for example, in some tests made by teachers for their own classrooms. The caring teacher and item writer will realize the disservice done to examinees by such misplaced attempts at humor. As has been previously emphasized, protecting the rights of examinees is an important part of good item construction and test use. One hopes that the informed item writer will never deliberately trivialize the measurement process for an examinee.

USE OF *ALL OF THE ABOVE* AND *NONE OF THE ABOVE* AS RESPONSE ALTERNATIVES

The use of *all of the above* and *none of the above* as response alternatives in multiple choice test items is tempting to many novice item writers, because they appear to fit easily into many multiple-choice test items and superficially make the item writer's task simpler. However, care should be taken that either response alternative is employed correctly.

Advantages of *All of the Above* and *None of the Above*

As properly used response alternatives, *all of the above* and *none of the above* offer distinct advantages. First among the advantages is that they can provide an appropriate discrimination between examinees who know an answer to an item and those who do not. The fact of their open-endedness tends to limit the possibility for guessing a single correct answer from among the response alternatives. Wood (1977) suggests that this feature of none of the above makes it especially well suited to test items that examinees may solve on the basis of the stem alone before searching through the response alternatives.

This is the case for many items involving arithmetic computation, as in Illustrative Item 4.27. By extension of this example, it is reasonable to conclude that the response alternatives *all of the above* and *none of the above* may be especially well suited to use in items involving computational or logic skills or rote memory, such as spelling, English mechanics, and particular facts like historical dates and events.

Illustrative Item 4.27.

Add
  54
 +14
 ‾‾‾

   A. 40
   B. 48
• C. 68
   D. none of the above

Another advantage of these two response alternatives is that they naturally flow into some items, as one can see in Illustrative Item 4.28. In this example, the examinee is instructed to consider the appropriateness of three actions that a citizen might use to change the draft law. There are seven combinations of actions that could be used as response alternatives. Obviously, listing all seven would be cumbersome and out of character with other items that have only four options. Hence, it is logical to list the correct combination of actions, two distractors, and then *none of these actions.* This is an example of appropriate use of the *none of the above* response alternative. Further, the reader will notice that the wording *none of the above* has been altered slightly to *none of these actions listed* in order to make the meaning more contextually related, a worthwhile technique to follow.

Illustrative Item 4.28.

Read the sentence and actions below and answer the question that follows.

A citizen might try to get the military draft law changed in these ways:

Action 1: supporting candidates for office who agree to change the draft law

Action 2: writing letters to editors of newspapers, giving arguments for changing the draft law

Action 3: writing letters in favor of the change to members of Congress and the president

Which action or actions are legal and appropriate for a United States citizen who is trying to get the law changed?

A. only 1

B. only 1 and 2

• C. 1, 2, and 3

D. none of the actions listed

Still another advantage of either the *all of the above* or *none of the above* response alternatives is their flexibility and ease of construction.

Cautions With *All of the Above* and *None of the Above*

While ease of construction is an advantage for these response alternatives, item writers should be careful not to let this fact cause them to overuse these phrases. Use them sparingly and only when it is justified by a particular circumstance. There is no discernible benefit to routinely employing *all of the above* or *none of the above* in every item in a test. In fact, doing so will probably frustrate examinees who may perceive these response alternatives as filler used by uninformed or lazy item writers.

A further caution is necessary when one is considering using *none of the above* in a best-answer item type: precise wording in such items is absolutely necessary. Loose language can lead to confusing the examinee, as in the faulty sample item given in Illustrative Item 4.29. This is a poorly constructed item because of the word not in the item's stem, making the *none of the above* response alternative confusing by creating a double negative.

Illustrative Item 4.29.

Which pair of terms does **not** correctly match a scientific instrument with what it measures?

    A. graduated cylinder: volume of a liquid

    B. spectroscope: composition of light

    C. ammeter: electric current

  • D. none of the these

Another consideration when using either *all of the above* or *none of the above* as response alternatives is to determine when to write an item so that these response alternatives are the correct ones. There is no general rule that will serve as a fast guide to this consideration: the decision must be made anew for each item. It is, however, a good idea to vary making the *all of the above* or *none of the above* a correct alternative or a plausible distractor.

Special Circumstances with *All of the Above*

The use of *all of the above* as a response alternative presents a special problem to the writer of test items, especially when four response alternatives are presented. With this alternative, an examinee may have sufficient knowledge of an item to know that two out of the four response alternatives are correct without having a corresponding knowledge of the third response alternative. The perceptive examinee will automatically select the *all of the above* option on the basis of only partial, rather than complete, knowledge of the item. This peculiar circumstance can be seen in Illustrative Item 4.30.

Illustrative Item 4.30.

Which statement is usually true of reptiles?

    A. They breathe air.
    B. They are cold-blooded.
    C. They have dry skin with scales.
  • D. All of the above.

Notice in this example that by considering any two of response alternatives A, B, or C, an examinee may go on to immediately select D, *all of the above* without any knowledge of the other response alternatives. This special circumstance does not represent sound measurement; rather, it probably reflects a learned contrivance by an examinee to respond correctly to this type of test item regardless of its content. The goal of sound measurement by test items is not served by this context-manipulating maneuver. For this reason, the item writer should use the *all of the above* response alternative only rarely and with special care.

Of course, the response alternative *all of the above* should not be used with the best-answer type of multiple-choice item. With only cursory consideration, one realizes that "best" is inherently contra dictory to *all of the above*.

All of the Above and *None of the Above* and Item Difficulty

The effect of using *all of the above* and *none of the above* as response alternatives on the difficulty level of test items is not easily determined. However, most researchers who study this aspect of test items more often report that using the response alternative *none of the above* increases the difficulty level (Boynton, 1950; Oosterhof and Coats, 1984; Rimland, 1960; Tollefson, 1987). This conclusion is, however, only a generalization and may not apply to any particular test item. In fact, studies into the difficulty level of test items in which the response alternative *none of the above* is used report mixed results.

Some early researchers in this area (Wesman and Bennett, 1946) compared passing rates of nursing school applicants on vocabulary and arithmetic items, half of which contained a specified correct answer while the other half contained the option *none of these*. Wesman and Bennett reported no significant differences in passing rates between groups of examinees, nor was there any significant effect on test reliability. While one may reasonably conclude that using *none of the above* as a response alternative probably increases an item's difficulty level, the item writer must determine for individual cases whether using *none of the above* is appropriate to achieve a desired difficulty level.

USING SPECIFIC DETERMINERS IN TEST ITEMS

Specific determiners are modifying words or phrases that limit the meaning of sentences or cause the meaning to be true or false only in extreme cases. In most instances, specific determiners are adverbs or adverbial phrases. The two specific determiners most often used by item writers are always and never, but there are many others, such as invariably, universally, constantly, in no case, and on no account. They are often contrasted to such modifiers as some, generally, often, typically, and mainly. The use of specific determiners in test items has been recognized for some time (e.g., Weidemann, 1926).

As a general rule, specific determiners should be avoided in test items, but they should not be banished from consideration altogether because, when used effectively, they can enhance item discrimination. Ebel (1979) suggested that if the sagacious item writer places specific determiners strategically in a sentence, they may confound the test-wise but uninformed examinee, thereby providing a better measure of the intended content. This manipulation is probably more appropriate for true-false items than it is for items in other formats.

Regretfully, incorrectly used specific determiners make their way into test items all too often. Novice item writers frequently rely upon them when preparing multiple-choice items to differentiate the correct response alternative from other options, and, in true-false items, as a way to limit the premise. As research has evidenced (Sarnacki, 1979), this practice is poor because test-wise examinees will immediately recognize such "over-qualification" to an item and use this as a strategy to answer, rather than relying upon their skills and knowledge of the item's content.

In sum, a specific determiner may be used in a test item, but only after the item writer has carefully considered how an examinee might react to it. One sometimes helpful item-writing strategy is to write the item in which a specific determiner is being considered two times, once using the specific determiner and once without it. By contrasting the two versions of the item, the writer will gain a perspective from which he or she can judge whether a specific determiner would enhance the quality of measurement by the item.

CONSTRUCTING COMPLEX RESPONSE ALTERNATIVES

Occasionally, it may be appropriate to use items with complex response alternatives. A complex response alternative for an item may be loosely thought of as any format for an item in which the response alternatives depend upon a combination of information, derived either from parts of the item stem or from other options. For example, in some cases particular response alternatives will depend upon combinations of information in the item's stem, as in Illustrative Item 4.31.

Illustrative Item 4.31.

Read the paragraph below and answer the question that follows.

These results might occur if the U.S. Postal Service raises the price of first-class postage to $5.00 a stamp:

1. People will mail fewer letters.

2. People will mail more letters.

3. The Postal Service will need more trucks.

4. The Postal Service will need fewer trucks.

Which are the most likely results of the increased postage?

    A. 1 and 3

•   B. 1 and 4

    C. 2 and 3

    D. 3 and 4

Another format with complex response alternatives is the multiple true-false. This item format contains a stem and response alternatives that appear in the traditional multiple-choice format, but with an important divergence. Rather than selecting a single perceived correct response, examinees are instructed to respond to each alternative as a separate true-false statement. An example of an item in the multiple true-false format is given in Illustrative Item 4.32. For perspective, a parallel illustration of a nearly identical item in the traditional multiple-choice format is displayed in Illustrative Item 4.33.

Typically, by the very nature of their complexity, items that involve complex response alternatives are more difficult to construct than are test items that are not so complex. This itself may be a consideration. When novice item writers attempt to construct items in this more-difficult format, a greater potential for error exists, such as unintended confusion in the language or unwanted hints. Chapters

---

Illustrative Item 4.32.

Read the question below and answer true (T) or false (F) to each of the alternatives.

What of the following descriptions of losing weight by jogging and exercise is technically correct?

__1. increasing maintenance metabolism
__2. decreasing net productivity
__3. decreasing biomass
__4. decreasing energy loss to decomposition
__5. increasing gross productivity

Illustrative Item 4.33.

What is the technically correct description of losing weight by jogging and exercise?

    A. decreasing maintenance metabolism
• B. decreasing net productivity
    C. increasing biomass
    D. decreasing energy lost to decomposition
    E. increasing gross productivity

5 and 6 discuss some stylistic and other considerations for constructing items with complex response alternatives.

TIME EXAMINEES NEED TO RESPOND TO ITEMS

Knowing the approximate length of time required by examinees to respond to an item is information useful to item writers. It can help writers gauge the numbers of items needed for a given testing time-limit as well as assist them in being sensitive to the examinees' needs. A commonly accepted maxim among test developers is that

children in the primary grades require about one-and-one-half minutes to consider a single multiple-choice item, while children in the
fourth grade and above need about one minute for a typical multiple-
choice item. Thus, the test developer or item writer can plan that, on
average, a fifty-item test will take examinees at least fifty minutes to
complete. This does not include the time necessary for getting
students seated, passing out materials, reading directions, collecting
materials, and other administrative chores.

Obviously, the one-minute-per-item rule-of-thumb will not apply to many individual items, especially if they have long reading
passages or require complex calculations or the scrutiny of detailed
graphic materials. Conversely, very short items, such as many items
requiring only recall of particular facts or items involving simple
addition or subtraction, will take less than one minute. Still, it is
often helpful to use this rule-of-thumb.

CONCLUSION

This chapter changed the focus of the item writer's task. Information previous to this chapter was primarily theoretical and was
intended to provide the writer with a thorough understanding of the
nature of and reasons for test items. In this chapter, the intent was to
describe and explain many practical aspects of constructing items.
The chapter began with a discussion of the importance of using good
writing in test items. The focus was on writing generally, rather than
offering a few rules which may or may not apply in a particular
situation. Several resources for learning elements of style were
cited. The next issue presented in this chapter was the use of taxonomic schemes for defining levels of cognitive processing. This
lengthy but important discussion was followed by several shorter
discussions covering array of issues important to the practical steps
of constructing test items.

Throughout each of the discussions in this chapter, a number of
examples, usually in the form of illustrative items, were displayed.

Some of these illustrative items were meant to portray weak strategies that should be avoided or used with special caution, while other illustrative items were cited as exemplars. By studying these examples, the diligent student will gain a full understanding of each of the points covered.

The next two chapters also present practical considerations for writing items, but they are concerns of a different kind than were addressed here. In Chapters 5 and 6, a number of stylistic considerations and formatting prescriptions are addressed. Chapter 5 describes these rules and guides for items in the multiple-choice format, and Chapter 6 focuses upon rules and guides for items in other formats, such as true-false, matching, sentence-completion, and cloze-procedure.

Chapter 5

Style, Editorial, and Publication Guidelines for Items in the Multiple-Choice Format

INTRODUCTION

When authors refer to style, they usually mean the expression of ideas in a smooth, orderly, pleasing manner. Each author develops an individual style of expression that allows for a personal presentation of his or her own thoughts and emotions. For editors, however, style connotes something different. Editorial style refers to the consistent use of a set of rules and guidelines. These rules and guidelines prescribe a consistent use of punctuation, abbreviations, and citations, a uniform and attractive format for tables, graphs, and charts, and a correct form for the many other elements that constitute written communication. Test-item writers are both authors and editors. As authors, they can express their ideas in novel, creative, and personal ways; as editors, they must be aware of and follow consistent editorial principles.

Chapter 4 focused on the role of item writer as author, describing the importance of good writing to producing meritorious test items and offering suggestions to improve one's writing style. This chapter addresses the editorial aspect of writing good items, introducing editorial rules and guidelines for the presentation of test items. These rules and guidelines will specify punctuation, spacing, alignment, and the appropriate use of charts, tables, and figures in test items. Additionally, several rules specify how to correctly cite terms commonly used in items, such as place names, titles, abbreviations, quotations, mathematical symbols, legal references, and the like.

Another, and important, section of this chapter describes the mechanics of how to prepare a test item for final publication. Publication does not only mean items that will be typeset and printed by a professional printing service; rather, it means the final presentation of a well-constructed test item, regardless of whether the product is professionally typeset, prepared on a personal computer with a word-processing, page-layout, or other desktop publishing program, or simply typed manually on a typewriter. For professional results, item writers must know when to use boldface type or italics, as well as what style and size of type are pleasing to the eye. These publication characteristics and many more such concerns are addressed in this chapter.

All of the remarks and examples in this chapter describe test items in the multiple-choice format. The following chapter presents parallel rules and guidelines as they apply to other item formats, specifically true-false, short-answer or sentence-completion, matching, and cloze-procedure. Of course, most of what is described in this chapter will apply to all item types. However, since the focus of this chapter is on multiple-choice test items, it will also address issues uniquely related to items in that format, such as their advantages and disadvantages.

The following topics are covered in this chapter:

- understanding the multiple-choice item format
- advantages and disadvantages of the multiple-choice format
- editorial format for multiple-choice items
- correct use and placement of directions

- specialized rules for formatting multiple-choice items
- type characteristics and appealing page layout.

UNDERSTANDING THE MULTIPLE-CHOICE ITEM FORMAT

The multiple-choice format for test items is characterized by an item with a stem sentence or phrase that presents a problem or asks a question, followed by usually two to five response alternatives, one of which appropriately answers the stem. Further, as has been described in earlier sections of this book, the stem should always be in the interrogative. The response alternatives may be complete sentences, sentence fragments, or even single words.

Although many of the discussions throughout this book use multiple-choice items as examples, one realizes upon inspection of this format that there is not just one style for all multiple-choice items. In fact, the multiple-choice item can assume a variety of types, including absolutely correct, best-answer, and those with complex alternatives. Features of multiple-choice items that are absolutely correct, best-answer, and those with complex alternatives were discussed in the preceding chapter. Wesman (1971) identified eight types for the multiple-choice item, although all of them could easily be placed into one or more of the three categories mentioned.

ADVANTAGES AND CRITICISMS OF ITEMS IN THE MULTIPLE-CHOICE FORMAT

Strengths of the Format

The multiple-choice format for test items has a number of strengths that make it particularly well-suited for assessing mental attributes. Perhaps principal among its advantages is the fact that it offers more flexibility for assessing a diversity of content and psychological processes than can be garnered from other item formats. Nitko (1983) remarked: "Among the various types of response choice items, the multiple-choice item can be used to test a greater variety of instructional objectives" (p. 193). And, Haladyna and Downing (in press) state that testing organizations and technical measurement experts prefer the multiple-choice format because its "sampling of content is generally superior when compared to other formats." This flexibility for accommodating a diversity of content means that the multiple-choice format can be used in a variety of assessment instruments, whether designed for educational or psychological assessment.

A further advantage of the multiple-choice format is that it allows for a precise interpretation which can lead to important evidence for content-related test validity. According to Haladyna and Downing (in press), "the use of MC formats generally leads to more content valid test score interpretations."

The advantage of multiple-choice items for content-related evidence for validity may be clearly demonstrated by comparing the format with another response mode, the essay. Consider the fact that the multiple-choice item does not require examinees to write their responses, which can become long and elaborate. When responses are written, as in essay examinations, an examinee can mask his or her limited knowledge of the subject being assessed by producing writing that obfuscates the issue. On the other hand, when measurement is accomplished through a set of multiple-choice items, examinees are less likely to be able to bluff their way through content-related material. Of course, this statement presumes measurement error has been minimized (e.g., no guessing, etc.).

Considering just the positive features of the multiple-choice item format, then, a set of well-constructed items in this format can provide very reliable assessment of an examinee's true ability. The format is flexible, sophisticated, and simple to use.

Criticisms of the Multiple-Choice Format

Items in the multiple-choice format also have negative aspects, some of which are the obverse of positive aspects of the format. For example, one positive feature of the format, that examinees need not produce a long, written response, can also be construed as a negative characteristic. By prescribing that examinees merely select one choice from among a very few alternatives, the multiple-choice format inhibits examinees from expressing creativity or demonstrating original and imaginative thinking. The critics charge that thorough discussion of events and their meaning is discouraged by reducing knowledge to only what can be accommodated by simple statements, since that is what fits most conveniently into the format.

Some detractors of standardized testing take the criticism that multiple-choice items inhibit creativity and reduce all important knowledge to superficial facts a step further by claiming that knowledge itself is "vulgarized" by the multiple-choice format. This vulgarization of knowledge is reified for these critics in the sense that multiple-choice items suggest there is one, and only one, correct answer to every problem.

However, this denunciation of the multiple-choice item is not universally accepted. In fact, there is overwhelming proof that valid interpretations of scores from tests containing multiple-choice items can be made. To review this proof, one need only examine the evidence for valid score interpretations from literally hundreds of well constructed tests. Further, the interpretations of test's scores are not limited to simple interpretations. Many times the score's interpretations are complex and sophisticated, lending further evidence that the criticism is unfounded. In separate essays, Wood (1977) and Ebel (1972) offer thorough and cogent defenses against this criticism.

Of course, the critics' charge can become all too accurate if items are poorly written. Regretfully, too many poor items exist. One hopes, however, poorly-prepared items will become increasingly rare. In a very real sense, this entire book is aimed at reducing the chances for the trivialization of knowledge which can occur with poorly-constructed test items. Preparing good test items requires not only all of the knowledge and background discussed in the preceding chapters, but also a familiarity with editorial format for items, information presented in the following section.

EDITORIAL FORMAT FOR ITEMS

Description of Editorial Style

Editorial style refers to the consistent use of rules and guidelines for punctuation and abbreviations, a uniform and attractive format for tables and other graphics, as well as proper citation and appropriate use of titles, names, dates, symbols, and many other special characters. For example, the mountain range bordering California and Nevada is correctly referred to as the Sierra Nevada (not Sierra Nevada Mountains or the Sierras). The Stone Age is capitalized but the nuclear age is not. Legal cases are cited as (including italics) *Plessy v. Ferguson.* And, time is properly noted as 3:15 P.M. and 12:00 noon or 12:00 midnight.

When constructing test items, writers should routinely and uniformly follow accepted editorial style. As a technical requirement for constructing test items, this rule is absolute.

Sources for Learning Editorial Style

No one can be expected to have full recall of the accepted form of the thousands and thousands of various citations, only one or two of which may be needed in any particular test item. Fortunately, the well-informed item writer need not attempt to memorize correct citations because there are several very good references to which he or she can turn for assistance. (Even the Chief of Protocol for the United States, who stands by the President's side and whispers into his ear the titles and correct forms of address for various world leaders, does not have all of them memorized, but often relies upon a specially prepared book!) Item writers can be instantaneously informed on hundreds of citations, abbreviations, and correct forms of address with just one reference: *The Chicago Manual of Style*—or, for short, *The Chicago Manual.* Its full citation is given below, along with that of alternate, but also excellent, sources which may serve as references to editorial style:

- Achtert, W. S., & Gibaldi, J. (1985). *The MLA style manual.* New York: Modern Language Association of America.

- American Psychological Association. (1985). *Publication manual of the American Psychological Association* (3rd ed.). Washington, D.C.: APA.

- Skilin, M. E., & Grey, R. M. (1974). *Words into type* (3rd ed.). Englewood Cliffs, NJ: Prentice-Hall.

- *The Chicago manual of style* (13th ed.). (1982). Chicago: University of Chicago Press.

Dozens of other source books (many excellent ones) are also readily available in libraries and bookstores. Regardless of the particular title of choice, such a reference will aid the item writer in achieving this aspect of his or her technical task.

Editorial Style for Graphics

Correct formatting of graphs, tables, charts, illustrations, photographs, and other such graphic material is another important ingredient in good item construction. There are precise standards for editorial style of graphic materials, and they too should be followed exactly. One should not presume that material in a graphic is "good enough" merely because the writer finds it appealing. Remember, consistency and uniformity of style help ensure that the graphic presentation is simple and clear.

As with other editorial stylistic concerns, a number of excellent sources exist to which one can turn for assistance in learning proper formatting of graphic material. Some of the better-known sources are as follows:

- Houp, K. W., & Pearsall, T. E. (1980). *Reporting technical information* (4th ed.). New York: Macmillan.
- *Illustrations for publication and projections* (ASA Y15. 1-1959). (1959). New York: American National Standards Institute. (Available from American National Standards Institute, Inc., 1430 Broadway, New York, NY 10018.)
- Strong, C. W., & Eidson, D. (1971). *A technical writer's handbook*. New York: Holt, Rinehart & Winston.
- Tufte, E. R. (1983). *The visual display of quantitative information*. Cheshire, CT: Graphics Press.

An additional note about the proper preparation of graphic material: Although selecting the appropriate type of graphic and formatting it correctly is exacting, even occasionally tedious work, it is nonetheless important, and the deliberate item writer will find it time well spent. Do not go lightly over this step when preparing test items.

Avoiding Biases in Language

Of course, good writers, whether preparing test items or in other writing, should avoid words that stereotype groups and language that may be offensive to individuals or outdated. This common-sense consideration is surprisingly difficult to keep in mind since most prejudices are subtle. Few writers deliberately use racist or offensive language in test items; but, subtleties of language can give rise to stereotypical or offensive language without the writer having intended offense. The following publications offer guidelines for reducing biases of ethnicity, age, gender, or disability:

- International Association of Business Communicators. (1982). *Without bias: A guidebook for nondiscriminatory communication* (2nd ed.). New York: Wiley.
- Maggio, R. (1987). *The nonsexist word finder: A dictionary of gender-free usage*. Phoenix, AZ: Oryx.

Sources for Specialized Editorial Circumstances

Several publications describe editorial style for specialized purposes. Publications that may be of use to writers of test items include the following.

For appropriate usage of mathematical expressions:

- American Institute of Physics. (1978). *Style manual* (3rd ed., rev.). New York: Author.

For the correct use of the metric system:

- National Bureau of Standards. (1979, December). *Guidelines for use of the modern metric system*. Dimensions/NSB, pp. 13–19.

For proper citation of legal procedures and proceedings:

- *A uniform system of citation* (13th ed.). (1981). Cambridge, MA: Harvard Law Review Association.

Although there are differences in many particular rules among various style manuals, item writers should uniformly follow one or the other of these guides to ensure clear, consistent presentation of printed test items.

USING DIRECTIONS CORRECTLY

Description of Directions

Directions for items are brief, single sentences instructing examinees how to respond after they have considered some relevant text or graphic, such as

- **Read the poem below and answer questions 24 and 25.**
- **Use the map below to answer questions 12, 13, 14, and 15.**

Typically, items that do not have a text or graphic do not require individual directions.

Directions for items are not the same as directions for an entire test, which may specify procedural or logistical concerns, such as time limits or the use of a soft-leaded pencil. Overall test directions are often read to examinees by a test administrator. Usually, they are placed at the beginning of an entire test and apply uniformly to all test items in the entire examination. Directions for items, on the other hand, refer to only a single item or group of items that share some passage or graphic. And, when directions apply to more than a single item, they offer the further advantage of permitting stems for items to be simplified.

Clear, concise directions are an important part of well-con-structed test items. Directions can specify the task for examinees by defining the activity required and focusing attention on relevant materials. Frequently, when responding to a test item, examinees must read a passage, study a diagram, or refer to a graphic. Unless the path from the text or graphic to the item's stem is brightly illuminated, examinees may not realize that a text or graphic accompanies a particular item.

Rules for Directions

The rules for writing directions are simple:

- Directions are only needed when a text or graphic accompanies an item.
- Directions should be clearly written and as concise as possible.
- Directions should appear above the relevant text or graphic and should refer the examinee's attention to the relevant item.
- Directions should appear in boldface type (for typeset tests or typewriters and word-processors with this capability).

These rules require elaboration for full understanding. Note that the first rule delimits directions for items to only those items that have an accompanying text or graphic. For all other items, directions are extraneous. Although unneeded directions may not be confusing to examinees, they add nothing and they tend to clutter the page.

A second rule for item directions—that the writing should be clear and concise—should be carefully noted. As much care should be taken in preparing the directions to an item as is spent in preparing the item itself. Table 5.1 presents a list of suggested wording for directions for a variety of situations. The suggested directions will apply to most situations. Item writers are encouraged to refer to this list and use the suggested wording when appropriate.

Table 5.1 Typical Directions for Items

A.   For text inserts

1.   Single paragraph:
Read the paragraph below and answer question 19.

2.   More than a paragraph:
Read the passage below and answer questions 7 and 8.

3.   Single sentence:
Read the sentence below and answer question 57.

4.   Poem:
Read the poem below and answer questions 3, 4, and 5.

B.   Graphic inserts

1.   Map
Use the map below to answer questions 1, 2, and 3.

2.   Diagram:
Use the diagram below to answer question 51.

3.   Table:
Use the table below to answer question 9.

4.   Graph:
Use the graph below to answer questions 42 and 43.

5.   Illustration (or picture):
Use the illustration ("**picture**" for lower vocabulary levels) **below to answer question 22.**

Another rule for item directions is that they should be located above the text or graphic to which they refer. It makes little sense to place text or graphic material first, where it may be read or skipped, and then instruct examinees in what they are to do. Misplacing directions can force some examinees to jump back and forth on the page between the text or graphic material, the directions, and the item itself. To facilitate the flow of information for examinees, the order should be: directions first, followed by the text or graphic material, and finally the item stem and response alternatives.

Illustrative Items 5.1 to 5.3 present examples of directions in correct editorial style. Illustrative Item 5.1 displays directions appropriately preceding text; 5.2 shows directions properly placed ahead of graphic material; and 5.3 displays directions correctly placed ahead of an item which has both graphic material and text.

Illustrative Item 5.1.

Read the passage below and answer the question that follows.

The driver and his mechanic were getting ready for the big race. The mechanic was making some last-minute adjustments to the engine. Bob, the driver, paced anxiously around the car. "Come on, Steve," he said. "Hurry up!"

"Haven't you ever heard the saying 'Better safe than sorry'?" Steve asked. "Some things just can't be rushed."

What probably happened next?

    A. Bob decided to drive a different car.

    B. Bob fired Steve because he was too slow.

• C. Steve finished his adjustments to the engine.

    D. Bob jumped in the car and drove off.

Illustrative Item 5.2.

Use the graph below to answer the question that follows.

Which statement describes the information presented in the graph?

    A. More butter pecan cones were sold than strawberry cones.
  • B. More vanilla cones were sold than strawberry cones.
    C. More strawberry cones were sold than vanilla cones.
    D. More vanilla cones were sold than chocolate cones.

Last, item directions should appear in boldface type. This draws attention to them so that there is less chance of their being missed by a nervous examinee. Also, it emphasizes their distinctness from the item stem. This printing requirement is reasonable, given the fact that today most typewriters, and nearly all word-processing programs and printers for computers, can accommodate boldface type.

Directions are easily accommodated in test items. Item writers should follow these rules for their correct and uniform use.

Illustrative Item 5.3.

Use the diagrams and the paragraph below to answer the question that follows.

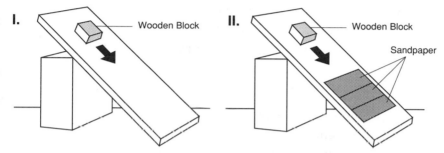

Lisa did an experiment in which she observed a small block of wood sliding down a long board. After trying this several times, Lisa taped sandpaper to the surface of the board. The block did not slide as far.

What stayed the same in this experiment?

- A. size of the block
  B. surface of the board
  C. distance the block moved
  D. time it took the block to come to a stop

SPECIALIZED STYLE RULES FOR MULTIPLE-CHOICE ITEMS

A number of editorial and stylistic guidelines should be followed when preparing items in the multiple-choice format. These rules are simple to follow, and item writers should adhere to them consistently. They may be stated as a series of editorial rules.

Avoid Repetition in Options

Like stems, options should be as brief as clarity permits, and unnecessary repetitions should be avoided, as in Illustrative Item 5.4. In this case, the phrase "It is added" is unnecessarily repeated in every response alternative.

Illustrative Item 5.4.

When is paprika added to the omelet?

    A. It is added before heating the skillet.

    B. It is added before cutting the ham.

    C. It is added while blending the ingredients

    D. It is added after cooking the omelet.

should be

    A. before heating the skillet

    B. before cutting the ham

    C. while blending the ingredients

    D. after cooking the omelet

Omit Articles in Options

Articles may usually be omitted at the beginning of options that are not complete sentences, as shown in Illustrative Item 5.5.

Illustrative Item 5.5.

What part of Grendel did Beowulf remove?

    A. a toe

    B. the nose

    C. the head

    D. an arm

should be

    A. toe

    B. nose

    C. head

    D. arm

Handling Measurement Units

Whenever possible, units of measure should appear in the stem rather than in the response alternatives, as in Illustrative Items 5.6 and 5.7. In 5.6, it is unnecessary to repeat the word "inches" in every option, the wording in the stem clearly refers only to inches. In 5.7, it is obvious from the meaning of the stem that the options are all expressions of square centimeters.

Illustrative Item 5.6.

What is the length of the line?

A. 2 inches
B. 3 inches
C. 4 inches
D. 5 inches

should be

What is the length of the line in inches?

A. 2
B. 3
C. 4
D. 5

Illustrative Item 5.7.

What is the area in square centimeters of a sheet of wall panel-ing measuring 112 centimeters by 242 centimeters?

$(A = l \times w)$

A.   354
B.   708
C. 13,552
D. 27,104

Note that this form is not possible when units are mixed, as in Illustrative Item 5.8. This is a case in which citing units is required for clarity.

Illustrative Item 5.8.

What is the approximate length of this line segment?

    A. 2 inches
    B. 3 inches
    C. 2 centimeters
    D. 3 centimeters

Unless the objective to be tested requires the understanding of standard abbreviations for units of measure, the units should not be abbreviated in the stem or response alternatives:

2 mm
should be
2 millimeters

When the length of a line or object is the variable to be measured (as opposed to being approximated), the distances should be precise. This rule may be shown by comparing two presentations of the same item: one without exact specifications in the graphic for measurement, thereby making it necessary for examinees to approximate, and the same item improved by the addition of vertical rules, creating precision in measurement. Note these differences in the two versions of Illustrative Item 5.9.

Illustrative Item 5.9.

What is the length of the key to the nearest eighth of an inch?

A. $2\frac{1}{8}$

B. $2\frac{1}{4}$

• C. $2\frac{1}{2}$

D. $2\frac{7}{8}$

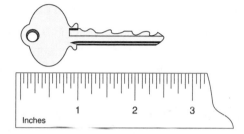

should be

What is the length of the key to the nearest eighth of an inch?

A. $2\frac{1}{8}$

B. $2\frac{1}{4}$

• C. $2\frac{1}{2}$

D. $2\frac{7}{8}$

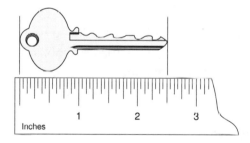

Use Third Person

Like stems, response alternatives should all be framed in the third person ("he," "she," or "it,") and particular care should be taken to avoid the second person ("you"). For example, notice in Illustrative Item 5.10 the rewording of the item's stem to the more accepted style.

Illustrative Item 5.10.

According to American Epileptic Society standards, what first aid should you perform when you witness someone having an epileptic seizure?

    A. You should keep the person on his back.

    B. You should turn the patient on his side.

    C. You should give the person something to drink

    D. You should put something between the person's teeth.

should be

According to American Epileptic Society standards, what first aid should be performed when someone has an epileptic seizure?

    A. keep the person on his back

    B. turn the patient on his side

    C. give the person something to drink

    D. put something between the person's teeth

Italics and Boldface

Italics are employed in accordance with conventional usage for foreign terms and for the names of books, plays, long poems, periodicals, paintings, films, musical works, ships, and like nouns. For example, Illustrative Item 5.11 correctly uses italics.

Illustrative Item 5.11.

Which is the best source for finding the 1980 population of Istanbul, Turkey?

- A. *The World Almanac*
-   B. *Compton's Picture Encyclopedia*
-   C. *The Guinness Book of World Records*
-   D. *Webster's School and Office Dictionary*

To consistently follow this rule, a manual of style, such as one of those cited earlier in this chapter, will probably be useful.

Contrary to conventional usage in writing, however, boldface rather than italic type is used to designate words as words, as, for example, in Illustrative Items 5.12 and 5.13. Note particularly that the word is not boldfaced in the text, which should read as naturally as possible, but only in the item's stem.

Illustrative Item 5.12.

Read the paragraph below and answer the question that follows.

After several weeks at sea, the ship ran into bad weather. The crew had to work hard and their tempers grew mean. When the captain discovered the first mate sleeping on the job, he was furious. Then he learned that the mate had passed out from overwork. Everyone on board was eager to see fair skies again.

What does **overwork** mean in this paragraph?

   A. hard work

   B. lack of work

   C. work above

• D. too much work

Illustrative Item 5.13.

Which word means the same as **amiable** in this sentence?

Because Phillip was an amiable person, he was nice to everyone.

• A. friendly

   B. bashful

   C. moody

   D. mean

The rule for boldface type should also be applied if the words appear in the response alternatives, as in Illustrative Item 5.14. Again, note that these words are not boldfaced in the text.

Illustrative Item 5.14.

Read the paragraph below and answer the question that follows.

Ms. Theodore is trying to weasel out of paying a legitimate bill by saying we did not do the work on her car properly. I cannot believe that our respected legal system would let someone who has an honest debt evade paying it.

Which is a loaded word in this paragraph?

- • A. **weasel** because it makes Ms. Theodore seem sneaky
  B. **properly** because it makes Ms. Theodore seem picky
  C. **bill** because paying bills is unpleasant
  D. **legitimate** because it is a formal word

Note that the rule extends to entire phrases, clauses, or sentences excerpted from a passage. To avoid confusion about what punctuation is included, quotation marks are not placed around the excerpt, as is shown in Illustrative Item 5.15

Illustrative Item 5.15.

Read the paragraph below and answer the question that follows.

> 1 I'd like to be like Nolan Ryan when I become an adult.
> 2 Bobby Grich was the last chance for the Twins from
> 3 Minneapolis, Minnesota and St. Paul, Minnesota nev-
> 4 ertheless he did his best. He gritted his teeth and
> 5 braced himself for what he felt was sure to be a
> 6 fastball, and no ordnary fastball the man on the mound
> 7 was 29 years old Nolan Ryan the fastest pitcher in
> 8 baseball. One of his pitches were electronicly timed at
> 9 100.2 m.p.h. Well, back to Bobby Grich at the stadium.
> 10 The count was 3-2, and it was the bottom of the ninth.
> 11 Ryan's team ahead by a run. The fastball that Grich
> 12 was so sure of was a tantelizing change-up that glides
> 13 over the outside corner Ryan threw the third strike.
> 14 Before he could collect himself and swing at it, Ryan
> 15 had done it pitched his fourth no-hit game and ties the
> 16 reocrd. The newspaper in his town stated, "Ryan was
> 17 the man of the hour."

What is the correct form of **that glides over the outside corner Ryan threw the third strike** in lines 12 and 13?

   A. that glides over the outside corner. Ryan throwed the third strike

   B. that glud over the outside corner. Ryan threw the third strike.

 • C. that glided over the outside corner. Ryan threw the third strike.

   D. The form is already correct.

Boldface is also used instead of italics in a stem to emphasize negatives like not or least when the meaning of the stem would be reversed if the word were omitted. Examples are given in Illustrative Items 5.16 and 5.17. Notice in 5.16 and 5.17 that if "not" or "least" were overlooked by an anxious examinee the meaning of the sentence would be interpreted as the opposite of its true meaning. Boldface type makes it less likely that an examinee will miss these important words.

Illustrative Item 5.16.

Which animal is **not** a reptile?

    A. snake
    B. turtle
    C. lizard
  • D. salamander

Illustrative Item 5.17.

For which essay would brainstorming probably be **least** effective when planning the first draft?

    A. "How to be happy"
    B. "Improving Cafeteria Menus"
    C. "We Can All Conserve Energy"
  • D. "Normal Human Body Temperature"

In some situations, however, boldface is not required for least, as for example, in Illustrative Items 5.18 and 5.19. Here, the meaning of the sentence would not be reversed if the word not or least were omitted; rather, the sentence would be nonsensical.

Illustrative Item 5.18.

What is the least common denominator of these fractions?

$$\frac{1}{3}, \ \frac{1}{4}, \ \frac{1}{2}, \ \frac{4}{5}$$

    A. 2
    B. 4
    C. 12
  • D. 60

Illustrative Item 5.19.

Which weighs the least?

    A. hectogram
- B. kilogram
    C. megagram
    D. gigagram

Mathematics items involving calculations are presented in imperative form and are indicated by boldface because they are considered directions, such as is shown in Illustrative Items 5.20 and 5.21.

Illustrative Item 5.20.

Add

$$\begin{array}{r} 29{,}647 \\ +\ 67{,}905 \\ \hline \end{array}$$

    A. 87,552
    B. 97,542
- C. 97,552
    D. 97,642

Illustrative Item 5. 21.

Solve and simplify

$$\frac{2}{7} + \frac{3}{7} =$$

A. $\frac{1}{7}$

B. $\frac{5}{14}$

• C. $\frac{5}{7}$

D. $\frac{6}{7}$

An alternative to this rule is to use this simple stem with all numerical operations: "Perform the following computation." Illustrative Item 5.22 presents this stem as an example.

Illustrative Item 5.22.

Perform the following computation

$$\begin{array}{r} 8,032 \\ - \; 3,938 \\ \hline \end{array}$$

• A.   4,094

B.   4,194

C.   5,094

D. 11,970

What and Which

Often which and what are interchangeable, as in these stems: "What [Which] constitutional principles conflict in this case?" Or, "Which [What] is the topic sentence of this paragraph?" Still, to the• fullest extent possible, a consistent use of what and which should be followed. Here are some guidelines: What usually implies an absolute answer; there are not degrees of correctness. For example: "What animal is this?" (Note that it can only be one animal.) Or, "What is the volume of this cylinder in cubic inches?" (Note that there is only one correct measurement.) This situation is also demonstrated in Illustrative Item 5.23, a circumstance in which there is one absolutely correct answer.

Illustrative Item 5.23.

What is the frequency in hertz of a sound wave with a velocity of 330 m/sec. and a wavelength of 2 meters?

   A.   6.6
   B.   16.5
 • C. 165
   D. 660

On the other hand, which is frequently used as an abbreviated form of "which of the following," thus limiting the realm of choice to the options listed below the stem: "Which animal is a carnivore?" (Note there are other carnivores but none on this list.) Or, "Which cylinder has the greatest volume?" (Note that other cylinders that are not depicted have greater volumes.) Illustrative Items 5.24 and 5.25 show this distinction between which and what.

Illustrative Item 5.24.

Which nationality was most prevalent among the early European settlers of Manhattan Island and the Hudson River valley?

    A. German

    B. Scottish

• C. Dutch

    D. Swedish

Illustrative Item 5.25.

What is the supplement of an angle that measures $21°$?

    A. $69°$

    B. $111°$

• C. $159°$

    D. $179°$

In a similar way, which may be preferable when referring to elements in a table, graph, diagram, illustration, or map, as is displayed in Illustrative Item 5.26.

Illustrative Item 5.26.

Use the graph below to answer question 77.

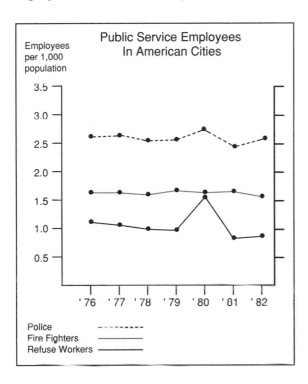

77. Which conclusion is supported by the graph?

    A. American cities employed 26,000 police officers in 1976.

    B. In 1980, American cities paid almost as much in salaries for refuse workers as they did for fire fighters.

  • C. The ratio of fire fighters to residents of American cities remained relatively stable from 1976 to 1982.

    D. The decline in the number of refuse workers from 1976 to 1982 is the result of more efficient trash collection.

Ordering Response Alternatives

Ordinarily, response alternatives should appear in random order. However, numerals are arranged in ascending order, and dates are given chronologically, as in Illustrative Items 5.27 and 5.28.

Illustrative Item 5.27.

Add

36
42
+17

  A. 85
  B. 86
  C. 93
• D. 95

Illustrative Item 5.28.

Use the time line below to answer the question that follows.

According to the time line, what was the approximate year of Abraham Lincoln's birth?

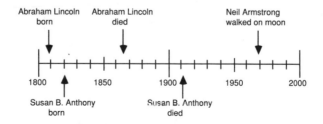

  A. 1800
• B. 1810
  C. 1820
  D. 1860

An exception should be made when such ordering provides clues to the correct response, as shown in Illustrative Item 5.29. In these cases, a random order is preferred.

Illustrative Item 5.29.

Which number is closest to zero?

    A. $\frac{2}{3}$

    B. $\frac{4}{7}$

•   C. $\frac{9}{64}$

    D. $\frac{1}{2}$

Aligning Numerals

Numerals should always be aligned according to the following rules. Numerals without decimal points are aligned, or justified, on their right sides, as in Illustrative Item 5.30.

Illustrative Item 5.30.

Add

$$\begin{array}{r} 34 \\ 28 \\ 15 \\ + 86 \\ \hline \end{array}$$

   A.   62

• B. 163

   C. 173

   D. 1423

Decimals are aligned vertically on the decimal point, as is displayed in Illustrative Item 5.31.

Illustrative Item 5.31.

Which number has the same value as 5.031 x 10³

- A.   0.005031
- B.   0.05031
- C. 503.1
- • D. 5031

Dollar signs should also be aligned vertically, as is seen in Illustrative Item 5.32.

Illustrative Item 5.32.

A dress that ordinarily costs $82 is now offered at a 20% discount. If sales tax is 5%, what is the total cost of the dress on sale?

- A. $ 6.51
- B. $65.60
- • C. $68.88
- D. $69.70

With the exception of money values, if decimals less than 1 are grouped with values greater than 1, a 0 is used to fill the one's place, as shown in Illustrative Item 5.33.

Illustrative Item 5.33.

The density of a cube of ice is 0.92 g/cm³ and its mass is 13.8 g. What is the volume of the cube in cm³?

   A.   0.15

   B.   12.6

• C.   15

   D. 126

Numerals of two digits or less may be spelled out in most cases. However, mathematics items should employ Arabic numerals for all numbers.

TYPE CHARACTERISTICS AND PAGE LAYOUT

Importance of Appearance

Considering the appearance and arrangement on the page of test items is a part of item construction. An attractive appearance will facilitate communication with examinees who may otherwise be distracted by sloppy page layout, difficult-to-read type, or poor-quality type. Additionally, insuring an attractive appearance for the test items that one has so carefully crafted should be a final step in a professionally produced product.

Formatting test items attractively can be readily done with to-day's technology. Many modern tests, even those that are "home made," are constructed with the aid of sophisticated word-processing and page-layout programs on personal computers. This is a boon to item developers because the increased sophistication in formatting capability permits great flexibility in many production features, such as selection of the typeface, and type size and the arrangement of items on the page.

This section will describe some suggestions for the appearance features of test items. This is not to imply that these guidelines are absolute; rather, they will provide some information which may be useful. When considering the typeface, size, and page layout, each item writer should consider the needs of a particular situation as well as the resources which he or she has available.

Suggested Typefaces for Items

Typeface is the style of type in which an item is printed. Any of several typefaces may be suited for tests, but for uniformity, it is recommended that item writers select one of three typefaces: Helvetica, Palatino, or Times Roman. These typefaces are standards throughout the printing industry, and any major-brand word-processor or modern typewriter will accommodate all of them. They are easy-to-read typefaces whose appearance will be instantly familiar to examinees. If one is preparing tests on a typewriter or other machine that does not accommodate these typefaces, then Courier type (the standard for most early typewriters) should be used.

When the choice of a typeface is made deliberately and artfully, it is doubtful that examinees will pay a second thought to the particular typeface chosen. This is as it should be, because if examinees did notice the type, it would almost certainly be a distraction. Attending to the detail of selecting a pleasing typeface and size, however, is a task of the skilled item writer. Except when otherwise noted, all of the illustrative test items in this book are printed in Helvetica type.

Helvetica type is a sans serif type. A serif is the little end mark, or curly-cue to letters. Letters that do not have a serif are called sans serif, or sometimes, block letters. The reader can easily spot Helvetica type by examining most of the illustrative items in this book. (There are a few items presented later in this chapter that are not printed in Helvetica; rather, they are printed in other typefaces for illustration.)

Alternatively, Palatino and Times Roman are serif typefaces. Both are attractive, and either can be used. The text in this book is printed in Times Roman. In some circumstances, these typefaces have advantages over Helvetica. For example, when Helvetica is printed in a large size, its block appearance can seem clumsy. In a large type size, the rounding curl of a serif adds a visual follow-through for the eye. Hence, it is recommended that when tests are to be printed in a large type size—as, for example, tests that are intended for use with very young children—Palatino or Times Roman should be used.

Suggested Type Size for Items

Type size is the physical dimension, from bottom to top, of the type. Except for specialized printing (signs and so forth), type size can range from one to 100 points. One-point type is so small as to be illegible (actually a type size this small is never used), and 100-point type is about one-and-a-half inches tall. But, most type lies somewhere between six-point and 48-point. The text of this book is printed in 12-point type. Often typefaces are measured in picas rather than point size. The conversion between the two is easily made: one pica equals 12 points.

For attractive test items, it is recommended that 10-point type be used for tests intended for adults or for students in grade 10 or above. For tests to be used with younger students who are still gaining proficiency in the visual acuity necessary for reading (from about grades 7 to 9), 12-point size is recommended. And, for tests that are intended to be used with very young children, who are just developing the visual acuity needed to read (from kindergarten to grade 6), 14-point type may be most easily recognized.

Table 5.2 presents a recommended typeface and type size for printing tests intended for various grade and age levels.

**Table 5.2   Recommended Typeface and Type Size for
Printing Tests Intended for Various Grade and Age Levels**

Grade Level or Age at Which Test is Intended for Use	Typeface	Type Size
K to Grade 6	Palatino	14
Grades 7 to 9	Helvetica	12
Grades 10 and above	Helvetica	10
Adult	Helvetica	10

The reader can compare the difference in these typefaces and type sizes by scrutinizing Illustrative Items 5.34 to 5.36.

Illustrative Item 5.34.

Read the paragraph below and answer the question that follows.

Not long ago a scientist quietly watched the daily habits of a pair of robins and their young. At three o'clock in the morning, the hard-working parents began feeding the babies. After their breakfast, the scientist saw the young mother bird wash and comb her young. Drawing each tiny feather through her bill, she removed every speck of dirt with her moist tongue. This was done every day until the young robins were old enough to clean themselves.

When did the mother robin wash the babies?

     A. at three o'clock
- B. after breakfast
     C. after they flew
     D. in the evening

Illustrative Item 5.35.

Read the paragraph below and answer the question that follows.

Not long ago a scientist quietly watched the daily habits of a pair of robins and their young. At three o'clock in the morning, the hard-working parents began feeding the babies. After their breakfast, the scientist saw the young mother bird wash and comb her young. Drawing each tiny feather through her bill, she removed every speck of dirt with her moist tongue. This was done every day until the young robins were old enough to clean themselves.

When did the mother robin wash the babies?

-     A.   at three o'clock
- • B.   after breakfast
-     C.   after they flew
-     D.   in the evening

Illustrative Item 5.36.

Read the paragraph below and answer the question that follows.

Not long ago a scientist quietly watched the daily habits of a pair of robins and their young. At three o'clock in the morning, the hard-working parents began feeding the babies. After their breakfast, the scientist saw the young mother bird wash and comb her young. Drawing each tiny feather through her bill, she removed every speck of dirt with her moist tongue. This was done every day until the young robins were old enough to clean themselves.When did the mother robin wash the babies?

    A.   at three o'clock

• B.   after breakfast

    C.   after they flew

    D.   in the evening

Placing Passage and Graphic Dependent Items Together

Another important aspect of appearance is the proper placement of items on the page. This aspect of appearance facilitates examinees' approaching the items in the clearest manner possible. The guidelines for this consideration are straightforward. In most cases, even when an item contains a long reading passage or a large graphic, the item's stem and response alternatives should appear on the same page as the text or graphic. In rare instances when an item requires more space than a single page, such as one that incorporates lengthy text or a very large map, the text or graphic can appear on one page and the item's stem and option on the next. In these cases, the text or graphic should appear on the verso (the left-hand or even-numbered) page, and the item's stem and options on the recto (right-hand or odd-numbered) page. Under no circumstances should examinees be forced to turn pages to refer to all parts of an item.

With these considerations addressed, when a test is finally produced it will reflect the quality of construction used for the items. Not only will this include the technical issues described earlier in this book, but it will also reflect the appearance. The following are sample pages—identified as Figure 5.1—that exemplify careful attention to these concerns.

Figure 5.1. Examples of how to place items with text or graphics in a test.

Reading/Language Arts

Read the paragraph below and answer question 17.

Have you ever looked up to see the antlike figures of men working on a huge building? Did it make your head spin and your palms sweat? Well, the Mohawk Indians think nothing of walking across a narrow steel beam that rises dozens of stories in the air. Their skill in building giant skyscrapers and bridges is known far and wide. The Mohawks are among the finest steelworkers in the world.

17. At what other job might a Mohawk Indian steelworker excel?

    A. architect
    B. tightrope walker
    C. ant farmer
    D. bridge operator

Read the paragraph below and answer question 18.

I know where the crystal flash is hidden. I was the one who climbed up the ladder and hid it. But I would never dare tell anyone. Hush! Here comes the princess.

18. What is the point of view in this paragraph?

    A. first person
    B. second person
    C. third person
    D. cannot be determined

Read the paragraph below and answer question 19.

It has been proven by a team of scientists that seals have an acute sense of hearing. Seals were trained to recognize different sounds. For instance, the sound of one bell meant food, and two bells meant no food. If the seals responded incorrectly, they were given a light tap. It was discovered that seals are very good learners. They were easily taught the difference between the sounds.

19. Which word is a synonym for **acute** as it is used in this paragraph?

    A. sharp
    B. loud
    C. weak
    D. unusual

20. Which sentence states a fact rather than an opinion?

    A. Blue jays are greedy, noisy birds.
    B. Blue jays are prettier than cardinals.
    C. Blue jays are a type of bird.
    D. Most people dislike blue jays.

Science

Use the table below to answer question 42.

Type of Light	Sun	Green	Blue	Orange
Average plant height at start of experiment	23 mm	22 mm	22 mm	21 mm
Average plant height one month later	51 mm	24 mm	41 mm	43 mm

42. The use of blue light resulted in a height increase of 95%. Which percentage correctly describes the increase under orange light?

   A. 47%
   B. 56%
   C. 70%
   D. 105%

Use the graph below to answer question 17.

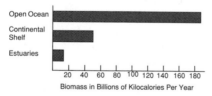

USABLE BIOMASS OF MAJOR OCEAN ECOSYSTEMS

Open Ocean
Continental Shelf
Estuaries

20 40 60 80 100 120 140 160 180
Biomass in Billions of Kilocalories Per Year

17. According to the graph, which statement is true?

   A. The open ocean has the greatest usable biomass.
   B. The estuaries have the greatest usable biomass.
   C. The continental shelf has the greatest usable biomass.
   D. None of the areas has more usable biomass than the others.

74. An automatic drip coffeemaker has a power rating of 1000 watts, and a stereo has a power rating of 80 watts. How many kilowatt hours are consumed when the two appliances are used continuously for 3 hours?

   A. 2.40
   B. 3.00
   C. 3.24
   D. 3240

75. Why does tire pressure increase when air is pumped into an automobile tire?

   A. The tire expands, increasing the inside surface area.
   B. More air particles exert more force while the inside surface remains almost constant.
   C. The force exerted for a given area of inside surface decreases when more particles are added inside.
   D. The force exerted y the particles inside the tire is reduced because the particles collide more with each other.

76. Which reaction will produce the greatest amount of energy?

   A. $^{235}_{92}U + ^{1}_{0}n \rightarrow ^{141}_{5}Ba + ^{92}_{36}Kr + 3^{1}_{0}n + energy$
   B. $4^{1}_{1}H \rightarrow ^{4}_{2}He + 2 + ^{0}_{1}e + energy$
   C. $CH_{4(g)} + 2O_{2(g)} \rightarrow CO_{2(g)} + 2H_2O_{(g)} + energy$
   D. $H_2O_{(g)} \rightarrow H_2O_1 + energy$

77. How many kilowatt-hours are used by a 4-watt electric wall clock in 30 days?

   A. 0.096
   B. 0.12
   C. 2.88
   D. 5.0

Mathematics

92. A right circular cone has a height of 12 inches and a base with a radius of 5 inches. What is the volume in cubic inches of the cone?

> Formula:
> $v = \frac{1}{3} h \, \pi \, r^2$

  A. 20π

  B. 100π

  C. $\dfrac{437\pi}{3}$

  D. 300π

93. What is the perimeter in centimeters of an isosceles triangle with sides of 11 centimeters and a base of 6 centimeters?

  A.   17
  B.   28
  C.   33
  D.   66

94. A right triangle has legs that are 6 inches and 8 inches. What is the length in inches of the hypotenuse?

  A. $3\sqrt{5}$

  B. $3\sqrt{13}$

  C.   10

  D.   15

95. Excluding the door and closet, how many feet of baseboard molding is needed for the perimeter of this room?

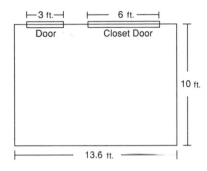

  A.   14.6
  B.   23.6
  C.   38.2
  D.   47.2

96. How many square yards of sod would be the minimum necessary to cover this yard?

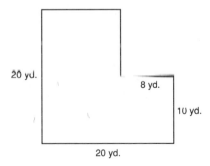

  A.   160
  B.   240
  C.   320
  D.   400

Mathematics

Use the diagram below to answer questions 88 and 89.

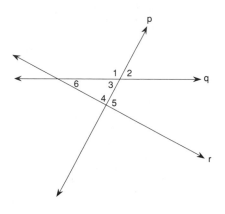

88. Which are vertical angles?

    A.   1 and 2
    B.   2 and 3
    C.   3 and 5
    D.   3 and 6

89. Which are supplementary angles?

    A.   1 and 3
    B.   2 and 3
    C.   3 and 4
    D.   4 and 6

90. What is the volume in cubic meters of this cylinder?

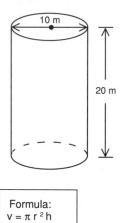

Formula:
$v = \pi r^2 h$

    A. 500π
    B. 1000π
    C. 2000π
    D. 2500π

91. What is the surface area in square centimeters of this wooden block?

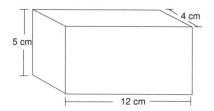

    A.   80
    B.   128
    C.   232
    D.   256

CONCLUSION

This chapter focused on design and formatting characteristics of test items in the multiple-choice format. It began with a thorough discussion of the multiple-choice format for items, citing advantages and criticisms. This was followed by a explanation of editorial guidelines and a description of specialized rules for formatting multiple-choice items. Finally, the appearance of finished page proofs for items was addressed, including appropriate type specifications and appealing page layouts.

By adhering to these editorial and style rules for formatting multiple-choice items, the item writer can produce items that will be uniform in format and consistent in style, and which can be presented to examinees in appealing fashion. Each of these is important considerations in the professional preparation of test items. Of course, many of the rules and guidelines presented can be applied to test items in other formats. How and when they should be applied will be described in the following chapter.

Chapter 6

Style, Editorial, and Publication Guidelines for Items in Other Common Formats

INTRODUCTION

Being familiar with the variety of formats in which test items can appear is one indication of a competent item writer. Familiarity with item formats means that writers understand the definition, structure, and advantages and criticisms for each of these item formats. It also means writers know the technical rules and the guidelines of editorial style for presentation of items in these formats. Whereas the preceding chapter presented information useful to understanding these features for items in the multiple-choice format, this chapter presents parallel discussions for items in several other popularly used formats, including true-false, matching, short-answer, sentence-completion, and cloze-procedure.

Of course, good writing is the dominant ingredient for any top-notch test item regardless of the particular format in which it may appear. Hence, this chapter (like its companion, Chapter 5) begins by discussing clarity of expression as an overarching guide to producing good test items. By now it should be clear to the reader that a broadly based discussion of the importance of good writing when preparing test items is preferable to arbitrarily picking out a few style rules, as is done with most lists of "dos" and "don'ts" for item writing.

But beyond merely asserting the fact that item writers must express themselves clearly, this chapter addresses clarity of expression by examining several examples of well and badly written test items in the various formats. Additionally, this chapter describes the structure for each of these item formats and notes strengths and criticisms. This knowledge will help one understand when and how a particular format may be appropriately used.

Further, as was done for items in the multiple-choice format in Chapter 5, this chapter presents several technical guidelines for formatting true-false, matching, short-answer, sentence-completion, and cloze-procedure items. This advice concerns technical characteristics of writing items in the various formats, such as when to use bold or italics in true-false items or how to display matching items clearly and attractively.

Finally, it was noted in Chapter 5 that many of the technical rules and guidelines of formatting and style are applicable to all items regardless of the particular format in which any single item may appear. An example of one such guideline is the recommendation of a specific typeface and type size for tests according to the age or grade level of the examinees. In reading those rules and guidelines in Chapter 5, one can readily see which ones may be applied to any item format. Accordingly, those rules and guidelines will not be repeated in this chapter.

The following topics are covered in this chapter:

- precision of language in test items
- true-false items
- matching items
- short-answer and sentence-completion items
- cloze-procedure items

PRECISION IN WORDING, AGAIN

Chapter 5 discussed the importance of good writing for multiple-choice test items. That discussion emphasized that not only is good writing necessary for clear communication, but through precise wording rigor of scientific thought is maintained. While that earlier discussion (which gave examples only from the multiple-choice format) will not be repeated here, it is worthwhile to examine more test items to illustrate the essential point of clarity of expression, but this time using examples in other formats.

To begin, consider Illustrative Item 6.1, which gives an example of imprecise wording in the true-false format. Does this item's stem mean that nine-year-olds more often play with other nine-year-olds than seven-year-olds play with their age peers? Or, does it mean that nine-year-olds are more likely to play with age peers and less likely to play with seven-year-olds? This ambiguity can be avoided with careful attention to word choice.

Illustrative Item 6.1.

Consider whether the following statement is TRUE or FALSE.

Nine-year-olds are more likely to play with age peers than seven-year-olds.

TRUE   FALSE

The next example of an item whose meaning could be misinterpreted because of poor wording is Illustrative Item 6.2, which is in the matching format. In this case, the descriptions of literary characteristics are worded so loosely that it is almost impossible to make distinctions among them. As these literary characteristics are presently worded, nearly any combination of matches between a literary characteristic and a literary term could be justified. Remember, the criterion for determining a correct answer to a test item is that a consensus of knowledgeable persons could be reached about the best response. As the literary characteristics in 6.2 are presently worded, even literary critics would probably argue about the correct response because the definitions are not sufficiently clear to match the characteristics precisely to one or another of the literary terms. Illustrative item 6.2 is also poor grammatically because three of the response alternatives are not complete sentences but one of them is. Because of these ambiguities, this item is unacceptable as currently written.

Illustrative Item 6.2.

Match the description of a literary characteristic on the left with its corresponding term on the right. The terms may be used only once. Record the letter of the term in the space to the left of its matching characteristic.

Literary Characteristic

__1. Figure of speech in which the actual thought is expressed in words that carry the opposite meaning.

__2. Under the guise of praise, a caustic or bitter expression of strong and personal disapproval is given.

__3. Writing whose purpose is the evoking of some kind of laughter.

__4. Writing that presents surprising contrasts, usually dealing with the foibles and incongruities of human nature.

Literary Term

A. Sarcasm

B. Wit

C. Irony

D. Humor

As a final example of the importance of precise wording for test items regardless of format, study an item that uses the short-answer format, Illustrative Item 6.3. This item is used for a test to certify the expertise of ballroom dance instructors. Several instances of imprecise wording contribute to making 6.3 seriously flawed. First, as currently worded, it is not a single item at all; rather, it is four parallel items embedded in a common stem. These should be separated for clarity.

Even more confusing to examinees, however, is the fact that the stem of 6.3 does not specify the type of response to the item that an examinee is expected to make. Should the response be a single word or two or a sentence, or should it be a complete paragraph or essay? Or should the response be made in the technical notation of choreographers? Additionally, the stem refers to "each section of the body" but responses A, B, and C each list more than a single body part. A further source of confusion for examinees is the fact that only the general case of ballroom dancing is specified. In fact, there are numerous types of ballroom dancing—such as the foxtrot, the waltz, the tango, the rumba, and many more—each of which requires different movements for various parts of the body. Working from only the cursory directions given, examinees could produce a wide array of responses, leaving consistency among interpretations suspect or spurious. An item with these flaws should not be produced by a knowledgeable item writer.

Illustrative Item 6.3.

Listed below are four sections of the body used in ballroom dancing. Describe how each section of the body is used.

A. upper arms and lower torso _____

B. arms and hands _____

C. legs and feet _____

D. head _____

The point to be seen from Illustrative Items 6.1, 6.2, and 6.3 is that regardless of the format in which an item is presented, good wording is essential. Without it, items cannot assess the abilities, aptitudes, and achievements that they are presumed to, and valid interpretations of test scores cannot be made.

UNDERSTANDING ITEMS IN THE TRUE-FALSE FORMAT

The true-false format is probably second only to the multiple-choice format in frequency of use in professionally produced tests, although there is no comprehensive count. It may be the most popular format of all for teacher-made tests. One reason for its popularity is its apparent simplicity, both conceptually and in ease of construction. After all, one may reason, the true-false format is nothing more than a single sentence which restates a fact and, seemingly, does not require any of the laborious attention to detail required to produce items in the multiple-choice format. But, one is cautioned not to underestimate the effort and attention to detail necessary to produce good true-false items. As we have seen throughout this book, constructing good test items, regardless of format, is a formidable task.

As with other item formats, the place to begin construction of true-false items is with understanding the format itself. Essentially, there are two types of true-false items: the *right-wrong* variety and the *yes-no* variety. Nitko (1983) listed five varieties of items in the true-false format, but beyond the two mentioned here, other types are contrivances that do not constitute any real distinctions.

The difference between the two types of true-false items is simple and can be easily recognized. True-false items of the right-wrong type are simple declarative sentences, while those of the yes-no type are worded in the interrogative. Examples of the right-wrong type and the yes-no type are presented in Illustrative Items 6.4 and 6.5, respectively. Further, and logically, responses to the right-wrong type are prescribed as *true* and *false*, while those to the yes-no type are prescribed as *yes* and *no*.

Illustrative Item 6.4.

Federal Identification Number cards—formerly Social Security Number cards—are not acceptable proof of identification for police purposes.

TRUE   FALSE

Illustrative Item 6.5.

If a glider and an airplane approach each other at the same altitude and on a head-on collision course, should the pilots of both aircraft veer right?

YES   NO

One modification of the true-false item is occasionally used by test developers, but is not recommended. In this flawed format, the examinee is directed first to respond to the stimulus as either true or false and then, if he or she perceives the answer to be false, to supply the correct answer. Illustrative Item 6.6 is an item of this type.

Illustrative Item 6.6.

Consider whether the following statement is true or false. Mark your answer by circling either TRUE or FALSE. If you marked FALSE, supply the correct answer in the space provided.

According to the U.S. Constitution, the President of the United States must be at least 30 years of age.

TRUE   FALSE _____

A rationale sometimes presented for this format is that such a multiple response will reduce the chance for guessing a correct answer from 50 percent to something less, thereby increasing overall test reliability. However, this rationale is not substantive, as will be explained in the section on guessing responses for items in the true-false format. Further, this type of item can uniformly be improved by presenting it either as an unmodified true-false item or as an item in the sentence-completion or short-answer format. Hence, lacking a sound rationale and given the preferred alternatives, this modified true-false format should be discontinued from use.

Advantages of the True-False Format

Test items in the true-false format are attractive to test developers because they offer many advantages. Principal among their advantages is that true-false items are simple, direct measures of learned content. A rationale for this statement is offered in the form of a syllogism by Ebel (1979), a chief proponent of the true-false format for test items:

1. The essence of educational achievement is the command of useful verbal knowledge.
2. All verbal knowledge can be expressed in propositions.
3. A proposition is any sentence that can be said to be true or false.
4. The extent of students' command of a particular area of knowledge is indicated by their success in judging the truth or falsity of propositions related to it.

While there are some technical considerations in true-false items that make it impossible (and undesirable) to express all educational outcomes in terms of true-false items, Ebel's logic is unlikely to be rejected in principle. Examination of this syllogism will reveals its veracity. The first two statements are generally accepted to be true, the third statement is true by definition, and the fourth statement is a logical consequence of the first three. *In toto*, the syllogism presents a strong rationale for the use of true-false items as valid measures of educational achievement.

As simple and direct measures of attainment, the true-false format can be used to cover a wide range of content. One can scarcely imagine a subject in which this format would be wholly inappropriate. True-false items can be prepared to cover factual knowledge as well as judgments and opinions; and, they can be used to assess knowledge from the very low level of simple recall to the more sophisticated cognitive processing levels. Ebel (1972) identified eleven areas in which this format may appropriately cover subject content:

1. generalizations in a subject area,
2. comparisons among concepts in a subject area,
3. causal or conditional propositions,
4. statements about the relationships between two events, concepts, facts, or principles,
5. explanations for why events or phenomena occurred,
6. instances or examples of a concept or principle,
7. evidential statements,
8. predictions about phenomena or events,
9. steps in a process or procedure,
10. numerical computations (or other kinds of results obtained from applying a procedure),
11. evaluative statements about events or phenomena.

The very comprehensive nature of this list is evidence of the flexibility of the format in accommodating a variety of content.

Another advantage of true-false test items is that they are comparatively easy to construct. The format requires only one sentence, and the item writer need not worry about the complexities introduced to an item by using response alternatives, as in the multiple-choice format. However, as noted in the earlier section of this chapter on the importance of good wording in this format, writers should not be lulled into thinking that true-false items are easy to construct. In fact, the precision in wording required for good true-false items is every bit as demanding as that needed for items in other formats.

Still another advantage of this format stems from the cumulative effect of the previously cited advantages. Because true-false items are comparatively shorter than most other item formats, they typically require less time for examinees to respond to them. Thus, more items in this format can be incorporated into tests than is possible with some other formats. As a result, a carefully planned test can cover a broader range of content in a given amount of test time than can be covered by tests using only other item formats.

Criticisms of the True-False Format

Despite these strong advantages for the true-false format for test items, some critics argue against using these items. Their criticisms of this format typically revolve around two concerns: 1) true-false items tend to rely heavily upon rote memorization of isolated facts, thereby trivializing the importance of understanding those facts; and, 2) tests containing true-false items lack reliability because examinees have a 50 percent chance of guessing the correct answer. Both of these criticisms warrant discussion.

The first criticism of true-false items can be paraphrased in a commonly asked question: do true-false items overemphasize isolated factual details? As with most important questions, the answer is neither yes nor no. Deciding whether test items should be measuring higher cognitive functions rests upon knowing the purpose for a particular test. In many instances, especially in licensing and certification examinations, a vast number of specific facts are essential for the successful mastery of a particular content. For example, airline pilots must memorize hundreds of facts—like the radio frequency used by the control tower at Los Angeles International Airport—that have no inherent meaning. Using true-false items as a means to assess such knowledge is efficient and sound. But there are other curricula with different goals—such as gaining a sense of the development of Western civilization—for which the significance is not in each particular factual detail but in the cumulative effect of all of the information known. Critics charge that true-false items cannot accommodate the measurement of such complex skills.

But true-false items need not call only for recognition of isolated factual details; good ones can present examinees with novel situations that emphasize understanding. They can assess an examinee's ability to draw inferences, do analysis, forecast likely occurrences, hypothesize a rule or principle, and evaluate the worth of an object or proposition. In fact, each of the cognitive processing levels presented in Chapter 3 can be assessed with test items in the true-false format. Evidence for this is given in Table 6.1, in which several types of statements of increasing sophistication are given, along with examples of true-false items for each. Study this table for examples of good true-false items that go beyond measuring the pedantic.

Also, notice in Table 6.1 that examples of introductory words or phrases are offered. These words and phrases can stimulate thinking when one is preparing true-false items. This table is parallel to Tables 4.1 and 4.3, presented in Chapter 4, in which suggestions for verbs and direct objects (cf. Table 4.1) and key abilities (cf. Table 4.3) useful for assessing specified cognitive levels were given.

From this discussion, one can see that it is the item writer's skill in correctly using true-false items, rather than an inherent defect in the format, that deserves the criticism. Although these items can measure important learning outcomes, as Table 6.1 shows, it is the item writer who determines whether the content for a particular item is substantive or trivial. Chapter 3 is devoted to explaining the importance of determining appropriate content for items, and that chapter is filled with strategies for how that can be accomplished, but another example here may be appropriate to relate the point to this particular format.

Table 6.1 Types of Statements that Might be Used to Write True-False Items

Type of Statement	Examples of Introductory words or phrases	Examples of true-false items
Generalization	All... Most... Many...	Most good true-false items are tests of information (T)
Comparative	The difference between...is... Both...and...require...	The difference between the raw scores corresponding to the 45th and 55th percentiles is likely to be smaller than the difference between the raw scores corresponding to the 5th and 15th percentiles. (T)
Conditional	If...(then)... When...	When one has a normal distribution the standard deviation and standard error are considered equivalent. (F)
Relational	The larger... The higher... The lower... Making...is likely to... How much...depends on...	Making a test more reliable is likely to make it less valid. (F)
Explanatory	The main reason for... The purpose of... One of the factors that adversely affect... Since... Although...	One of the factors that adversely affect the reliability of an objective test is the amount of guessing the students do in answering it. (T)
Exemplary	An example of... One instance of...	An example of a "factual information" question is to ask how horsepower of an engine is calculated. (F)
Evidential	Studies of...reveal...	Studies of the marking standards and practices of different faculty members reveal that they tend more toward uniformity than toward diversity. (F)
Predictive	One could expect... Increasing...would result in...	One could expect to increase the reliability coefficient test from .30 to .60 by doubling its number of items. (F)

(continued)

Table 6.1 (continued)

Type of Statement	Examples of Introductory words or phrases	Examples of true-false items
Procedural	To find...one must... In order to...one must... One method of...is to... One essential step...is to... Use...of... The first step toward...	One method of ensuring that scores from a 100-item test and scores from a 25-item test will carry equal weight is to multiply the latter scores by 4. (F)
Computational	(Item includes numerical data and requires computation or estimation.)	The range of the scores 2, 3, 4, and 6 is 5. (T)
Evaluative	A good... It is better to...than... The best...is... The maximum...is... The easiest method of...is to... It is easy to demonstrate that... It is difficult to... It is possible to... It is reasonable to... It is necessary to...in order to... The major drawback to...is...	It is difficult to obtain reliable scores from a group in which the range of abilities is very wide. (F)

From *Essentials of Educational Measurement* (pp. 183-185) by R.L. Ebel, 1972, Englewood Cliffs, NJ: Prentice-Hall.

Consider two true-false items, Illustrative Items 6.7 and 6.8. The subject for both items is Broadway, the street in New York; but, the content for the two items is drastically different. In the first, 6.7, the content is obviously picayune and inconsequential to most people; but, the second, 6.8, is substantive and could be appropriate content for an item. The responsible item writer must judge for every item produced whether the content is trivial or meaningful.

Illustrative Item 6.7.

Consider whether the following statement is TRUE or FALSE.

Broadway, in New York City, extends from near the lower tip of Manhattan northward through the length of Manhattan and the Bronx to beyond the city line.

TRUE   FALSE

Illustrative Item 6.8.

Consider whether the following statement is TRUE or FALSE.

Broadway, in New York City, is practically synonymous with American theater.

TRUE   FALSE

The second commonly voiced criticism of true-false items is that they are subject to enormous error because examinees can blindly guess at them and expect to get half of them right. This criticism reflects either a lack of information or the presence of misinformation about the statistics which comprise much of testing, in this case binomial theory.

The statistics of testing which address this criticism may be most easily explained by describing a sample testing scenario. In this scenario, presume that an examinee guesses blindly on every item—

a situation that is atypical. If the test were only one item long, then the examinees would have a fifty-fifty chance of receiving a perfect score. However, if the test were two items long, the chances are reduced by a factor of two, leaving only a 25 percent chance of receiving a perfect score. If the test contains five true-false items, the examinee's chances of receiving a perfect score are three percent; and, for a ten-item test, they are less than one percent. On a test of 100 items, the chances are less then a million trillion, trillion— less odds than winning every state's lottery!

On this same test, the examinee's chances of getting even three-quarters of the items correct are fewer than one in ten thousand. Nitko (1983) illustrated this point by preparing a table (presented here as Table 6.2) that displays the chances of getting 60, 80, or 100 percent of the items correct solely by blind guessing.

Table 6.2 Chances of Getting Percentages of T-F Items Right

Number of T-F Items on the test	60% or better	80% or better	100%
5	50 in 100	19 in 100	3 in 100
10	38 in 100	6 in 100	1 in 1,000
15	30 in 100	2 in 100	3 in 100,000
20	25 in 100	6 in 1,000	1 in 1,000,000
25	21 in 100	2 in 1,000	3 in 100,000,000

From *Educational Tests and Measurement* (p. 175) by A.J. Nitko, 1983, New York: Harcourt Brace Jovanovich. Reprinted by permission.

Of course this scenario would rarely occur, for examinees seldom, if ever, guess blindly on every item. This fact is well known among measurement specialists since tests containing only true-false items generally have high reliability coefficients (Nitko, 1983). One study of true-false items reported that examinees, on the average, blindly guess on only about five percent of the items (Ebel, 1968b). Further, examinees respond to items—true-false, multiple-choice, and other formats—with varying degrees of information, including complete information, partial information, misinformation, blind guessing, as well as a variety of other reasons (cf. Hughes and Trimble, 1965).

Hence, neither of the two common criticisms of true-false items is in itself sufficient to reject the format. In fact, as we have seen, it can be a valuable assessment technique when correctly prepared by a skilled item writer.

Comparison of True-False and Multiple-Choice Items

The differences, as well as the similarities, between items in the true-false format and those in the multiple-choice format are easily determined. Some obvious differences between the formats, for example, are the number of options available for examinees to choose from, and the fact that true-false items are always of the absolutely correct type and cannot be best-answer variety. Multiple-choice format may be of either type. Also, true-false items are usually easier to construct than are multiple-choice items, as has been described. These are the principle differences between the two formats.

In contrast to these superficial differences between the true-false and multiple-choice formats, the similarities are quite significant. In fact, it can be argued that multiple-choice items are a variation of the true-false format. A side-by-side comparison of the two formats reveals this lineage. Instead of only one true or false stem (as in the true-false format), multiple-choice items consist of one statement followed by several false statements and one true statement. This can be seen by examining a single proposition written in both formats, as in Illustrative Items 6.9 in the multiple-choice format and 6.10 to 6.13 in the true-false formats.

Illustrative Item 6.9.

According to the U.S. Constitution, who may introduce fiscal bills in Congress?

    A. president of the United States

    B. member of the Supreme Court

    C. member of the Senate

    D. member of the House

Illustrative Item 6.10.

According to the U.S. Constitution, the president of the United States may introduce fiscal bills in Congress.

    TRUE   FALSE

Illustrative Item 6.11.

According to the U.S. Constitution, a member of the Supreme Court may introduce fiscal bills in Congress.

    TRUE   FALSE

Illustrative Item 6.12.

According to the U.S. Constitution, a member of the House of Representatives may introduce fiscal bills in Congress.

    TRUE   FALSE

Illustrative Item 6.13.

According to the U.S. Constitution, a member of the Senate may introduce fiscal bills in Congress.

    TRUE   FALSE

Because both formats for items use propositions, the rewriting of items from the multiple-choice format into the true-false format can be routinely done, including items that tap the most complex cognitive processes. For example, Illustrative Item 6.14, an item in the multiple-choice format that assesses a subtle inference skill, is rewritten into the true-false format in Illustrative Items 6.15 to 6.18.

Illustrative Items 6.14 to 6.18.

Read the poem below and answer questions 1 to 5.

THE SUN

1 I'll tell you how the sun rose, —
2 A ribbon at a time.
3 The steeples swam the amethyst,
4 The news like squirrels ran.

5 The hills untied their bonnets,
6 The bobolinks begun.
7 Then I said softly to myself,
8 "That must have been the sun!"

9 But how he set, I know not.
10 There seemed a purple stile
11 Which little yellow boys and girls
12 Were climbing all the while

13 Till when they reached the other side,
14 A dominie in gray
15 Put gently up the evening bars,
16 And led the flock away.

Illustrative Item 6.14.

---

1.   To what do lines 14-16 refer?

    A.   what the rising sun looked like

    B.   what the poet did after she watched the sun set

    C.   what the setting sun looked like

    D.   little boys and girls climbing steps over a fence

Illustrative Item 6.15.

---

2.   Do lines 14-16 refer to what the rising sun looked like?

    YES NO

Illustrative Item 6.16.

---

3.   Do lines 14-16 refer to what the poet did after she watched the sun set?

    YES NO

Illustrative Item 6.17.

---

4.   Do lines 14-16 refer to what the setting sun looked like?

    YES NO

Illustrative Item 6.18.

---

5.   Do lines 14-16 refer to little boys and girls climbing steps over a fence?

    YES NO

Of course, not every true-false item that could be a correspondent for a response alternative of a multiple-choice item would be used in any test. To do so would create needless redundancy. Only the most important ones need have a correspondent true-false item. It is only done here to illustrate the point that every well-written response alternative could have a corresponding true-false item.

Further, the two formats are not always interchangeable. In some situations, only two alternatives may logically be presented, as in contrasting two specific features of a product, or comparing two variables of a hypothesis. An example of this is given in Illustrative Item 6.19.

Illustrative Item 6.19.

Consider whether the following statement is TRUE or FALSE.

Normal atmospheric pressure at sea level is 30.00 inches of mercury.

TRUE   FALSE

And, true-false items cannot automatically replace multiple-choice items that are of the best-answer variety. Most best-answer multiple-choice items are not based strictly on propositions, and hence they may be more appropriately assessed by presenting examinees with an array of choices.

The question of which format is preferred is mostly a matter of judging from the context and needs of a particular situation. The little research to guide one in making such a decision suggests that reliabilities and concurrent validities are similar for well-written true-false and multiple-choice items (Frisbie, 1973). Certainly, if one incorporates the information presented in this book about these two formats into such decisions, one will have a thorough background from which to make informed choices.

Rules for Presenting True-False Items

Since most true-false items are only brief statements followed by either the alternatives *true* and *false* or *yes* and *no*, the rules for presenting them clearly and attractively in tests are also short. First, as with most other items, a simple direction to examinees should precede the item itself. Second, as is the case for all directions, these should be in boldface type. Third, a simple direction will suffice in most instances, such as the following:

Consider whether the following statement is TRUE or FALSE.

If the item is stated as an interrogative and requires a *yes* or *no* response, this direction will suit:

Consider whether the following question is correct (YES) or incorrect (NO).

The item writer may also need to add further directions if there is a particular way in which examinees should mark their responses or a certain place where they must record them. For example, the directions given above may be extended to include this sentence:

Indicate your response by circling YES or NO.

Or,

Indicate your response by writing the letter T (for TRUE) or F (for FALSE) in the space provided to the left of each item.

Often, these directions will apply to all items on a test. When this is the case, they should appear at the beginning of the test or be read aloud by the test administrator. This must always be done if examinees are recording their responses on a separate answer document.

UNDERSTANDING ITEMS IN THE MATCHING FORMAT

Matching items are not conceptually difficult. They consist merely of a set of premises, a set of associated responses, and some directions for drawing the most appropriate correspondence between them. Often the association between the premises and the responses is the labels, or names, that one list gives the other. Illustrative Item 6.20 is an example of a matching item format in which one list simply names the other.

Illustrative Item 6.20.

Match the category of material from the left column with an example of that material from the right column.

1. fabric   a. acetate

2. wood   b. lignum vitae

3. paneling   c. fiberboard.

4. paper   d. gauze

5. plastic   e. filet

6. lace   f. onionskin

Cautions For Matching Items

Matching items are especially useful when a large number of specific facts are called for, as is the case with the historical contexts presented in Illustrative Item 6.21. However, care should be taken when preparing such matching items to make the content substantive and not merely pedantic. By now, the reader should be well aware of this caution, since it has been mentioned repeatedly.

Illustrative Item 6.21.

Match the epoch from the left column with its corresponding date in the right column.

1. Byzantine Empire   a. fifteenth century

2. Crusades   b. ninth century

3. Italian Renaissance   c. seventh century

4. Reformation Era   d. eleventh century

5. Medieval Monasticism   e. sixteenth century

One criticism of the matching format is that it is almost exclusively constrained to low-level, factual content. However, inspection shows this criticism is not entirely accurate. While understandings, judgments, and evaluations cannot easily be accommodated by this format, in some situations sophisticated thinking is required to complete accurately a matching item, as in Illustrative Item 6.22. This matching item displays a situation in which the content is not inherently difficult, but a sagacious judgment is needed to respond correctly. The examinee must use a complex thinking skill to synthesize the relevant knowledge about each category and judge whether a particular characteristic is properly associated with it.

Illustrative Item 6.22.

Match the categories from the left column with the corresponding characteristic in the right column.

1. SENSATION   a. condolence

2. AFFECTION   b. rocks

3. SPACE   c. incombustibility

4. PHYSICS   d. hearing

5. MATTER   e. interval

Although matching items can sometimes assess high-level thinking skills, most often they are used to assess very low levels of cognitive processing. Because of this characteristic use of matching items to evaluate low-level skills, it is recommended that they be used sparingly, and probably in combination with items in other formats. A particular test should probably not contain only matching items. Again, the item writer must determine on an individual basis whether a particular content can properly be formatted as a matching item.

Directions for Matching Items

Matching items require explicit directions if examinees are not to be confused about how or where to respond. If examinees should simply mark a letter or number from one column in a space provided next to the second column, then the directions are implicit in the format. As is the rule for all item directions, those for matching items should be set in boldface type.

If, however, examinees are instructed to mark their responses to a matching item on a separate answer document, then directions assume special importance, and must be precisely worded. The consequences for examinees of mismarking an item are compounded by the multiple responses of the format, which could cause confused examinees to miss all matches included in the item because the first one was misplaced. The following sample direction is recommended for matching items on tests where examinees use a separate answer document:

Match the term from the left column with its corresponding characteristic in the right column. Record your answer by marking on the answer sheet the letter (i.e., a, b, c, d, or e) of the characteristic that matches the numbered term in the left column.

Slight modifications in this recommended wording should be made to accommodate a particular item as well as the lay-out of the answer document. The most important point, however, is that the wording be clear and concise. Directions should communicate to examinees necessary information about how and where to respond to items, and they should not interfere with examinees' thinking about the items.

UNDERSTANDING SHORT-ANSWER AND SENTENCE-COMPLETION ITEMS

Since short-answer items and sentence-completion items share a similar format, both conceptually and in many operational aspects, they are discussed together in this section. The few differences between them will be pointed out. Short-answer and sentence-completion items are both constructed-response items. The reader will recall from Chapter 2 that constructed-response test items are ones in which examinees must write out the response to an item, typically in one or two words or a short sentence. They are usually contrasted with selected-response items like multiple-choice, true-false, and, to a lesser degree, matching. Short-answer and sentence-completion items are often informally called "fill-in-the-blank" questions, but that term is avoided by test professionals.

Narrow Focus of the Format

By their nature, short-answer items and sentence-completion items ask mainly for factual recall since their format allows only for information or data that can be reported in a single word or two or a phrase. In this regard, they are much more limited in their applicability to wide-ranging tests of achievement, aptitude, or ability than are multiple-choice, true-false, or even matching item formats. Nevertheless, the trained item writer will not view this narrow focus of short-answer and sentence-completion items as a reason for not considering them. Rather, the writer should view the narrow focus as merely a characteristic of this item format. With such a perspective, these items can be used appropriately.

When to Use Short-Answer and Sentence-Completion Items

One correct use of short-answer and sentence-completion items is in assessing areas that require a great deal of factual recall. Many areas of vocational or technical training are appropriate for assessment by items in the constructed-response formats. For example, fields that call for recognizing numerous machine parts or for using complex computer-programming skills would probably be suitable for tests that contain short-answer and sentence-completion items.

Further, many fields require a background of specialized factual knowledge before one can reach the more sophisticated levels of understanding or appreciation. Astronomy is one such area in which the student must have an enormous store of factual information as a background against which an understanding is built.

Another place in which short-answer and sentence-completion items could be used is when machine scoring is not possible, as with many teacher-made tests intended for use in a teacher's own classroom. With these item formats, a great deal of information can be assessed while still conveniently allowing for hand-scoring of the answers.

Special Considerations for Short-Answer and Sentence-Completion Formats

One presumed advantage for items in the short-answer or sentence-completion format—"presumed" because there seems to be little research on this point—is that guessing by examinees is reduced over what it might be in some other item formats. However, one is cautioned from over-reliance on this as an advantage because, as was discussed in Chapter 4 and mentioned above in the description of the true-false item format, examinees rarely guess blindly on an item.

In creating short-answer and sentence-completion items, the item writer should be certain that the beginning portion of the sentence will logically lead an examinee to one—and just one— correct response. For example, consider Illustrative Item 6.23, in which the sentence may make sense with multiple endings.

Illustrative Item 6.23.

Rain is produced by_____clouds.

This item is poor because, accordingly to meteorologists, a variety of cloud types produce rain. The examinee could easily respond with a correct cloud type, but it may not be the one that the teacher had in mind as the intended response. For this reason, the wording used in 6.23 should not be followed. Illustrative Item 6.24 represents a simple rewriting of 6.23 into acceptable language. In 6.24 the wording is made precise by the addition of a delimiting phrase, so that only a single cloud type could correctly be inserted.

Illustrative Item 6.24.

During thunderstorms, rain is produced by _____clouds.

A variation on the issue of wording these items so that only a precise answer will fit occurs when the desired answer is a number. In these instances, examinees are asked to perform a calculation or computation and supply the correct answer. A problem arises in considering how far a decimal should be carried. Unless a specific direction, such as, "Decimals should be carried out to two places," is clearly stated, examinees will be confused. An example of such confusion could occur in Illustrative Item 6.25. For this reason, it is better to limit numerical short-answer and sentence-completion items to responses that are whole numbers, as in Illustrative Item 2.26.

Illustrative Item 6.25.

The comonly accepted value for pi (P) is _____ .

Illustrative Item 6.26.

The average weight of the St. Louis Zoo's three famous ele-
phants—Bertha (who weighs 3,623 pounds), Mama (who tips the
scales at 5,101 pounds), and Mia (who carried a record 6,243
pounds)— is _____.

Occasionally, an errant item writer will attempt to use a single
stem combined with predefined and hypothetical situations for a
series of short-answer or sentence-completion items. This situation
is illustrated by Illustrative Item 6.27, taken from a certification test
administered to baseball umpires. This format could alternatively be
labeled the "Yogi Berra format" because of its twists in logic,
structure, and syntax. While it is interesting to try to make sense out
of the possible meanings of this item, it is not well written, and this
format should be avoided by the skilled item writer.

Illustrative Item 6.27.

The next question refers to live- or dead-ball situations which
involve the placement of runners. In each situation,

  (A) tell whether the ball remains alive or is ruled dead
  (B) if the ball is ruled dead, place all runners including the
       batter
  (C) if the ball is ruled dead, indicate who, if anyone, is called
       out on the play

There is one out and a runner is on second base. The batter hits
a ground ball which the pitcher deflects and the ball hits the base
umpire working in the infield. The second baseman picks up the
ball and throws out the runner who had rounded third base.

  (A) _____
  (B) _____
  (C) _____

Converting Short-Answer and Sentence-Completion Items to Other Formats

Finally, it should be recognized that many short-answer and sentence-completion items can be easily converted into more meaningful true-false or multiple-choice test items. This conversion can be readily seen by considering the following sample items. Illustrative Item 6.28 is a short-answer item; its content is presented in Illustrative Item 6.29 as a true-false item, and again presented as a multiple-choice item in Illustrative Item 6.30.

Illustrative Item 6.28.

The name of the largest dinosaur ever discovered is _____.

Illustrative Item 6.29.

Megalosaurus is the largest dinosaur ever discovered.

TRUE   FALSE

Illustrative Item 6.30.

What is the name of the largest dinosaur ever discovered?

A. Triceratops
B. Megolosaurus
C. Brontosaurus
D. Diplodocus

One should note, however, that the conversion from short-answer or sentence-completion format into the true-false or multiple-choice formats is only possible with items requiring low-level recall of factual material. This is due to the limitation of the short-answer or sentence-completion format mentioned above. Additionally, notice that the conversion is only possible in one direction: from short-answer or sentence-completion to multiple-choice. A multiple-choice item cannot be converted into a single item in the short-answer or sentence-completion format without laboriously contorting a sentence's syntax.

An understanding of the features and limited utility of the short-answer or sentence-completion format will guide the careful item writer in deciding when and how to use this format. Despite the shortcomings, items in these formats can occasionally be useful. They also provide a contrast that may aid one in understanding other item formats which are more appropriate for assessing complex cognitive skills. One such format, the cloze-procedure, is described in the following section.

UNDERSTANDING CLOZE-PROCEDURE

The cloze-procedure is a technique for assessing examinees' reading ability. In this format, test items are embedded within a passage. Some words from the passage are deleted, and the examinee is instructed to supply them by selecting an appropriate word from among a list of alternatives. The passage looks something like a fill-in-the-blank exercise, while the response alternatives look like multiple-choice (cf. constructed-response and selected-response). Illustrative Item 6.31 is an example of cloze-procedure. This item is a sample passage from the *Degrees of Reading Power* (DRP) program, probably the most widely recognized test to use cloze-procedure.

Illustrative Item 6.31.*

Bridges are built to allow a continuous flow of highway and railway traffic across water lying in their paths. But engineers cannot forget that river traffic, too, is essential to our economy. The role of_____1_____ is important. To keep these vessels moving freely, bridges are built high enough, when possible, to let them pass underneath. Sometimes, however, channels must accommodate very tall ships. It may be uneconomical to build a tall enough bridge. The _____2_____ would be too high. To save money, engineers build movable bridges.

1. a) wind   b) boats   c) wires   d) wires   c) experience
2. a) levels   b) cost   c) weight   d) waves   e) deck

In the swing bridge, the middle part pivots or swings open. When the bridge is closed, this section joins the two ends of the bridge, blocking tall vessels. But this section _____3_____ . When swung open, it is perpendicular to the ends of the bridge, creating two free channels for river traffic. With swing bridges, channel width is limited by the bridge's piers. The largest swing bridge provides only a 75-meter channel. Such channels are sometimes too _____4_____ . In such cases, a bascule bridge may be built.

3. a) stands   b) floods   c) wears   d) turns   e) supports
4. a) narrow   b) rough   c) long   d) deep   e) straight

Bascule bridges are drawbridges with two arms that swing upward. They provide an opening as wide as the span. They are also versatile. These bridges are not limited to being fully opened or fully closed. They can be _____5_____ in many ways. They can be fixed at different angles to accommodate different vessels.

5. a) crossed b) approached c) lighted d) planned   e)positioned

In vertical lift bridges, the center remains horizontal. Towers at both ends allow the center to be lifted like an elevator. One interesting variation of this kind of bridge was built during World War II. A lift bridge was desired, but there were wartime short-ages of the steel and machinery needed for the towers. It was hard to find enough _____6_____. An ingenious engineer designed the bridge so that it did not have to be raised above traffic. Instead it was _____7_____. It could be submerged seven meters below the surface of the river. Ships sailed over it.

6. a) work   b) material   c) time   d) power   e) space
7. a) burned   b) emptied   c) secured   d) shared   e) lowered

*From *DRP Handbook* (p.2) Touchstone Applied Science Associates, 1986, New York: The College Board.

The cloze-procedure attempts to assess reading comprehension by providing longer, and hence more "real world," reading experiences during assessment than is possible with other item formats. This "real world" focus is an attempt to directly addresses the problem in measurement that the precise nature of the relationship between reading tasks—as assessed by test items—and the level of cognitive functioning required to respond to reading items is unknown (Kirsch & Guthrie, 1980). As an answer to the problem, cloze-procedure seeks to provide a substantive method that provides meaningful evidence for valid interpretation of psychological constructs.

Writing good cloze tests is exceedingly difficult. The item writer cannot merely select or write any passage and randomly delete words, but must instead consider the context for each deleted word. The context provides the only clue to examinees for choosing the correct alternative. This means that item writers must write or select passages which contain all of the information examinees need to be able to respond correctly to the embedded items. If this is not the case, examinees' prior knowledge of the subject matter could be a confounding variable in their ability to respond. The only feature of interest for the assessment of reading comprehension is an examinee's ability to comprehend the prose; the content itself is not of special interest. The difficulty of the text should be the only limiting factor to reading comprehension.

Illustrative Items 6.32 and 6.33 present two examples from the DRP that display the difficulty of cloze items as related to the complexity of the passage. Both passages are similar in content and have exactly the same items, but 6.31 is much more difficult for examinees because the reading level of the prose is higher. Examination of these two examples reveals self-evident differences.

Illustrative Item 6.32.*

Hard Version of Passage

Henry Ford was the trailblazer of mass production in the automotive industry. When Ford began manufacturing, automobiles were usually assembled like houses, with the chassis fabricated at stationary locations where mechanics gathered around, attaching various parts. Assistants were constantly required to fetch materials, a practice that consumed numerous man-hours. Ford studied these production methods and was concerned. Such a great waste of _____1_____ was disturbing.

1. a) gas   b) oil   c) space   d) time   e) steel

Ford had observed slaughtered hogs transported on a revolving chain past stationary employees, a process which eliminated the necessity for superflous motion, and from this developed his concept of continuous assembly lines. Why not _____2_____ cars the same way? Why not bring the job to the man, rather than vice versa? In implementing the assembly line, he subdivided the work into the simplest possible tasks. As unskilled man could achieve considerable productivity with minimal instruction. So the need for _____3_____ was reduced.

2. a) select   b) move   c) name   d) test   e) sell
3. a) wealth   b) glass   c) paint   d) water   e) training

Ford recognized that whenever work was carried out by hand every piece would inevitable differ somewhat from the others; furthermore he understood that one indispensable key to mass production lay in the interchangeability of components. Therfore he increasingly substituted machines for men. That way, the product was more _____4_____. Because parts could be substituted for one another, automobiles could be turned out faster.

4. a) complete   b) uniform   c) powerful   d) natural   e) comfortable

Seeking greater efficiency, Ford installed conveyor belts at waist level to eliminate crouching. The new _____5_____ was indeed an improvement. Not needing to bend, men became less fatigued and more productive. Moreover, Ford provided positive incentives by increasing wages to five dollars a day, an unprecedented level of compensation. Nobody else was _____6_____ as much. Ford could afford to do so because of the great popularity of the Model T.

5. a) wheel   b) price   c) body   d) height   e) motor

6. a) driving   b) delaying   c) paying   d) buying   e) demanding

By 1925, however, as the greater convenience and better appearance of other manufacturers' products reduced Ford's competitive advantage, sales dropped. Ford's colleagues beseeched him to overhaul the design. He _____7_____. The fundamentally unchanged Model T continued its popularity decline until 1927, when promduction finally ended.

7. a) lied   b) refused   c) managed   d) searched   e) benefited

---

*From *The DRP: An Effectiveness Measure in Reading* by B.L. Koslin, et al., (p. 23), n.p.: Touchstone Applied Science Associates.

Illustrative Item 6.33.*

Easy Version of Passage

Henry Ford was a leader in the automobile business. He changed the way that cars are built. He was the first person to make cars the modern way. This way is known as mass production.

Ford began making cars around 1900. He studied the way that cars were built then. This is what he saw. The chassis or frame for the new car was set in one place in the factory. It stayed there. The whole car was built in that one place. First only the frame stood there. Then more parts were added. And more. The workers ran around the shop to get the parts. They brought them to the car. They put them on. Bit by bit the car was built.

Ford saw all this. But he didn't like it. The workers had to keep going back and forth for parts. Back and forth. Again and again. Too many minutes and even hours were wasted. Ford was concerned. Such a great waste of ____1____ was disturbing. "There must be a better way," he thought.

1. a) gas   b) oil   c) space   d) time   e) steel

Ford remembered something he had seen in a meat factory. First the hogs had been killed. Then they were carried on a belt or chain that ran around the factory. The hogs were brought to the workers on the chain. The workers stood still. This gave Ford an idea. The idea was to make cars on assembly lines. He had seen hogs carried along on a chain. Why not ____2____ cars the same way? Why not bring the work to the man? That would be better than having men run back and forth to do their work.

2. a) select   b) move   c) name   d) test   e) sell

So Ford build an assembly line. Each car was carried along on a revolving belt. It passed from worker to worker. Each man did his job. Ford had divided up the job of building a car. He had divided the work into many simple tasks. Each task was very easy. It did not require much skill. So the need for ____3____ was reduced. Even a man with little skill could learn to do this job. He needed very little instruction. Then he could do his job well.

3 . a) wealth   b) glass   c) paint   d) water   e) training

Cars were made mostly by hand in those days. Few machines were used. Ford understood something important about parts. He knew that hand-made parts would always differ fom each other. They might be alike. But never exactly the same. Not if they were made by hand. Ford, though, wanted to use parts that were exactly the same. He wanted the parts to fit any car. He thought this would be helpful in making a low-cost car.

Only machines could make identical parts. So Ford took jobs that men used to do by hand. He made machines to do the jobs. He used machines to build parts. The machines could make parts that were more alike. That way, the product was more ____4____. Any part could be used in any car. Cars could be turned out faster.

4. a) complete b) uniform c) powerful d) natural e) comfortable

Ford wanted to make things even better. He wanted to turn out cars even faster. So he raised the level of the belt that carried the cars. He put the belt at waist level. This new ____5____ was indeed an imporvement. The workers did not need to bend anymore. They did not get as tired. They could do more work. They could turn out more cars.

5. a) wheel   b) price   c) body   d) height   e) motor

Ford did something else that pleased the workers. He raised wages to $5 a day. That was the highest salary anywhere. Nobody else was ____6____ as much. But Ford was able to do it. His cars were being sold quickly. He was making a lot of money. People loved his Model T car.

6. a) driving   b) delaying   c) paying   d) buying e) demanding

But by 1925 sales fell. Other companies were making cars too. The other cars rode better. They looked nicer. Many people were choosing other cars. The men in Ford's company were worried. They spoke to him. They begged him to change the Model T. He ____7____. He did not want to make any major changes. So sales of the Model T kept falling. Fewer and fewer were sold. In 1927, Ford built his last Model T car.

7 a) lied   b) refused   c) managed   d) searched   e) benefited

*From *The DRP: An Effectiveness Measure in Heading* by B.L. Koslin, et al., (p. 24), n.p.: Touchstone Applied Science Associates.

There is no set rule for how to select words for removal in cloze tests. Roid and Haladyna (1982) report that a typical cloze method is to delete every fifth word from a hundred-word passage, but the DRP selects key words regardless of their position in the passage. Unfortunately, there seems to be no generally accepted criterion other than using one's intuitive judgment.

It is important, however, that the selected words be common words. That is to say, the examinees should be able to recognize the words removed as well as all of the response alternatives. Were this not the case, cloze-procedure could be merely a test of vocabulary. Of course, antonyms, synonyms, and homonyms would not be good distractors. Further, all of the response options should work grammatically in the sentence if it were read in isolation. The point of the procedure is that when the context is also considered, only one of the response alternatives should make sense.

Each of these techniques for removal of words is designed to reduce the likelihood of guessing by examinees. Collectively, the strategies for constructing cloze tests promote valid interpretations for the scores. According to the *DRP Handbook* (College Entrance Examination Board, 1986), there is an inherent strength for content-valid interpretations of scores derived from close-procedure items because ". . . a student who comprehends the prose in a passage ought to be able to answer the items correctly; . . . in order to select the correct response, the student must understand the prose; and . . . choosing wrong answers signals a failure to comprehend" (p. 3).

The cloze-procedure is certainly one of the most widely researched of all item formats. The reliability of cloze tests has been well documented (cf. Finn, 1978; Hively, Patterson, & Page, 1968; Roid & Haladyna, 1982). An excellent discussion of the validity and reliability of the cloze method is offered by Koslin, Zeno, and Koslin (1987). And, Bormuth (1971) offers a discussion of readability methods for evaluating passages as likely candidates for the procedure.

As originally conceived by Taylor (1953), cloze items were presented to examinees as sentence-completion items wherein they would supply the missing word for each blank space. While this approach had intuitive appeal, the idea of cloze tests remained unverified until Bormuth (1970) suggested a more rigorous theory for their development and use. His work remains seminal in the development of the procedure.

Bormuth proposed a procedure for transforming sentences into a series of who, what, when, where, and why questions. The idea was to provide uniformity among questions so that difficult questions would not be asked about easy prose, nor easy questions asked about difficult prose. This item-generating procedure was advanced by Finn (1978) and Roid and Haladyna (1978). The technique is technically complex, and the interested reader is referred to Roid and Haladyna's (1982) excellent description of generating prose-transformation items.

CONCLUSION

This chapter has paralleled the discussions presented in Chapter 5 for items in the multiple-choice format, with the focus here on items in the true-false, matching, short-answer, sentence-completion, and cloze-procedure formats. Each format has been described in turn, with a basic description of each, followed by a discussion of its advantages and criticisms, and finally an explanation of peculiarities and unique considerations to bear in mind when constructing an item in that format. As was mentioned in the introduction, many of the editorial rules for formatting items described in Chapter 5 also apply to items in these formats. Taken together, Chapters 5 and 6 describe thoroughly the information an item writer needs to prepare items in these commonly used formats.

The next chapter changes the focus from generating items to analyzing them. Item analysis presents one with systematic procedures for determining the quality of items. As will be stressed in the succeeding chapter, an item once written is still unfinished; it needs to be analyzed to determine whether it achieves its desired objective. Such analysis is also an important part of constructing good test items.

Chapter 7

Judging the Quality of Test Items: Item Analysis

INTRODUCTION

An item merely written is not complete. Once an idea for a test item has been conceived and articulated according to the rules for writing good items, the important task of determining its quality remains. If it is flawed, it must be improved or discarded. To accomplish such analysis for items, the writer must employ a precise methodology to systematically uncover information about an item, and then make judgments about it based on that information. In educational and psychological assessment, such judgments revolve around detecting and reducing errors in measurement, which can be in the form of either systematic bias or random error. This chapter explores the concept of measurement error first by explaining it and then by discussing strategies for determining the degree to which it may exist and how the sources for error can be reduced. By alleviating the causes of measurement error, the quality of particular test items correspondingly increases.

Two basic approaches can be used to unearth errors in measurement: through judgments by knowledgeable people using established criteria and through appropriate statistics. A variety of procedures exists for both, and both can address systematic bias as well as random error. This chapter describes the most widely practiced forms of these approaches for detecting both kinds of measurement error.

Throughout this chapter, the reader should keep in mind that many of the techniques of item analysis are grounded in either classical or modern test theory. In most instances, describing the theory in detail is beyond the scope of this book; therefore, this chapter will frequently refer the reader to other sources devoted to measurement theory for more thorough explanations.

Additionally, throughout this chapter various statistics will be cited as useful for analyzing particular data. The formulas for these statistics are not described in this book, because in most test-development contexts, the calculations required by the mathematical algorithms are accomplished with the aid of a computer. Many statistical programs are available for both large and small computers that will compute these statistics. While computers are not required for figuring most of the statistics presented in this book—in fact, many can easily be done either by hand or with the aid of only a pocket calculator—they are commonly used and do make the task more convenient. Instead, this chapter focuses on understanding the aims and reasons for a particular analytical look at items, as well as learning the procedures needed to accomplish it.

The following topics are covered in this chapter:

- measurement error
- item analysis
- validating the content of items
- judgmental approaches to item analysis
- item statistics
- item parameters
- item bias

MEASUREMENT ERROR

The reader has already been introduced to the concept of measurement error in Chapter 2, where it was discussed in relation to describing the purpose for test items. It was explained there that error is inherent in measuring educational achievements and psychological constructs. Here, the description of measurement error focuses upon techniques for detecting its presence and reducing the sources from whence it arose. These unwanted sources could be wording in items that is confusing to examinees, information in items that is not factually accurate, lack of congruence between an item and the objective it is intended to assess, and more. While measurement error cannot be completely eliminated in psychological assessment as it is currently practiced, keeping the sources of error to a minimum will contribute to making items better.

Description of Measurement Error

Measurement error can be simply described as the amount of deviation an examinee's score on a set of test items would exhibit if the test was administered to that examinee an infinite number of times, under identical conditions. The more those scores disperse, the greater the error of measurement. Of course, in real life, no examinee is given a set of test items an infinite number of times, so the measurement error must be estimated from a single administration. But, it can be estimated with precision. The precision with which a score is estimated is expressed in the term *standard error of measurement*. Theoreticians conceive of this relationship with the following equation:

True score = Observed score − Measurement error

where: *True score* is the score an examinee would obtain if no error was present, and

Observed score is the score an examinee actually received during a real-life test administration.

The true score is conceptualized as the mean score the examinee would have received by averaging his or her score from the infinite number of test administrations theoretically done. The standard error of measurement may be graphically represented as the distribution of scores around the true score for an individual. Figure 7.1 displays this graphical representation for two examinees, one of low ability and one of high ability.

Figure 7.1 Display of standard error of measurement for different abilities.

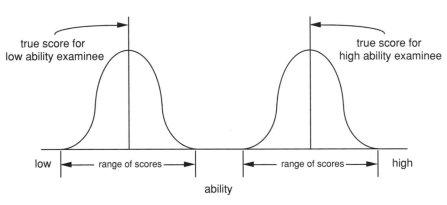

These highlighted points about measurement error are important to understand if one wishes to use properly the techniques of item analysis. The reader should be aware, however, that this description of measurement error scarcely touches the surface of the theory behind this topic. Researchers have written extensively about the theory of measurement error, from Thorndike's 1904 classic *An Introduction to the Theory of Mental and Social Measurements*, to the excellent 1986 text by Crocker and Algina, *Introduction to Classical and Modern Test Theory*. In between, dozens of fine books were written that describe in detail test theory and errors of measurement (e.g., Cronbach, 1984; Ebel & Frisbie, 1986; Gulliksen, 1950; Lindquist, 1936; Lord, 1952; Lord & Novick, 1968; Nunnally, 1978) to which the interested reader is referred.

Keeping Measurement Error in Perspective

One should realize, however, that the presence of error in psychological assessments is not so serious a problem as it first appears. There are a number of reasons why this is so. First, it is easy to overstate the importance of error in mental measurements because seemingly little is understood about psychological processes and how they may be assessed. This is in itself not too great a problem when one considers that our understanding of many aspects of the physical realm is similarly limited. In fact, psychological measurements are probably no more plagued by error than are measurements in other areas of science. Furthermore, some small amount of measurement error probably does not harm most scientific investigations, whether in the physical realm or the psychological domain.

Another reason why the importance of error in measurement is often exaggerated is that the terminology and methods used for describing it can have an imposing appearance to persons unfamiliar with the statistics involved. Since many aspects of measurement error can be conveniently expressed in mathematical terms—and later in this chapter we will explore some of the techniques for doing so—it is difficult for untutored persons to regard such numbers with perspective. Mathematical models for describing measurement error, with their specialized nomenclature and elaborate, Greek-lettered symbols, are seemingly impressive. This makes it easy to overstate their importance.

While it is worthwhile to keep the issue of measurement error in perspective, the skilled item developer identifies and reduces sources of error throughout the item-construction process. By identifying and reducing the sources for measurement error, the quality of the items will be correspondingly improved. Therefore, it is important to learn about error in this context and discover strategies that will help to reduce it, while simultaneously keeping perspective on the concepts of measurement error.

UNDERSTANDING ITEM ANALYSIS

Item analysis is the process by which test items are examined critically. Its purpose is to identify and reduce the sources of error in measurement. Writers routinely perform item analysis so that they may gauge the quality of items and discard those which are unacceptable, repair those which can be improved, and retain those which meet criteria of merit.

Item analysis is accomplished in either of two ways: through numerical analysis on by judgmental approaches. In numerical item analysis, the statistical properties of particular test items are examined in relation to a response distribution. This definition requires that someone has already prepared a numeric description of test items *after* they have been administered to a group of examinees, as is done in a field trial for examination development. The primary purpose for field trials of items is, of course, to collect appropriate data for reviewing them.

While the field trial of items is necessary to gather the data for analysis of individual items, this text does not discuss the process of conducting a field trial. A field trial is itself a procedure involving myriad considerations, such as how items should be ordered on a test form or distributed among various test forms, how to determine an appropriate sample, and necessary considerations of the size of that sample. Although these issues are important to constructing a good test instrument, they are more properly concerns for test developers rather than item writers, and therefore they are not addressed here. The reader can easily identify sources in which these issues are fully addressed, such as Allen and Yen (1979), Crocker and Algina (1986), Nunnally (1987), Thorndike (1982), and many others.

Judgmental approaches to analyzing items involve asking people to comment on particular items according to some criteria. The persons asked for comment might be content-area experts, editorial specialists, or even examinees. Judgmental reviews have two guiding principles: each reviewer must be qualified for the task, and the task itself must be a systematic process. In this context, *a systematic process* means that a methodology is defined and that criteria for the review are available. Both numerical analysis and judgmental review are important ways for writers to learn about the items they have written. Each of these avenues to analyzing items will be explored in appropriate sections of this chapter.

VALIDATING THE CONTENT OF ITEMS

It was explained in Chapter 3 that evidence for valid test-score interpretations is not inherent in the item-construction process but must be gathered through a systematic validation study. Such a study will typically be an examination of content-related evidence for validity. The procedures used for gathering content-related evidence for validity can also be of enormous help in determining the quality of test items. The item writer can use the information uncovered through this systematic study to examine and improve items.

A content-validation study usually seeks to establish a consensus of informed opinions about the degree of congruence between particular test items and specific descriptions of the content domain that is intended to be assessed by those items. This typically requires convening a panel of expert judges who rate the item-to-content congruence according to some established criteria.

Two principal methods are used to gather the opinions of experts about the congruence between a content domain and specific test items. In the first method, judges are given the objective descriptions and test items that have already been matched by the intention of the item writer. In other words, the item writer, who will have constructed an item intentionally to reflect a particular domain or objective, will tell the judges which item is supposed to be matched with which description. The role of the judges, then, is to confirm or reject the opinion of the item writer.

Of course, an appropriate form for recording the opinions of the judges will be needed. The form for recording judges' ratings should allow for more than just a yes-versus-no matching by permitting judges to record degrees of congruence—typically, one designation recording a strong match, a second designation noting a moderate match or uncertainty, and a third designation denoting a poor match or no match at all. These three categories are all that is necessary; finer discriminations are of little practical value and could needlessly complicate the consensus-building process. Also, a space on the form should be provided where judges can comment on the rationale for a given opinion. An example of such a form is given in Table 7.1.

Another, and stronger, approach to gaining consensus among expert judges of item-objective congruence is to refrain from informing the judges beforehand of the item writer's intended match. In this approach, the judges are simply given the items and the objectives without any indication of which item is meant to be matched with which objective. Each judge will indicate his or her perceived match on a rating sheet, and a project coordinator will tally the responses. A consensus of judges' opinions as to a particular item-objective match is considered content-related evidence for validity. Table 7.2 offers a sample of a rating form that can be used for this data-gathering technique. Variations may be made in the forms displayed in Tables 7.1 and 7.2 to suit particular circumstances.

As a further means of enhancing the rigor of this judging process, the judges may be assigned to a "blind" panel, that is, they do not meet in face-to-face sessions, nor do they know the identity of the other panelists. Opinions of the panelists are gathered by a project coordinator through telephone or mail contacts. Because the panelists do not meet, the consensus would presumably be uncontaminated by specious persuasion, or by the effects of personal prestige, rank, or charisma.

In most instances four or five judges rating each test item will suffice; however, if a large number of items are to be rated, the items may be split into two or more groups, and four or five judges for each group of items will be needed. For tests that have a cut-off score

Table 7.1   Item-Objective Congruence Rating Form

Name _____

Instructions: Read Objective #1 below. Next, read the first item in the test booklet. Consider carefully the degree to which the item is congruent with the skill. Rate the congruence according to this scheme:

> H = high degree of congruence
> M = medium degree of congruence
> L = low degree of congruence or uncertainty

If you have comments about the congruence of this item, record them in the space provided. After you have finished with this item, proceed to the second item, and thereafter to all subsequent items, rating each in the same manner.

Objective #1
Use mathematical techniques to solve real-life problems.

	Rating	Comment
Item #1	_____	_____
Item #2	_____	_____
Item #3	_____	_____
Item #4	_____	_____
Item #6	_____	_____
Item #9	_____	_____

Objective #2
Use the properties of two- and three-dimensional figures to perform geo-metrical calculations.

	Rating	Comment
Item #3	_____	_____
Item #5	_____	_____
Item #8	_____	_____
Item #10	_____	_____
Item #11	_____	_____

Table 7.2 Judge's Summary Sheet for the Items/Objectives Matching Task (Sample)

Items/Objectives Matching Task

Reviewer: _____ Date: _____

Content Area: _____

First, read carefully through the lists of domain specifications and test items. Your task is to indicate whether or not you feel each test item is a measure of *one* of the domain specifications. It is, if you feel examinee performance on the test item would provide an indication of an examinee's level of performance in a pool of test items measuring the domain specification. Beside each objective, write in the test item numbers corresponding to the test items that you feel measure the objective. In some instances, you may feel that items do not measure any of the available domain specifications. Write these test item numbers in the space provided at the bottom of the rating form.

Objective	Matching Test Items
1	
2	
3	
4	
No Matches	

From R. K. Hambleton "Validating the test scores" (p. 225) in R. A. Berk (Ed.), *A Guide to Criterion-Referenced Test Construction,* 1984, Baltimore: The Johns Hopkins University Press.

and significant consequences for examinees, then more judges—possibly as many as ten or even fifteen—are recommended. Under no circumstance should one person be the sole judge in a content-validation study, especially the person who wrote the test item. Unrecognized prejudices, chauvinistic perspectives, or other biases can too easily go unnoticed when one judges one's own work.

The judges should be both expert in the subject area they are assessing and trained for the matching task. A judge's subject-area competence is requisite to his or her selection because any subject has many details that could go unnoticed by a novice. Training the judges for the matching task is equally important, for the task requires more skill than may be imagined at first glance. Chapter 4 included a thorough discussion of strategies for arriving at an item-objective match and could be used as a training guide.

Quantifying Results of Judge Opinions

Once the relevant data from the judges' evaluation of items has been gathered, the information must be analyzed and interpreted. This means determining whether a consensus of opinions has been achieved. The item writer, seeking to get feedback about the quality of items, must decide how many judgments matching a particular test item to a specific objective must coincide in order to declare that a consensus of opinion has been achieved. There is no precisely established number, but the consensus should be quite evident; e.g., if there are five judges, four must agree, or if there are ten judges, eight must agree.

Although simply tabulating the number of opinions that agree is undoubtably the most popular method, other procedures are sometimes preferable. Some of these methods require quantitative approaches and may be more precise than tallies. For example, if there is the presumption (often made) that for every test item there should be one, and only one, clear match to a skill or objective, an index of the item-objective congruence may be derived (Rovinelli and Hambleton, 1977; Hambleton, 1980). For this procedure, judges would be instructed to assign a +1 if there is a strong match between an item and an objective, a 0 if a judge is uncertain whether congruence exists, and a -1 if the item does not match the objective. The rating form displayed in Table 7.1 is an example of a form that accommodates this quantification scheme.

A formula indicating that any particular item, k, is congruent with a specific skill or objective, i, can be applied to the judges' ratings. This formula is:

$$I_{ik} = \frac{(N-1)\sum_{j=1}^{n} X_{ijk} + N \sum_{j=1}^{n} X_{ijk} - \sum_{j=1}^{n} X_{ijk}}{2(N-1)n}$$

In this formula, I_{ik} is the index value, i and k are as described above, N is the number of skills or objectives, and n is the number of judges. The X_{ijk} is simply the rating assigned by a particular judge for the congruence between a given item and a specific objective. The Σ is of course the symbol for summation.

Although rather imposing at first glance, this formula is actually straightforward and can be easily worked through with a set of data. For example, suppose a test has 36 items that are intended to assess five specific objectives. For this example, suppose the item-objective congruence rating of interest is between the test's first item and the test's second objective. (In other words, "How well does item #1 match objective #2?") Now, imagine nine judges have rated the item for its congruence to the objective. One of the judges rated the item as a poor match (or -1), one of the judges rated the item as a moderate match (or 0), and seven of the judges rated the item-objective match as strong (or +1). The sum of the nine judges' ratings is 6 (i.e., (-1) + 1(0) + 7(+1) = 6). Applying these numbers to the item-objective congruence formula yields the following:

$$I_{ik} = \frac{(5-1)6 + 5(6) - 6}{2(5-1)9} = \frac{(4)6 + 30 - 6}{2(4)9} = \frac{24 + 30 - 6}{(8)9} = \frac{48}{72} = .67$$

This formula will yield an index score from +1 to -1. A +1 would be obtained if all the judges agree that there is a strong item-objective match. Conversely, if none of the judges agree that an item is matched to one and only one skill or objective, the formula will yield an index of -1.

For the item writer, this index can provide information useful for gauging the quality of an item in either of two ways: by using the item-objective congruence index either as a relative standard or as an absolute standard. When the index is viewed as a relative standard, the statistic for any particular item is judged in relation to its power (i.e., its proximity to +1) compared to the power of the index for the other items considered. For example, if the index value were computed for each of 50 items and it proved to be comparatively low for, say, six, of the items, then the six would be suspect and should be reviewed.

To use the index in an absolute sense, the item writer must establish a criterion level for the index, above which items would be passed, and below which items would be reviewed for their success in fulfilling a test's objective. This criterion level may be set by deciding the poorest level of judges' rating that would be acceptable. In the computational example above there were nine judges. The criterion might be that at least seven of the judges should rate the item as strongly congruent to a given objective. This standard would yield a criterion for the index of .78. Hence, .78 would be the floor value for accepting the congruence for any particular match of an item with an objective. In the example above, the index was .67—below the .78 criterion—indicating that the content of that particular item should be examined by the item writer for its appropriateness as a measure of the objective.

Alternative Quantification Schemes

Klein and Kosecoff (1975) describe a variation of this tally method which includes examinees' performance data in the congruence process. This procedure may be slightly more rigorous than merely tallying judges' ratings; however, it is probably less precise than computing an item-objective index. Also, Polin and Baker (1979) offer an item-review scale consisting of six dimensions: domain description, content limits, distractor limits, distractor domain or response criteria, format, and directions plus a sample item. A rater reviews an item and scores it on each of the six dimensions according to prescribed criteria. This procedure is intended to provide information useful to discovering the relationship between "what test writers have wrought and the original test specification" (p. 2). Although an exploratory study of this methodology produced mixed results, the approach does represent a useful attempt to judge content-related evidence for validity.

USING LEADING QUESTIONS IN ITEM ANALYSIS

Judgmental approaches to analyzing items can be very effective methods for improving items. Obviously, the item-congruence index discussed in the preceding section is a judgmental approach, but there are other methods involving judgment as well, such as the technique of asking leading questions to appropriate people. For example, if the items are be included on a test for assessing school children, asking teachers to review and discuss items informally with the item writer is often worthwhile. No particular form is needed for this discussion, but some guiding questions might focus the task. Such questions might include the following:, "In your opinion, will this item be confusing to students?"; "Do you notice any language that might be offensive on stereotyping to students?"; "Do you believe the distractors are plausible?"; "Are there any vocabulary words in the item that you imagine will be unfamiliar to students at this age or grade level,"; "Are the graphics clear?"

Another group to whom the item writer can turn is persons in the same category as future examinees. If a test is being developed for, say, fifth-graders, the opinions of students who are in the fifth grade can be valuable. Again, the same guiding questions used with teachers can be used for discussion with students.

There are two principal disadvantages to this technique of informal discussion. First, it is often difficult to manage the logistics for such visits. They may be hard to arrange in schools, because teachers and administrators could view this as an interruption of valuable instructional time. Or, if the test is to be used for licensing, one frequently does not know beforehand who will take the test and an appropriate group cannot be easily identified.

The second disadvantage to the technique of informal discussion is that it consumes enormous amounts of time. It is the author's experience that in a typical 50-minute classroom period, perhaps only three or four test items will be discussed. This drawback might be alleviated if the writer were to select from a pool of freshly prepared items only a few for discussion, and then consider the other items based on what has been said by students about the selected items.

Regardless of the logistical difficulties in managing an informal discussion of items, the practice can be extremely valuable to improving items and has been used with students as early as the second grade. In fact, students of all ages frequently demonstrate remarkable insight into the reasons for asking a particular question, and they can diagnose specific flaws in items and suggest improvements.

While informal discussion of items with an appropriate group is not a widely practiced technique for analyzing items, it is highly recommended. It can yield specific improvements in items and—perhaps even more importantly—it can help the writer become sensitive to examinees in ways that may be difficult to describe but are nevertheless extremely valuable.

ITEM STATISTICS

A number of statistics can be used to indicate particular features of test items. Researchers (Crocker & Algina, 1986) categorize these indices by the parameters which are commonly examined:

1. Indices that describe the distribution of responses to a single item (i.e., the mean and variance of the item responses),

2. Indices that describe the degree of relationship between response to the item and some criterion of interest, and

3. Indices that are a function of both item variance and relationship to a criterion.

Some of the commonly used statistics for describing these item parameters are *p*-values, *variance*, and a variety of *item discrimination* indices, such as the point-biserial estimate of correlation, the biserial correlation coefficient, and the phi correlational estimate. Each of these statistical indices is important for a specific purpose in item analysis, and each will be described.

The Proportion Correct Index

Probably the most popular item-difficulty index for dichotomously scored test items is the *p*-value. The *p*-value is merely a shorthand way of expressing the proportion of examinees who responded correctly to a particular item. It may be most clearly explained by using a few simple examples. Suppose a given item was administered to 100 examinees, and 80 of them responded correctly. In such a case, the *p*-value is .8, indicating that 80 percent of the examinees responded correctly to the item. If another item were administered to a group of 311 examinees and 187 of them responded correctly, the *p*-value would be .60 (i.e., $187 \div 312 = .60$). Table 7.3 presents a simple table of *p*-values for a hypothetical five-item test.

Table 7.3 *P*-Values for a Five-Item Test

Item Number	p-value
1	.68
2	.45
3	.91
4	.36
5	.48

The *p*-value for an item does not by itself indicate whether an item is good or bad; rather, it merely represents a difficulty index relative to the particular group of examinees to whom the item was administered. If the same item were administered to a different group of examinees, the *p*-value would probably not be identical.

The group-referent aspect of the *p*-value is termed *sample dependence*, meaning that any given *p*-value is dependent upon the particular group to whom the item was administered. This sample dependence characteristic for the index can be easily seen by imagining that a given item is administered to third-grade students and again to sixth-graders. Since these two groups are not from the same total population, the *p*-values yielded by the two groups would probably be different. The item would have two *p*-values, one indicating its difficulty relative to third-graders, and the other showing its difficulty for students in the sixth grade. Each *p*-value depends upon which sample of examinees is tested. This is what is meant by saying the *p*-value is sample dependent.

Of course, if a sample of examinees is carefully selected to represent a larger population, then the *p*-value for the sample can be interpreted as similar to a value that would have been obtained had the item been administered to the entire population. (Subject to the limits of the sampling design.) Conversely, if a group of examinees is not selected from a larger population by a method that allows generalizations, then the index is meaningful only to that particular group of examinees.

It is important to understand the sample-dependence feature for *p*-values because it is one of the most salient aspects of *p*-values. As we shall see later, other statistics have been developed which attempt to define a difficulty index independent of a particular sample of examinees.

Using *P*-values for Item Analysis

P-values are of enormous help to a writer during item analysis. By understanding *p*-values and interpreting them correctly, the writer can see how an item is performing in relation to a given group of examinees, as was displayed in Table 7.3. However, they can also be used to give the item writer a more complete description of an item's performance. For instance, p-values can aid in detecting some common writers' mistakes, such as making apparent wording in an item that is evidently confusing to examinees, recognizing flawed distractors, and identifying inadvertently miskeyed items. The index can allow the writer to see how an item is performing for examinees within the same population who differ in ability. Each of these uses for the p-value will be explained in turn, but first, the p-value must be displayed in a manner that facilitates such interpretations.

While Table 7.3 presented p-values for a group of items in a test, in item analysis work, p-values are typically displayed singly. Additionally, for item analysis, a p-value is computed for each response alternative: the correct option and all of the distractors. Further, when p-values are displayed in this manner, it is customary to also report the number of examinees who omitted the item. Table 7.4 presents an example of p-values reported for every response alternative to a single test item as well as the number of examinees who omitted the item.

Table 7.4 *P*-Values for a Single Test Item

Response Alternative	A	B	C*	D	omits	Total
Number	28	17	197	41	3	286
p-value	.10	.06	.69	.14		

*correct response

As can be seen in Table 7.4, the p-values reveal much data useful to writers trying to improve items. In this instance, the correct response is indexed at .69, indicating that for most tests of general achievement the item is neither too difficult nor too easy for this group of examinees. Also, as a group, examinees have selected all of the distractors, which may signify that none is rejected out-of-hand. Often, this is a good indicator of the quality of an item; however, since comparatively few examinees (six percent) selected option B, it may be worthwhile to examine this distractor for possible improvements.

It is common in most general assessments of academic achievement for a test developer to specify limits for item difficulty. Often, such limits for p-values are that the set of items on the test can range from a low of .40 to a high of .80. There are, of course, many instances when other limits for item difficulty will be appropriate. The writer should be aware of the test developer's limits for item difficulty values, as they can guide the writer in deciding which items should be reviewed.

Now, note the p-values for another item, displayed in Table 7.5. In this instance, p-values reveal several flaws in the item. Apparently, examinees find this item confusing since their responses are widely scattered among the response alternatives. The correct response, A, attracted fewer examinees (27 percent) than did one of the distractors, C (45 percent). And distractor B was apparently so implausible than no one responded to it. Also, a comparatively large number of examinees omitted responding to the item, which may be another indication that the item is confusing. Taken together, these findings suggest a seriously flawed item.

Table 7.5 *P*-Values for a Poor Test Item

Response Alternative	A*	B	C	D	omits	Total
Number	77	0	130	63	16	286
p-value	.27	.00	.45	.22		

*correct response

Lest the reader imagine that an item so fraught with error would not be produced by serious item writers, the reader should be aware that flaws in items frequently do not become apparent until they are subject to the scrutiny of item analysis. Remember, constructing good test items is not a process that ends with the initial writing; it demands rigorous scrutiny of the item as well.

Miskeyed Items

Another useful feature of *p*-values for item development work is for identifying items that have been miskeyed. Regretfully, miskeying items is all too common in item preparation. In many instances it is an understandable lapse. Sometimes the tedium of producing many items can cause writers to be lax in attending to detail, and an item will be miskeyed. At other times, the ambiguity of ill-conceived or poorly worded items is not immediately noticed, and the correct response may not be apparent. Occasionally, when a particular item is designed to assess a complex cognitive-processing skill, the subtleties of language or the difficulty of the content result in miskeying items.

Miskeyed items often become obvious when the item writer examines a table of *p*-values that display widely different results from what had been anticipated. For example, Table 7.6 displays statistics for a sample test item in which the item writer perceived one correct response (B), but examinees uniformly selected another

Table 7.6 *P*-Values for a Miskeyed Test Item

Response Alternative	A	B*	C	D	omits	Total
Number	202	31	28	25	0	286
p-value	.71	.11	.10	.9		

*correct response

response alternative (A). In this case, the item is a good item, but one that had been miskeyed.

Comparing *p*-values for High- and Low-Achieving Subpopulations

Sometimes it is useful to compare subgroups of the examinee population to determine how an item is performing. For this analysis, the population is often divided into two groups, a high-achieving group and a low-achieving group. Typically, the groups are examinees whose total score on a test comprise the top 27 percent of all examinees, and those whose scores place them in the bottom 27 percent of the examinees. The figure 27 percent is chosen because it is used in some computational algorithms for determining internal reliability indices and Kelly (1939) demonstrated that this number will provide a stable index of differences between high and low ability groups. For this analysis, the principal focus is on determining how well the item is functioning for the extremes of the ability range. Table 7.7 displays item data for this analysis.

Table 7.7. *P*-Values for Examinee Subgroups on a Single Test Item

Response Alternative	A	B*	C	D	omit
upper 27%	.29	.61	.08	.02	1
lower 27%	.31	.27	.31	.11	6
difference	-.02	.34	-.23	-.09	

*correct response

Note that the item statistics displayed in Table 7.7 reveal that the difference between the examinee subpopulations is 34 percent for the correct response. This is a rather large difference which may signify that the item was not especially difficult for high-ability examinees (the top group) but was quite difficult for low-ability examinees (the bottom group). For many kinds of assessments, this difference is a desirable feature for an item. Also, heed the fact that the difference between the groups for all other response alternatives is a negative value. Such negative values indicate that fewer high-ability examinees selected the distractor than did low-ability examinees. Again, usually, this is a positive feature for an item. Still, writers should pay attention to the fact that the difference between the groups for response alternative A is a scant .02 percent. This suggests that option A should be reviewed.

Comparing Several Subpopulations

Frequently in item analysis several segments of a population of examinees are compared. Each segment, or subpopulation, of the total group of examinees represents an ability stratum. Ideally, the examinees are grouped into segments, or subpopulations, by their performance on an outside criterion, such as another measure of analogous content with similar reliability. In practice, however, such external measures are rarely available; hence, the test itself is usually used as a measure of examinees' ability. For this purpose, the total test score is used.

When the total population to whom the test has been administered is large (about 200 examinees or more), typically five groups are formed, each representing about 20 percent of the distribution of scores on the test. A sample of responses reported by fifths of the population distribution is presented in Table 7.8, which will be described momentarily.

The procedure for splitting the population is straightforward. First, a frequency distribution of scores is prepared. Then, exact scores are noted at the 20th, 40th, 60th, and 80th percentile points, yielding five ranges of scores. Test scores within each of these ranges become the criterion into which particular examinee scores are grouped. Because most populations exhibit skewed distributions, not every group will have precisely 20 percent of the examinee population, but most groups should be fairly close to 20 percent.

Often, when the examinee population is divided into fifths, it is useful to display *p*-values graphically. Such a representation makes it easy to identify the relative position of each segment of the examinee population. Flaws in items that may go otherwise unnoticed, are revealed by viewing the number of examinees for each distractor for the various subpopulations, as well as the *p*-values. Table 7.8 displays a graphical representation of an item with the corresponding numbers for each subpopulation and overall *p*-values.

Table 7.8 Graphical Representation of an Item Including Item Statistics

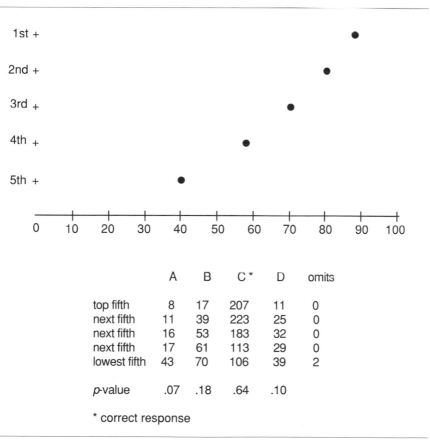

	A	B	C *	D	omits
top fifth	8	17	207	11	0
next fifth	11	39	223	25	0
next fifth	16	53	183	32	0
next fifth	17	61	113	29	0
lowest fifth	43	70	106	39	2
p-value		.07	.18	.64	.10

* correct response

Notice in 7.8 that the top fifth of the population (that is, the highest scorers on the total test) also achieved the highest number of correct responses on this particular item, followed by the next fifth who achieved the next-highest number of correct responses, and so forth, until the lowest fifth is shown achieving the lowest number of correct responses. For a group-referenced interpretation, this item seems to be behaving very well since one would anticipate that the examinees who are most able in the tested construct would also have the greatest proportion correct on any particular item. Notice also that the lower-ability groups increasingly chose an incorrect response alternative.

Table 7.9 similarly displays data for a different item. Notice, here that the item is not performing very well and needs to be revised. As can be seen, no examinee, regardless of ability, selected distractor A. It adds no information to the test and should be dropped or modified. Also, more examinees at every level of ability selected response alternative C rather than the intended correct response, B. This could indicate poor wording. And, as shown in the graphical representation, the two lowest achieving groups outperformed the highest achieving group. This is a clear sign to examine the item for confusing wording or for observing the phenomenon of proactive inhibition (a concept discussed in Chapter 4). In either case, this item needs major repair. It does show, however, an example of using graphical representation and numerical analysis for improving items.

Item Discrimination Indices

Discrimination is another important concept for judging the quality of items. Actually, we were examining discrimination for items in the preceding section, but it may not have been conceptually understood. Discrimination for items may be conceptually understood as the relationship between the difficulty of an item and the ability of the examinees. Simply put, *item discrimination* is an index for determining differences among individual examinees on the subject matter or psychological construct being assessed. It relies

Table 7.9 Graphical Representation of a Poorly Performing Item.

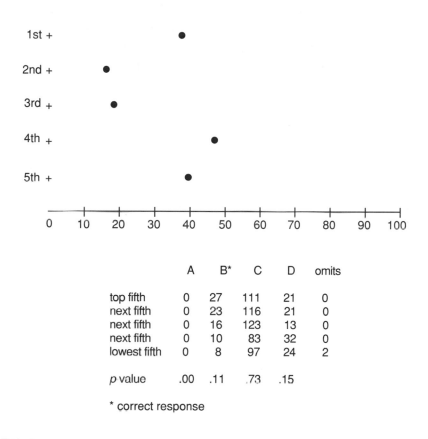

	A	B*	C	D	omits
top fifth	0	27	111	21	0
next fifth	0	23	116	21	0
next fifth	0	16	123	13	0
next fifth	0	10	83	32	0
lowest fifth	0	8	97	24	2
p value	.00	.11	.73	.15	

* correct response

upon a fundamental assumption, which is that examinees who exhibit mastery of the subject or high ability in the construct are
presumed to be more likely to answer any particular item about that
subject or construct than examinees who exhibit low mastery or
ability. Conversely, items that either all examinees responded to
correctly or all examinees missed do not discriminate. Items that do
not discriminate yield no information about differences between
individuals.

Mathematically, item discrimination defines an item's difficulty as a function of the examinee population's ability in the construct being assessed. In other words, discrimination is related to difficulty for a particular ability. The relationship may be readily seen by examining the graphical representation of four items. Figures 7.2 to 7.5 display such graphical representations of items at four levels of item discrimination: high discrimination, moderate discrimination, no discrimination, and negative discrimination.

The item represented in Figure 7.2 would usually be considered to be a good item because it is highly discriminating. It distinguishes among examinees who are of high ability and got the item correct and those who are lower in ability and did not respond correctly to the item. Notice in 7.2 that as examinee ability increases, there is a corresponding increase in the difficulty. The data shown earlier in Table 7.4 would be for this highly discriminating item.

Figure 7.2. Characteristics of a highly discriminating test item.

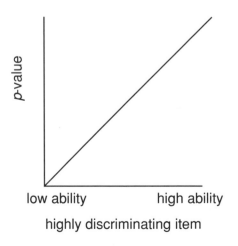

highly discriminating item

Figure 7.3 presents data for an item which discriminates moderately well. It shows differences among examinees but not as sharply as the item in 7.2.

Figure 7.3. Characteristics of a moderately discriminating test item.

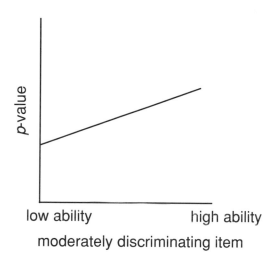

moderately discriminating item

Figure 7.4 displays a graphical representation of an item that shows no differentiation between high and low achievers. Probably, this is an item that either all examinees got correct or all incorrect. Typically, such items add little or no information to a test and are rejected. However, zero discriminating items should not be rejected summarily. There are some items that assess skills so important to a particular test's objective that one would expect all examinees to respond correctly.

Finally, Figure 7.5 is a graphical representation of a negatively discriminating item. In items of this type, more low-ability examinees answered this particular item correctly than did high-ability persons. This usually means that the item is poorly worded or in some way confusing to examinees who have greater knowledge of the content. Here, it is likely that proactive inhibition is operating for the item. Negatively discriminating items are almost always in need of repair by the writer, or they should be discarded.

Figure 7.4. Characteristics of a non-discriminating test item.

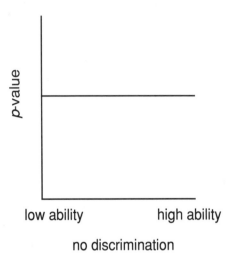

no discrimination

Figure 7.5. Characteristics of a negatively discriminating test item.

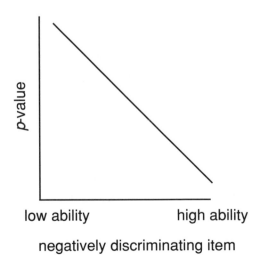

negatively discriminating item

Although, generally speaking, discrimination is a positive item attribute, judgment must be used in deciding when an item discriminates optimally. In some easy mastery-type items, it is appropriate for items to be highly discriminating at just one level of ability, as was seen in the earlier example of an item on an airline pilot's certification test in which examinees are requested to identify the radio broadcast frequency used by the control tower at Los Angeles International Airport. At other times, very good items may discriminate less restrictively.

Still, such judgments about optimal discrimination could be arbitrary without guidance. Fortunately, several statistical procedures are available that can quantify the discrimination of an item. These are especially useful statistics in item analysis because they often will guide the item writer to specific items needing improvement.

The Point-Biserial Measure of Correlation

One index of discrimination is the *point-biserial correlation coefficient*. As a measure of correlation, the point-biserial coefficient estimates the degree of association between two variables: a single test item and a total test score. As before, for most purposes of item analysis, the total test score is considered a reasonable measure of examinees' ability. It is often the only measure of ability available to the item writer when he or she is considering the quality of items. When the test item is inherently dichotomous (i.e., scored in only one of two possible categories, such as correct or incorrect) and the total test score is inherently continuous (that is, the scores range from low to high), the point-biserial statistic is most useful for examining the relative performance of an item between two groups.

The point-biserial estimate of correlation is a *product-moment correlation coefficient*. To understand this term and its advantages for analyzing items, one must realize that moments are thought of as standard score deviations about a mean. The deviates themselves are referred to as the first moments of a distribution; the squared deviates are the second moments; cubed deviates are the third; and so forth. Since standard scores have a mean of zero, one standard score away from the mean is the first deviate. By this conceptual approach, and by calculus, point-biserial coefficient of correlation is the association of two sets of standard scores. The advantage of this arrangement of data is that the relationship between an item score and a total test score is on a common base so that they may be meaningfully correlated.

With this statistic, the item writer can gauge the discriminating value of a test item. For example, consider the data displayed in Table 7.10. Here, several test items are arranged in descending order of their difficulty. The discrimination value for each item, as established by the point-biserial statistic, is also cited. Generally speaking, items with higher point-biserials are more highly discriminating. Conversely, items with relatively low point-biserials are less discriminating. As a general practice, items with negative point-biserials are either dropped from further consideration or revised.

Item writers will use the information yielded by the point-biserial correlation in conjunction with p-values to examine the quality of particular items. When an item has a difficulty index within a range deemed appropriate for the goals of a test (often, $.40 \leq p \leq .80$) and is relatively highly discriminating, the item is judged to be sound. For example, notice in Table 7.10 that the first item (test item #3) is too easy for our criterion and also discriminates poorly. Hence, this item is diagnosed as flawed and needs review. Item #14, the most difficult item in the set, also needs review. It is apparently confusing to most examinees since the few examinees who got the item correct came from no apparent ability group. Item #9, however, seems to be operating well; its difficulty is within the acceptable range, and its relative discriminating power is high.

Table 7.10 Difficulty and Discrimination for a Hypothetical Test

---

Item	*P*-Value	Point-Biserial
3	.94	-.09
1	.86	.06
16	.75	.12
9	.73	.45
2	.68	.15
11	.62	-.21
15	.60	.31
7	.55	.46
8	.51	.45
14	.28	-.21

In using the point-biserial coefficient of correlation for item analysis, it is often helpful to contrast the coefficient for the correct response alternative with that of the distractors. Accordingly, computing this statistic for each of the response alternatives—the correct response as well as the distractors—is commonly done. Discrimination for a single item is presumed to exist if the coefficient for the correct response is a positive number while the same statistic for the incorrect response alternatives is negative. Table 7.11 displays the statistics for a test item that exhibits this circumstance. By this criterion, it is a good test item since it exhibits a high level of discrimination.

Shortcomings of the Point-Biserial Estimate

Despite the fact that the information yielded by the point-biserial correlation is often used in item analysis, the statistic is not problem-free. With only casual analysis, one can realize that the particular item score being analyzed has itself contributed to the total test score, or ability measure. This leads one to wonder whether the

Table 7.11   An Item Displayed with *P*-Values and Point-Biserial Indices

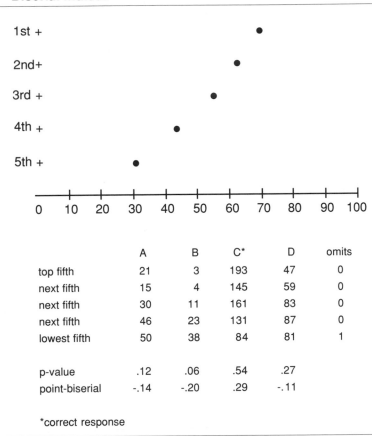

	A	B	C*	D	omits
top fifth	21	3	193	47	0
next fifth	15	4	145	59	0
next fifth	30	11	161	83	0
next fifth	46	23	131	87	0
lowest fifth	50	38	84	81	1
p-value	.12	.06	.54	.27	
point-biserial	-.14	-.20	.29	-.11	

*correct response

information is actually spurious and may therefore be misinterpreted. Logically, this point is correct, but in practice it is not a serious problem since the effect of a single item on the total score for a set of items is minimal, especially when the number of items is comparatively large, say, 25 or more.

When very precise estimates are required, or when the number of items is fewer than 25, the point-biserial estimate may be corrected for spuriousness. The formulas for calculating the correction are not especially complex, but they are computationally long, and they are seldom employed for the purposes of item analysis. (They are used in some multivariate analyses.) Therefore, they are not described here; instead, the interested reader may readily find them in any of several sources (e.g., Allen & Yen, 1979; Henrysson, 1963; Nunnally, 1978; Thorndike, 1982).

A further problem with the point-biserial correlation coefficient is that when the distribution of scores in the total test group is continuous, the range for the statistic is restricted to less than +1 and greater than -1. In fact, the point-biserial range is a function of the point at which the ability groups are split. This anomaly of numbers can be most easily comprehended when one considers the point mentioned above that very easy items and very difficult items provide relatively little differentiation between high-ability examinees and low-ability examinees. Despite these technical limitations (which will be elaborated upon momentarily), the statistic remains useful for item analysis and is the generally preferred statistic for examining item discrimination by traditional item analyses.

The Biserial Estimate of Correlation

Another statistic that can be used for analyzing items for discrimination is the *biserial estimate of correlation*. It is closely related to the point-biserial correlation, with an important difference. The distinction between these two measures exists in the assumptions. Whereas the point-biserial statistic presumes that one of the two variables being correlated is a true dichotomy, the biserial estimate of correlation assumes that both variables are inherently continuous. Further, the assumption is made that the distribution of scores for both variables is normal. For computational purposes, however, one of the variables has been arbitrarily divided into two groups, one low and the other high. In item analysis, the two groups are examinees who responded correctly to a given item and those who did not.

For practical purposes in item analysis, the strength of this statistic lies in its ability to overcome the limitations of the point-biserial statistic discussed above. When it can be assumed that the construct being assessed is normally distributed among the examinee population, the biserial range is limited from −1 to +1 absolutely. This means that examinees of either very low ability or very high ability are better represented in the correlational estimate. Thus, if the writer is considering items at the extremes of the difficulty range, the biserial estimate of correlation is preferred to the point-biserial statistic.

The Phi Coefficient

The *phi coefficient of correlation* is another estimate of a correlational relationship that can be used for analyzing test items. Like other correlation coefficients, it yields an estimate between +1 and −1. However, it differs from the two previously discussed correlation estimates because it assumes a genuine dichotomy in both variables to be correlated. The principal focus of the phi coefficient is to determine the degree of association between an item and some criterion, like some program feature, gender, or some other demographic characteristic.

During item analysis, it is often convenient to correlate two items, giving the effect of treating each item as a criterion for the other item. For this analysis, it is necessary to present the data for the two items in terms of the joint proportion-response distribution for the two items. Table 7.12 displays this data for two items in which 30 percent of the examinees got both items correct and 20 percent answered neither item correctly.

For analyzing items, the value of the phi coefficient lies in its utility for comparing the degree of stability in responses to the same item by examinees at different points in time. For example, if the item writer wishes to consider whether some variable such as gender is correlationally related to how a group of examinees perform mathematics items from differing test administrations, the phi coefficient is the appropriate statistic. This information is especially useful to writers wishing to improve items on a test that is undergoing revision.

Table 7.12 A Four-fold Table Presenting Responses to a Single Item Administered Two Times

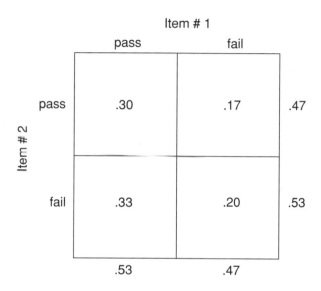

Using the Phi Coefficient With Pre- and Post-Instructed Groups

One technique of analyzing items is to compare the performance of two groups on the same items. One group is selected as the "criterion group"—that is, an appropriate group whom one expects to be able to respond correctly. In the case of mastery-specific learning, the criterion group would be the group who has received instruction. For any item, then, the performance of the uninstructed group is compared against that of the criterion group. Ideally, both groups would be tested simultaneously, and the only difference between them would be the specific instruction. The phi coefficient can be applied to analyzing differences between the groups.

This technique has been in use for some time (e.g., Cronbach & Meehl, 1955; Klein & Kosecoff, 1976; Millman, 1974b); however, it has substantial limitations. First, and perhaps most obvious, is the fact that rarely are instructional programs so well organized around a single set of clearly elaborated objectives that the item writer could identify two appropriate groups. This is a problem of establishing a criterion.

A second disadvantage is the procedural difficulty of testing two similar groups, one of which has received the instruction while the other has not. This can lead to an adjustment in which the same group is tested before and again after instruction. However, this adjustment introduces a lengthy, and often impractical, delay between testings. Despite these difficulties, when a criterion can be reasonably set and appropriate groups are available, this is a strong techniques for analyzing items.

Shortcomings of the Phi Coefficient of Correlation

One especially significant limitation of the phi coefficient occurs because this estimate of correlation, like its relatives the point-biserial and biserial measures of association, is derived from the traditional Pearson coefficient of correlation. Since all product-moment correlations are expressed in the form of a standard score, two variables with identical standard scores will necessarily correlate perfectly. Hence, the phi coefficient will always be exactly $+1.00$ when the p-value for the two groups are equal.

ITEM PARAMETERS

It has been emphasized throughout this book that the modern view of test items considers not only the particular subject content addressed by an item, but also the psychological construct that examinees must employ to solve the problem. The discussion of the purpose for test items in Chapter 2 provides a thorough treatment of the rationale for this approach, and most of Chapter 3 was devoted to an explanation of putting this theory into practice. This theory of a latent trait approach to testing has a serendipitous effect for item analysis: the ability to present test items graphically in a way that makes it easy to view several important characteristics simultaneously. This is accomplished by mapping *item trace lines*, or functions, for test items. Technically, Figures 7.2 to 7.5 in this chapter can be considered item trace lines, but in practice item trace lines are more often computed for items analyzed with latent trait approaches.

Item trace lines are typically called *item characteristic curves* (ICC), and they present information about one, two, or three *parameters*, or mathematical boundaries, for each item. Generally speaking, these parameters are

1. Parameter A, indicating the "steepness" of the item trace line and representing the probability of responding correctly to an item increasing as one goes up the scale as a measure of discrimination among varying ability levels,

2. Parameter B, defining the difficulty of the item by noting the point at which a latent variable (e.g., psychological construct) falls—this is also the left-to-right shift of the curve—and, sometimes,

3. Parameter C, showing the beginning, or base, of the curve, suggesting the probability of guessing (also called "chance" or "pseudo-chance") a correct response on the item for very-low-ability examinees.

Although item characteristic curves were briefly mentioned in Chapter 2, it will be useful to display several curves here for the purpose of examining these particular item parameters. Figure 7.6 presents a item characteristic curve. Note that the graph plots "percent success" along the ordinate (Y axis) and the examinee attribute (viz., ability) along the abscissa (X axis). Three other features of note are: 1) the slope of any curve is monotonic, that is, it always rises and is never exactly horizontal; 2) an "inflection point" (which can be shown by drawing a horizontal line from a point on the curve

Figure 7.6. Trace line for a single item.

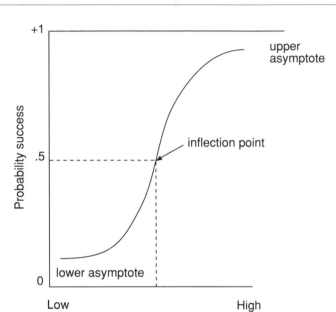

Examinee ability

to the Y axis) is determined by the left-to-right shift of the curve (Parameter B); and 3) the two asymptotes, lower and upper, may approach but never actually reach 0.00 and 1.00 respectively. An item trace line is technically termed a *monotonic normal ogive*. Ogives are merely a specialized graphical representation of a frequency distribution.

Because all three features—discrimination, difficulty, and guessing (or pseudo-chance)—for an item can simultaneously be displayed graphically, ICCs are especially useful for analyzing items. Accordingly, it will be instructive to examine the curves for several items so that differences among them can be noted and their utility discussed. Figure 7.7 displays ICCs for two items which are similar in many respects but differ in difficulty.

Figure 7.7. ICC of two similar items of different difficulty.

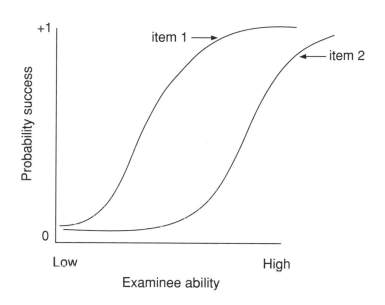

Notice in the figure that items 1 and 2 have similar shapes, indicating that the two items discriminate at about the same rate; however, since the curve for item 2 is shifted further to the right than that for item 1, item 2 discriminates at a higher level of ability. One can conclude, therefore, that these two items have equal discriminating power but that item 2 is a much more difficult item. The informed item writer could use this information to decide whether item 1 or item 2 would be appropriate for a particular group of examinees. For example, item 1 might be appropriate for use with average-achieving third-graders, whereas item 2 may be appropriate only for especially able third-graders or perhaps for fourth-graders.

Next, examine ICCs for two different items, items 3 and 4, in Figure 7.8 Notice that the ICC for item 3 is very flat, indicating that the item discriminates very little, regardless of the ability level of examinees. Typically, items that display the characteristics shown in item 3 are poor and need repair or elimination. Last, notice the very steep slope of the ICC for item 4. This item discriminates very well, but at only one point along the ability continuum. Under certain circumstances such sharp discrimination is appropriate, but more often item writers will consider this slope too steep for making distinctions among examinees and will repair or discard the item. For most tests, item writers will seek items whose ICC is of the smooth, lazy-S form displayed in Figure 7.7.

Figure 7.8. ICCs for two different items.

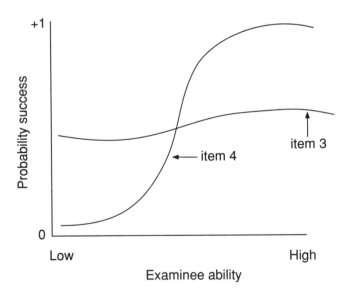

Examining Item Characteristic Curves with Item Response Theory

It should be clear from the discussion thus far about item characteristic curves that they are merely a specialized form of a frequency function and that they can be computed using the methods described; but, this is not the only way to compute item characteristic curves. A much more elegant, but technically complex, approach is to use the rationale and methods of latent trait theory to examine ICCs. Simply put, latent traits are examinee characteristics, or hypothetical constructs, that cause a consistent performance on a test of any given cognitive skill or achievement or ability.

Latent trait theories have been developed and applied under several rubrics, but we shall use the one that most clearly emphasizes the psychologically based nature of latent trait theories, *item response theory* (IRT). It is from IRT that the item ICC may be most meaningfully used in item development. However, while theoretically satisfying, ICC techniques are also the most difficult to understand conceptually and are extremely complex procedurally. Computer processing of data, often involving large samples of examinees, is the only practical way IRT methods may be exploited. Nonetheless, in those instances when IRT is available to the item writer, it can provide powerful data for item analysis.

The issues involved in item response theory are too encompassing to detail here, nor are computational algorithms germane; rather, the focus here is on understanding how to use ICCs that have been computed by IRT methods for item development. Several excellent descriptions of the theory and methods of IRT are available. A technical introduction is given by Birnbaum (1968), and developments in latent trait theory and related issues are discussed by Hambleton (1979), and by Hambleton and Swaminathan (1985). A primer of IRT is given by Warm (1978); also, an excellent introduction to the models of IRT is provided by Crocker and Algina (1986). As one can easily imagine, a vast and growing body of literature is devoted to this important topic.

ITEM BIAS

Item bias is a particularly significant topic in reviewing test items for quality because it is used by those who argue that tests are unfair, inconstant, contaminated by extraneous factors, and subject to misuse and abuse. For this reason, in addition to the focus on improving items generally, the careful item writer will pay special attention to bias in items. As with many other concepts in writing items, bias is not something inherent in test items; rather, it arises from specific sources of error variance. Hence, addressing bias in items involves searching for a particular kind of error variance and then seeking to eliminate or reduce the sources of error.

Further, bias can be either internal to a test or external. Internal bias is concerned with particular characteristics of items, and it shall be our only focus. External bias is more a matter of determining the appropriate uses for test scores, such as for selection or placement into programs, and usually involves an entire test rather a particular item. External bias, by definition, sets the score of a test in a statistical comparison with a criterion. While a very important topic to test developers and test users, external bias is not a matter that the writer of items can directly address without reference to the broader issues of entire test scores and their reference to outside measures; therefore, it will not be covered in this discussion. For a thorough treatment of external bias, the interested reader may refer to Jensen's *Bias in Mental Testing* (1980) and to a special issue of the *Journal of Educational Measurement* (1976) devoted to the topic.

For the writer to examine bias in individual test items in a meaningful way, he or she must understand fully the concepts covered by the term and must also realize what is not included. To begin, item writers should understand that the term *bias*, when used in item analysis, is conceptually distinct and operationally different from the concepts of fairness, equality, prejudice, preference, or any of the other connotations sometimes associated with its use in popular speech. In item analysis, *bias* is a technical term whose meaning will become evident momentarily. The reader interested in exploring the sociological aspects of bias in tests can consult any number of books, journals, and periodicals for discussion (e.g., *Ability Testing: Uses, Consequences and Controversies, Parts I and II*, National Research Council, Committee on Ability Testing, 1982; and *Bias in Mental Testing*, 1980).

As has been mentioned, in item analysis bias has a precise, mathematical definition. According to Osterlind (1983), "bias is defined as a systematic error in the measurement process. It affects all measurement in the same way, changing measurement—sometimes increasing it and other times decreasing it. . . . It is a technical term and denotes nothing more or less than the consistent distortion of a statistic" (p. 10-11).

This mathematical definition for bias may be readily understood when one examines a common occurrence of systematic distortion at the U.S. Bureau of Standards, the official store for U.S. measurements. At the Bureau, measurements of weight are kept in two metrics: the kilogram and the K20. It has been empirically determined that these two measures are not precisely equal. The K20 is estimated to be 19 parts in a billion lighter than the kilogram. Therefore, all measurements at the Bureau done by K20 are systematically off (or biased) by this very small amount. Since some measurements require extreme accuracy, the Bureau compensates for this measurement bias by revising K20 measurements up by 19 parts in a billion. Regardless of compensating remedies, the example shows a systematic error in measurement, or bias.

In test theory, an item is said to be *unbiased* when the probability of success on the item is the same for equally able examinees regardless of a particular subgroup's membership. In other words, if an item is designed to assess reading comprehension for all fifth-graders, any two children from this population *who are of the same ability* should have an equal chance of responding correctly to the item. Characteristics beyond the fact that they are both fifth-graders should not matter, whether gender, ethnic heritage, or whatever. If members of one subpopulation consistently score lower or higher than members of another subpopulation (assuming, of course, that individual members between the groups have equal ability), then there is a consistent distortion, and bias exists.

One naive but widely held notion concerning bias should be quickly dispelled: Bias is not the mere presence of a score difference between groups. It is grossly inappropriate to simply compare *p*-values between two groups, note that the *p*-value for one group is higher than for the other, and conclude that bias is present. Were this true, every item on every test could be "biased" against or in favor of one subpopulation or another, and "bias" could be repeatedly inferred by merely redefining the groups. The logic of this argument would have every item "biased" for tall persons, or overweight persons, or either of the two genders, or persons of one or another ethnic heritage, or any other variable that could be named. This thinking confuses the issue of bias either with the fact that real differences between groups are extant, or with concerns about curricular validity of the instrument, equal opportunity to learn the subject materials, violations of standardizations of testing conditions, and the like.

The techniques of bias detection have evolved considerably in a short period of time. But the most significant advancement of bias-detection strategies accompanied the rising interest in IRT in the late 1970s and into the 1980s. Today, techniques involving item response theory are generally considered the most robust, or technically meritorious, approach to detecting items that exhibit a systematic distortion (Lord, 1980).

Unfortunately, these procedures involve exceedingly complex statistics, require very sophisticated computer programs which must perform vast numbers of calculations, and are very difficult to implement because the mathematical algorithms need enormous sample sizes from each subpopulation to produce stable item-parameter estimates. This final condition means that for bias detection work, IRT can be used in only a few very large-scale testing programs because when the variable to be investigated is ethnic heritage (the usual case), it is rare to have a population with sufficient numbers of examinees in each of the subpopulations. Nevertheless, item-bias detection using these techniques is important, even if only conceptually available to most item writers. Therefore, the technique will be described, if only briefly. Osterlind (1983) offers a more complete discussion of this technique, as well as surveying a variety of other bias-detection strategies.

The technique for IRT item-bias detection is to compare the differences in the ICCs for groups. The area between the equated ICCs is an indication of the degree of bias present in an item. In other words, for a particular item, an ICC is computed for each group. The two ICCs are placed on the same scale by a simple linear transformation, and then compared. This method can be easily presented graphically, as in Figures 7.9, 7.10, and 7.11.

Figure 7.9. Hypothetical equated item characteristic curves for two groups different in discrimination.

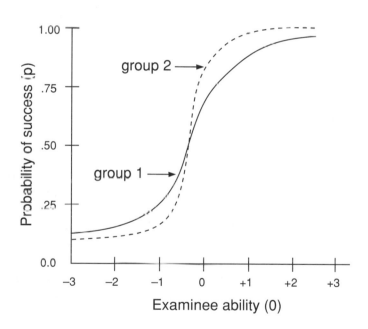

Notice in Figures 7.9, 7.10, and 7.11 that in each instance only a single item is considered. There are two ICCs, one from each sub-population. Each figure displays an item that operates differentially between groups for different reasons. In 7.9, the differing slope for the item reveals differential performance in discrimination for each group; in 7.10, the left-to-right shift shows differences in difficulty for each group; and, in 7.11, differences are displayed in all three parameters for each group.

Figure 7.10. Hypothetical equated item characteristic curves for two groups different in difficulty.

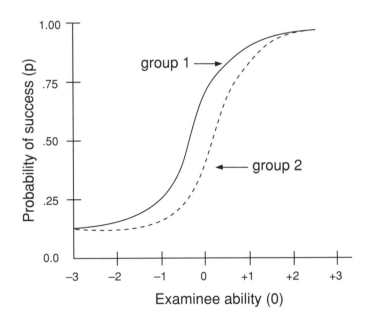

This information is very useful to item writers. Not only is it known that an item performs differently for various groups, but the nature of the differential performance is revealed. With such knowledge, writers can eliminate items or improve them, knowing where they need to focus their efforts—whether on making the item easier or more difficult, or on trying to produce an item that is more highly discriminating among ability levels, or on attempting to reduce the effects of guessing for very-low-ability examinees.

Figure 7.11. Hypothetical equated item characteristic curves for two groups different in discrimination, difficulty, and pseudochance.

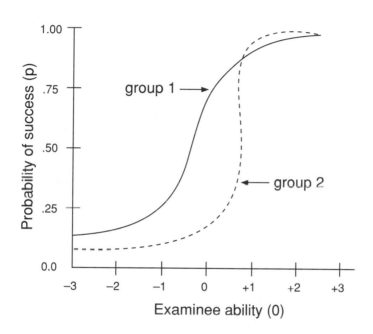

Simple but Incomplete Bias-Detection Strategies

One very simple, albeit incomplete, technique for detecting bias in items compares the rankings of item difficulty values between two groups. If the items for the two groups do not rank similarly, a differential performance may be inferred. It should be understood, however, that comparing rank order of item-difficulty indices between groups is an incomplete strategy for concluding bias exists in test items. It is, nevertheless, a useful technique as an early indication of whether particular items behave differently between groups. And, it is one that item writers can use for preliminary examination of particular items.

To set up the procedure of relative rankings for items, the *p*-value rankings for each of two or more groups are computed. These values are placed side-by-side to facilitate comparisons (Table 7.13).

Table 7.13   Rank Order of Item Difficulty for a Hypothetical Test

Item	Rank Order for Item Group I (*p*-value)	Rank Order for Item Group II (*p*-value)
1	3rd (p = .62)	2nd (p = .64)
2	1st (p = .93)	1st (p = .81)
3	4th (p = .55)	3rd (p = .51)
4	2nd (p = .71)	5th (p = .19)
5	5th (p = .28)	4th (p = .38)

$p = .40.$

Suppose the data for a five-item test are distributed as in 7.13. Notice in the table that item 2 is the easiest for both groups, regardless of the fact that a substantially higher percentage of examinees in Group I responded correctly than did examinees in Group II (i.e., PI= .93 versus PII= .81). The pattern for responses, however, is not continued for item 4. This item is only second in difficulty ranking for Group I, but it is the most difficult of all the items from Group II. Thus, the suspicion is raised that Item 4 does not behave similarly between the two groups. Bias may be present in the item to a degree that consistently underestimates the performance of Group II. All other items appear to rank in a pattern similar for both groups, so no other item is suspected of aberrance.

A rank-order correlation coefficient, typically Spearman's rho, between the two sets of values can be computed for further confirmation of aberrance. For correlations of this kind, one would look for a correlational estimate of .8 or higher to judge the similarity in rankings of item-difficulty values between the two groups. In the example, the coefficient of correlation is .40. The comparatively low level of correlation supports the suspicion of bias by this method. (Of course, this data is computed only for illustrative purposes, and is distorted by the very few items considered.)

Mantel and Haenszel (1959) suggested a procedure with more technical merit that involves applying the chi-square statistic to matched groups. Although their work appeared early in the literature of bias-detection approaches, its value was not fully recognized until recently. This may be due to the fact that although the Mantel-Haenszel procedure is quite simple, it provides a powerful approximation of the IRT methods described above.

Another advantage of the Mantel-Haenszel procedure (cf. Holland and Thayer, 1986) is that it involves the computation of only a chi-square statistic and is, therefore, not limited like IRT to use only with very large groups of examinees. The chi-square approach proposed by Marascuillo and Slaughter (1981), which is also based on a chi-square statistic and is very similar to the Mantel-Haenszel, offers this same advantage.

Procedurally, one establishes strata of ability groups based on the total test score by considering natural breaking points in the total population's distribution of scores. Typically, three or four ability strata are established. The number of persons from each subpopulation to be considered who passed and failed the item is then determined. These frequencies are then set in a series of 2 X 2 contingency tables. Table 7.14 displays data for a hypothetical distribution of scores that have been broken into four ability strata.

The chi-square statistic is then computed and tested for significance. If a value significantly above chance is attained, differential item performance is inferred. The item should then be discarded or reworked.

Thus, examining items for bias is important to the item writer. It provides information that can be helpful in identifying poor items, and it may provide clues as to how a particular item can be improved. The skilled item writer will use these bias-detection strategies to advantage when conducting item analysis.

Table 7.14 Contingency Tables for Two Groups at Four Total Score Intervals on One Test Item

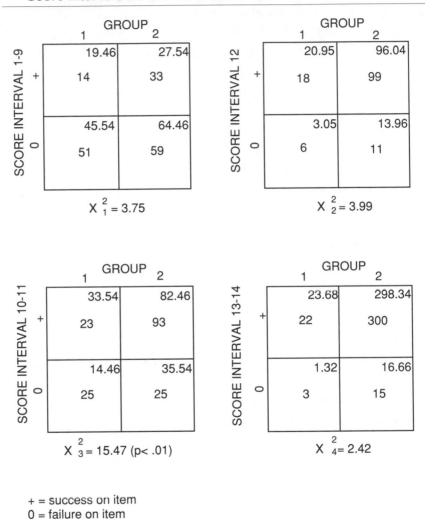

+ = success on item
0 = failure on item

Judgmental Approaches to Bias Detection

In addition to the mathematical definition for bias described in the preceding section, the writer should be sensitive in his use of language to gender, cultural, ethnic-heritage, and other differences.

Language that may offend persons of either gender or persons from any ethnic-heritage or religious group may not manifest numerical differences and could go undetected by statistical approaches to detecting bias in items. Further, changing roles for persons force changes in language. For example, at one time it was nearly universal to refer to medical doctors with the masculine pronoun *he* and nurses with the feminine *she*. Such distinctions are no longer applicable. Or, persons with physical disabilities were once called *handicapped*. Today, more enlightened attitudes generally prevail, and terms such as *physically challenged* are preferred. Chapter 5 cites sources to which one can turn for more information on reducing offensive and stereotyped language.

It is important that item writers gather differing opinions representative of the two genders, of persons from differing ethnic heritages, and of other groups to address the issue of sensitivity in language. Such review process does not require a complex methodology. In most cases, for the purpose of improving items, it is adequate to have persons representing the relevant viewpoints review items informally, preferably in honest, open discussions. This does not mean such a review should be haphazard. The reviewers will need criteria. The criteria might be a list of guiding questions, such as the following: "Does the language offend either gender, or persons of various ethnic heritages, or others?"; "Does the language stereotype either gender or persons of various ethnic heritages, or others?"; "Does the language set a tone that reflects out-of-date attitudes for either gender or persons of various ethnic heritages, or others?."

This kind of review will likely yield the writer, who is trying to improve the language of the items more useful information if it is gathered through discussion, rather than asking reviewers to complete a form. When such a discussion is conducted in the spirit of improving language, the item writer will usually find these reviewers invaluable in reducing this kind of bias in test items.

CONCLUSION

It was mentioned at the outset of this chapter that constructing a test item is not complete until the item has been thoroughly scrutinized for its quality. This chapter provides the writer with the tools necessary for such scrutiny. As can be seen, these tools include the techniques of conducting a validation study relevant to the preparation of the items, as well as methods for defining items in mathematical terms so that they may be examined by appropriate statistics.

When these tools are understood, the item writer will be prepared to gauge his or her work; when the tools are properly used, the writer will have taken a very important step in identifying good test items and poor ones. When the good items are recognized and the poor items are removed or improved, the writer will have taken the final step in the long and difficult journey of constructing good test items.

The next chapter is the concluding one. It focuses less on specific constructing test items than on discussing some overarching considerations, especially ethical and legal concerns for item writers.

Chapter 8

Ethical, Legal Considerations, and Final Remarks for Item Writers

INTRODUCTION

This concluding chapter identifies and explains some elements of item construction that do not conveniently fit into any of the previously discussed categories yet are important, even overarching, elements of constructing good test items. These features include ethical concerns, considerations related to using copyrighted materials and obtaining copyright protection for one's own items, and concerns for preparing or modifying items for use with people who have handicapping conditions. The chapter concludes with a final remark on the task of constructing meritorious test items.

The following topics are covered in this chapter:

- ethical concerns for item writers
- copyrights for test items
- preparing or modifying items for people who have handicapping conditions
- final comments on constructing test items

ETHICAL CONCERNS FOR ITEM WRITERS

Item writers need to adopt the highest standards of ethics when constructing test items. Ethical values are concerned with right conduct. For item writers, right conduct is not relative to a given situation; rather, it is an absolute standard which must be adhered to in all cases. Ethical behavior is needed by the item writer in several specific circumstances, such as when the writer wishes to use items that were originally prepared by another person, or wishes to incorporate another author's text or graphic material into an item, or is entrusted with the security of test items.

The first circumstance involving ethical conduct occurs when an item writer wishes to utilize another writer's items, either as reference or for modifications and use. Often writers, when constructing items of their own or preparing to do so, will refer to test items written by another person. This practice is helpful to writers for a variety of reasons, including giving them a sense of context for writing specific items. And, writers may have a reason to modify another's items to suit a particular circumstance, such as for research that examines a given hypothesis. Referring to or modifying another's items is, in and of itself, neither bad practice nor unethical behavior. However, permission should be sought and obtained. Usually, permission is obtained by a single letter or telephone call in which the writer explains to the original author the specific items wanted and the purpose. Sometimes permission may require more involved procedures, such as a legal contract. Obtaining permission when items are copyrighted is discussed in the following section.

There are no exceptions to this rule of ethical behavior for item writers. If permission cannot be obtained, such as when the author cannot be located or permission is denied, the items should not be used.

Another circumstance which calls for item writers to exhibit high standards of ethical behavior occurs frequently in item construction. This is the case in which the writer wishes to incorporate another author's text or graphic material into an item being otherwise originally written. For example, when preparing items in the language arts domain, it may be desirable to excerpt a passage or a poem from a longer literary work; or when constructing items to assess skills in the social sciences, a chart, map, political cartoon, or other graphic may be useful to incorporate into an item. As before, this practice is appropriate and often desirable; but it should be done only after permission from the author has been obtained.

A less-recognized but common circumstance that calls for item writers to exhibit ethical behavior of the highest order concerns the security of items, whether written by oneself or by another. Items left in accessible, unguarded places can be tempting objects for theft by potential examinees. This is not an indictment against exam-inces; rather, it speaks to the need for right conduct by item writers. After all, the accessibility to items is under the control of the author. He or she is given a trust of confidentiality. This is akin to trusting one's bank to keep one's money safe from theft. The bank assumes a responsibility for safely protecting your money. The writer, too, has a responsibility to use all reasonable diligence to ensure that items are not lost, whether by theft or misplacement. Security for items is also a service to examinees. When items have been misap-propriated and are reviewed beforehand by examinees, the error of measurement in a test is aggravated, and the best possible measure of an examinee's ability cannot be obtained. Thus, ethical behavior by item writers to ensure security for items will aid in protecting the right of examinees.

Obtaining Copyrights for Materials

The experienced writer will know that using another's work is legal and ethical so long as proper permission has been obtained and the appropriate citation is given. Also, test developers and item writers should protect their own investments of time, expertise, and expense for producing test items. For such considerations, test developers and item writers should be informed about statutory copyright protection.

As one may suspect, copyrights can become complex and technical. For example, there is a legal definition of copyrights, and explicit conditions for obtaining a copyright, as well as precise terms for the endurance of a copyright, and specific requirements for who may file. Because these terms and conditions would require lengthy, technical explanation, this section does not explain them. Instead, this section discusses situations in which the item writer may need to research copyright matters or seek legal advice. There are several sources to which item writers and others can turn to become informed about particular aspects of copyrights. The first place to turn for assistance is the Copyright Office of the Library of Congress, which publishes a number of brochures and booklets explaining points of copyright law. In addition, several other good sources are available, including the following publications:

- Strong, W. S. (1984). *The copyright book*. Cambridge, MA: MIT Press.

- Advark Developmental Labs. (1988). *Copyrights, trademarks, and patents*. Houston, TX. [Computer program: Macintosh Hypercard Application].

There are three specific instances when copyright information may be needed: 1) when the test developer wishes to use intact items from another source, 2) when the item writer wants to incorporate text or graphic materials in an item being constructed, and 3) when either the test developer or the item writer wishes to obtain a copyright for items they have originally prepared. Each circumstance has peculiarities unique to it.

In the first instance, when a test developer, item writer, or other person wishes to use complete test items that are taken from another test or other source, permission must be obtained. This is unequivocal, regardless of whether or not the author obtained a copyright for the material. Certainly, by now the reader appreciates the fact that constructing test items is a labor of enormous effort, and ethically, if not also legally, using another person's test items requires his or her permission. When the items are copyrighted, it may be a violation of law not to obtain permission.

Permission can be obtained by writing the publisher or author. A permission letter should include a copy of the test items or a complete citation, indicating every item to be used, and information about where and how it will be used. This may include such pertinent details as whether the item is to be used in a classroom test, or in a test that is to be marketed for sale, or for an instrument that is part of a research project, or elsewhere. Typically, such requests are not for a single item, but for a collection of items, as from a completed test or from a bank of items. Often, it may be helpful to discuss the details of this request with the publisher. A fee for using the copyrighted materials is customary. Many style manuals include a sample letter for requesting permission to use copyrighted materials (e.g., The Chicago Manual of Style, 13th Edition, 1982).

The second instance, when item writers wish to incorporate some text or graphic material into an original item, is very common. As the reader certainly is aware, many test items have reading passages from literary works, cartoons from newspapers and periodicals, charts, tables, and graphs from many sources, and like material. Here, again, permission should be obtained, even if a passage is excerpted and only a few lines are used.

The third circumstance in which item writers should be informed about copyrights is when the test developer or item writer wishes copyright protection for his or her own work. Nearly all professionally produced tests that are published and marketed for sale have been copyrighted. And, many items that are in banks of items have also been protected by a copyright. Writers should adopt the habit of seeking the protection of a copyright for their work. The reason is self-evident: The effort extended to construct the item deserves the protection of a copyright.

Obtaining a copyright is not difficult and usually does not require legal advice. Item writers can complete the necessary application forms themselves. Applications for copyright, registration forms, and other relevant information can be obtained from the Copyright Office, Library of Congress, Washington, D.C. 20559. For initial copyrights, one should write and request Circular 2, "Publications on Copyright." The Copyright Office is not permitted to give legal advice.

Preparing and Modifying Items for People Who Have Handicapping Conditions

People who have handicapping conditions are becoming involved with testing and assessment issues with increasing frequency. This circumstance demands attention from all of the parties involved in testing: the test developer, the examinee, and the test user. Writers of test items can play an especially important role in ensuring that the assessment of educational or psychological skills and constructs for people who have handicapping conditions is accomplished with the same skill and care as assessments developed originally for the general population.

When suggesting modifications to items for testing people who have handicapping conditions, the item writer most often has only common sense and intuition as a guide. Regretfully, there is very little research into alternative items, adaptive formats, and novel presentation of items to people who have handicapping conditions. Rudner (1978) produced a significant study into item bias using standardized tests with the hearing impaired. But, there seems to be little research beyond Rudner's work. This dearth may be partly due to the relatively small number of people who require such specialized considerations. For a given testing situation, typically only a few people a year require modifications. Still, in this important area, there are several questions of basic research that need investigation, including these: "Do items presented differently to people who have handicapping conditions than to the general population affect the same cognitive function?"; "How do modifications to items impact valid score interpretations?"; "Is the reliability of the test's scores changed?" and more.

There is a growing awareness of the need for research in this crucially important area. This is evidenced by the fact that the Standards (AERA/APA/NCME, 1985) devotes an entire section exclusively to consideration of test development and test use for assessing the abilities of people who have handicapping conditions. And, today most tests produced for a national audience suggest that appropriate accommodations be made to test people who cannot take the exam under usual circumstances.

Often item modifications that are necessary for testing people who have handicapping conditions can be made. For example, specialized equipment can automatically enlarge the size of type in a printed test, enabling some visually impaired persons access to the assessment. Under these circumstances, the time limits for administration may need to be lengthened. Also, other specialized equipment can transform typed letters into braille, making tests available to even more people.

Physical aspects responding to test items are also a consideration when modifications to items are required. For example, some people with motor-skill dysfunction cannot complete the usual answer document. Specialized adaptations are needed in these cases. Sometimes even a trained recorder is required. Or, nonverbal tests may be needed for assessing persons with hearing impairments, particularly in accommodating people who are prelingually deaf.

The overriding concern for the item writer when suggesting modifications to items for testing people who have handicapping conditions is the benefit of the test taker. It is recommended that any modification to items be discussed with the test taker, with relevant persons who know the examinee, as well as with persons who are professionally competent to understand the particular handicapping condition, before a decision is made whether to pursue such modifications. And, consultation with persons who have expertise in psychometrics is needed. Merely altering the circumstances for administration, without understanding fully the effect this may have on the interpretation of the item, is a disservice to the examinee.

Common sense and intuition can help one make sagacious decisions about the appropriateness of specific modifications. And, again, such modifications should be attempted only when it is to the benefit of the examinee.

CONCLUDING COMMENTS ABOUT CONSTRUCTING TEST ITEMS

From the outset of this book, it has been emphasized that constructing test items is a complex task, requiring both technical skill and creativity. By careful study of the various points identified and explained in the eight chapters of this book, one can gain the requisite technical proficiency. Creativity, however, is an element of item construction that can only be identified; it cannot be explained. Item writers, as individuals, will bring their own sense of art to the task.

Further, as the reader can appreciate, constructing test items demands an enormous amount of energy, far more energy than is popularly recognized. Producing test items of merit is slow, arduous, and demanding work. Still, persons who use the information in this book and elsewhere and their own creativity, coupled with hard work, can produce test items of merit. Meritorious items will contribute to sound measurement of examinee attributes. In turn, sound measurements, properly interpreted, will yield better information for making informed decisions. Better-informed decisions can only be to the benefit of examinees.

References and Indexes

References

Allen, M. J., & Yen, W. M. (1979). *Introduction to measurement theory*. Monterey, CA: Brooks/Cole.

American Educational Research Association, American Psychological Association, & National Council on Measurement in Education. (1985). *Standards for educational and psychological testing*. Washington, DC: Author.

American Educational Research Association. (1955). *Technical recommendations for achievement tests*. Washington, D. C.: Author.

American Psychological Association, American Educational Research Association, & National Council on Measurement Used in Education. (1954). *Technical recommendations for psychological tests and diagnostic techniques*, 51 (Supplement). Washington, D. C.: Author.

American Psychological Association. (1966). *Standards for educational and psychological tests and manuals*. Washington, D. C.: Author.

Anastasi, A. (1988). *Psychological testing* (6th Ed.). New York: Macmillan Publishing.

Angoff, W. H. (1988). Validity: An evolving concept. In H. Wainer, & H. I. Braun (Eds.), *Test validity*. Hillsdale, NJ: Erlbaum.

Baker, E. L. (1974). Beyond objectives: Domain-referenced tests for evaluation and instructional improvement. *Educational Technology, 14*, 10-16.

Berk, R. A., & Boodoo, G. M. (Eds.). (n.d.). *Educational measurement resource bank*. Washington, D.C.: National Council on Measurement in Education.

Binet, A., & Simon, Th. (1917). *A method of measuring the development of the intelligence of young children*. In C. H. Town (Trans.). Chicago: Medical Book.

Birmbaum, A. (1968). Some latent trait models and their use in inferring an examinee's ability. In F. M. Lord, & M. R. Novick (Eds.), *Statistical theories of mental test scores*. Reading, MA: Addison-Wesley.

Bloom, B. S. (Ed.). (1956). *Taxonomy of educational objectives, handbook 1: The cognitive domain*. New York: McKay.

Bloom, B. S., Hastings, J. T., & Madaus, G. F. (1971). *Handbook on formative and summative evaluation of student learning*. New York: McGraw-Hill.

Blumberg, P., Alschuler, M. D., & Rezmovic, V. (1982). Should taxonomic levels be considered in developing examinations? *Educational and Psychological Measurement, 42*, 1-7.

Bormuth, J. R. (1970). *On the theory of achievement test items*. Chicago: University of Chicago Press.

Bormuth, J. R. (1971). *Development of standards of readibility: Toward a rationale criterion of passage performance*. Chicago: University of Chicago. (ERIC Document Reproduction Service No. ED 054233)

Boynton, M. (1950). Inclusion of 'none of these' makes spelling items more difficult. *Educational and Psychological Measurement, 10*, 431-432.

Budescu, D. V., & Nevo, B. (1985). Optimal number of options: An investigation of the assumption of proportionality. *Journal of Educational Measurement, 22*, 183-196.

Buros, O. K. (Ed.). (1972). *The seventh mental measurements yearbook*. Highland Park, NJ: Gryphon Press.

Campbell, D. T., & Fiske, D. W. (1959). Convergent and discriminant validation by the multitrait-multimethod matrix. *Psychological Bulletin, 56*, 81-105.

College Entrance Examination Board. (1986). *DRP handbook*. Washington, D.C.: Author.

Costin, F. (1970). The optimal number of alternatives in multiple-choice achievement tests: Some emperical evidence for a mathematical proof. *Educational and Psychological Measurement, 30*, 353-358.

Crocker, L., & Algina, J. (1986). *Introduction to classical and modern test theory*. New York: Hold, Rinehart, and Winston.

Cronbach, L. J. (1970). Review of [On the theory of achievement test items]. *Psychometrika, 35*, 509-511.

Cronbach, L. J. (1971). Test validation. In R. L. Thorndike (Ed.), *Educational measurement* (2nd ed.). Washington, DC: American Council on Education.

Cronbach, L. J. (1980). Validity on parole: How can we go straight? In W. B. Schrader (Ed.), *Measuring achievement: Progress over a decade*. (Proceedings of the 1979 ETS Invitational Conference, pp. 99-108). San Francisco: Jossey-Bass.

Cronbach, L. J. (1984). *Essentials of psychological testing* (4th ed.). New York: Harper & Row.

Cronbach, L. J. (1988). Five perspectives on the validity argument. In H. Wainer, & H. I. Braun (Eds.), *Test validity*. Hillsdale, NJ: Lawrence Erlbaum.

Cronbach, L. J., & Meehl, P. E. (1955). Construct validity in psychological tests. *Psychological Bulletin, 52*, 281-302.

Cunningham, G. K. (1986). *Educational and psychological measurement*. New York: MacMillan.

Ebel, R. L. (1951). Writing the test item. In E. F. Lindquist (Ed.), *Educational measurement*. Washington, D. C.: American Council on Education.

Ebel, R. L. (1962a). Obtaining and reporting edivence on content validity. *Educational and Psychological Measurement, 16*, 269-281.

Ebel, R. L. (1962b). Content standard test scores. *Educational and Psychological Measurement, 22*, 15-25.

Ebel, R. L. (1968a). The value of internal consistency in classroom examinations. *Journal of Educational Measurement, 5*, 71-74.

Ebel, R. L. (1968b). Blind guessing on objective achievement tests. *Journal of Educational Measurement, 5*, 321-25.

Ebel, R. L. (1969). Expected reliability as a function of choices per item. *Educational and Psychological Measurement, 29*, 565-570.

Ebel, R. L. (1972). *Essentials of educational measurement* (2nd ed.). Englewood Cliffs, NJ: Prentice-Hall.

Ebel, R. L. (1979). *Essentials of educational measurement* (3rd ed.). Englewood Cliffs, NJ: Prentice-Hall.

Ebel, R. L. (1983). The practical validation of tests of ability. *Educational Measurement: Issues and Practice, 2*, 7-10.

Ebel, R. L., & Frisbie, D. A. (1986). *Essentials of educational measurement* (4th ed.). Englewood Cliffs, NJ: Prentice-Hall.

Echternacht, G. J. (1972). The use of confidence testing objective tests. *Review of Educational Research, 42*, 217-236.

Eysenck, H. J. (Ed.). (1982). *A model for intelligence*. Heidelberg: Springer-Verlag.

Finn, P. J. (1978, March). *Generating domain-referenced test items from prose passages*. Paper presented at the annual meeting of the American Educational Research Association, Toronto.

Flannagan, J. C. (1962). Symposium: Standard scores for aptitude and achievement tests: Discussion. *Educational and Psychological Measurement, 22*, 35-39.

Forsythe, G. B., McGaghie, W. C., & Friedman, C. P. (1986). Construct validity of medical competence measures: A multitrait-multimethod matrix study using confirmatory factor analysis. *American Educational Research Journal, 23*, 315-326.

Frisbie, D. A. (1973). Multiple-choice versus true-false: A comparison of reliabilities and concurrent validities. *Journal of Educational Measurement, 10*, 297-304.

Frisbie, D. A., & Sweeney, D. C. (1982). The relative merits of multiple true-false achievement tests. *Journal of Eductional Measurement, 19*, 29-35.

Garrett, H. E. (1937). *Statistics in psychology and education.* New York: Longmans, Green.

Gilman, D. A., & Ferry, P. (1972). Increasing test reliability through self-scoring procedures. *Journal of Educational Measurement, 9*, 519-521.

Glaser, R., & Nitko, A. J. (1971). Measurement in learning and instruction. In R. L. Thorndike (Ed.), *Educational measurement* (2nd ed.). Washington, DC: American Council on Education.

Grier, J. B. (1975). The number of alternatives for optimal test reliability. *Journal of Educational Measurement, 12*, 10-113.

Grier, J. B. (1976). The optimal number of alternatives at a choice point with travel time considered. *Journal of Mathematical Psychology, 14*, 91-97.

Gronlund, N. E. (1988). *How to construct achievement tests* (4th ed.). Englewood Cliffs, NJ: Prentice-Hall.

Guilford, J. P., & Fruchter, B. (1978). *Fundamental statistics in psychology and education* (6th ed.). New York: McGraw-Hill.

Guion, R. M. (1977). Content validity--The source of my discontent. *Applied Psychological Measurement, 1*, 1-10.

Gulliksen, H. (1950). *Theory of mental tests.* New York: Wiley.

Guttman, L. (1944). A basis for scaling qualitative data. *American Sociological Review, 9*, 139-150.

Haertel, E., & Calfee. (1983, Summer). School achievement: Thinking about what to test. *Journal of Educational Measurement, 20*, 119-132.

Haladyna, T. M., & Downing, S. M. (in press). A taxonomy of multiple-choice item writing rules. *Applied Measurement in Education.*

Haladyna, T. M., & Downing, S. M. (in press). The validity of a taxonomy of multiple-choice item writing rules. *Applied Measurement in Education.*

Hambleton, R. K. (1979). Latent trait models and their applications. In R. Traub (Ed.). *New directions for Testing and Measurement* (volume 4): *Methodological Developments.* San Francisco: Jossey-Bass.

Hambleton, R. K. (1980). Test score validity and standard setting methods. In R. A. Berk (Ed.). *Criterion-referenced measurement: The state of the art.* Baltimore: John Hopkins University Press.

Hambleton, R. K. (1984). Validating the test score. In R. A. Berk (Ed.). *A guide to criterion-referenced test construction.* Baltimore: John Hopkins University Press.

Hambleton, R. K., & Eignor, D. R. (1978). Guidelines for evaluating criterion-referenced tests and test manuals. *Journal of Educational Measurement, 15*, 321-327.

Hambleton, R. K., & Novick, M. R. (1973). Toward an integration of theory and methods for criterion-referenced tests. *Journal of Educational Measurement, 10*, 159-170.

Hambleton, R. K., & Swaminathan, H. (1985). *Item response theory: Principles and applications*. Boston: Kluwer-Nijhoff.

Hanna, G. S. (1975). Incremental reliability and validity of multiple-choice tests with an-answer-correct procedure. *Journal of Educational Measurement, 12*, 175-178.

Hannah, L. S., & Michaelis, J. U. (1977). *A comprehensive framework for instructional objectives: A guide to systematic planning and evaluation*. Reading, MA: Addison-Wesley.

Hattie, J. A. (1981). *Decision criteria for determining unidimensionality*. Unpublished doctoral dissertation, University of Toronto.

Hays, W. L. (1988). *Statistics* (4th ed.). New York: Holt, Rinehart, and Winston.

Henrysson, S. (1963). Correction of item-total correlation in item analysis. *Psychometrika, 28*, 211-218.

Herman, J. L. (1988). Item writing techniques. In J. P. Keeves (Ed.). *Educational research, methodology, and measurement: An international handbook*. New York: Pergamon.

Herrnstein, R. (1971). IQ. *Atlantic, 228*, 43-64.

Hively, W., Patterson, H. L., & Page, S. A. (1968). A "universe-defined" system of arithmetic achievement tests. *Journal of Educational Measurement, 5*, 275-290.

Holland, P. W., and Thayer, D. T. (1986, April). *Differential item differences and the Mantel-Haenszel procedure*. Paper presented at the annual meeting of the American Educational Research Association, San Francisco.

Hughes, H. H., & Trimble, W. E. (1965). The use of complex alternatives in multiple choice items. *Educational and Psychological Measurement, 21*, 117-126.

Hunt, E. B. (1980). Intelligence as an information processing concept. *British Journal of Psychology, 71*, 449-474.

Jensen J. R. (1980). *Bias in mental testing*. New York: The Free Press.

Jensen J. R. (1982a). The chronometry of intelligence. In Sternberg, R. J. (Ed.). *Advances in the psychology of human intelligence* (Vol. 1), 255-310. Hillsdale, N. J.: Erlbaum.

Jensen J. R. (1982b). Reaction time and psychometric *g*. In Eysenck, H. J. (Ed.). *A model for intelligence*. New York: Springer-Verlag.

Joint Committee on Standards for Educational Evaluation. (1981). *Standards for evaluations of educational programs, projects, and materials.* New York: McGraw-Hill.

Kane, M. T. (1982). A sampling model for validity. *Applied Psychological Measurement, 6,* 125-160.

Katz, M. (1972). Selecting an achievement test: Principles and procedures. In V. H. Noll, D. P. Scannell, & R. P. Noll (Eds.), *Introductory readings in educational measurement.* Boston: Houghton-Mifflin.

Kelly, T. L. (1939). Selection of upper and lower groups for validation of test items. *Journal of Educational Psychology, 30,* 17-24.

Kirsch, I. S., & Guthrie, J. T. (1980). Construct validity of functional reading tests. *Journal of Educational Measurement, 2,* 81-93.

Klein, S. P., & Kosecoff, J. P. (April, 1975). *Determining how well a test measures your objectives* (CSE Report No 94). Los Angeles: University of California, Los Angeles, Center for the Study of Evaluation.

Koslin, B. L., Zeno, S., & Koslin, S. (1987). *The DPR: An effectiveness measure in reading.* n.p.: Touchstone Applied Science Associates.

Krathwohl, D. R., Bloom, B. S., & Masia, B. (1964). *Taxonomy of educational objectives, handbook II: The affective domain.* New York: McKay.

Lefrancois, G. R. (1988). *Psychology for teaching* (6th ed.). Belmont, CA: Wadsworth.

Lindquist, E. F. (1936). The theory of test construction. In H. E. Hawkes, E. F. Lindquist, & C. R. Mann (Eds.), *The construction and use of achievement test examinations.* Boston: Houghton-Mifflin.

Lord, F. M. (1952). *A theory of test scores* (Psychometric Monograph. No. 7). Psychometric Society.

Lord, F. M. (1963). Formula scoring and validity. *Educational and Psychological Measurement, 23,* 663-672.

Lord, F. M. (1977a). Reliability of multiple-choice tests as a function of number of choices per item. *Journal of Educational Psychology, 35,* 175-180.

Lord, F. M. (1977b). Optimal number of choices per item--a comparison of four approaches. *Journal of Educational Measurement, 14,* 31-38.

Lord, F. M. (1980). *Applications of item response theory to practical testing problems.* Hillsdale, NJ: Erlbaum.

Lord, F. M., & Novick, M. R. (1968). *Statistical theories of test scores.* Reading, MA: Addison-Wesley.

Madaus, G. F., Woods, E. M., & Nuttall, R. L. (1973). A causal model analysis of Bloom's taxonomy. *American Educational Research Journal, 10,* 253-262.

Mantel, N., & Haenszel, W. (1952). Statistical aspects of the analysis of data from retrospective studies of disease. *Journal of the National Cancer Institute, 22,* 719-748.

Marascuillo, L. A., & Slaughter, R. E. (1981). Statistical procedures for identifying possible sources of item bias based on X2 statistics. *Journal of Educational Measurement, 18*, 229-248.

McDonald, R. P. (1980a). The dimensionality of tests and items. *British Journal of Mathematical and Statistical Psychology, 33*, 205-233.

McDonald, R. P. (1980b). Fitting latent trait models. In D. Spearitt (Ed.), *The improvement of measurement in education and psychology*. Proceedings of the invitational seminar for the Fiftieth Anniversary of the Australian Council of Educational Research, Melbourne.

McDonald, R. P. (1982). Linear versus non-linear models in item response theory. *Applied Psychological Measurement, 6*, 379-396.

Mehrens, W. A., & Lehmann, I. J. (1987). *Using standardized tests in education* (4th ed.). New York: Longman.

Merz, W. R. (1980). *Methods of assessing bias and fairness in tests* (Technical Report IZI-79). Sacramento, CA: Applied Research Consultants.

Messick, S. (1975). The standard problem: Meaning and values in measurement and evaluation. *American Psychologist, 11*, 263-272.

Messick, S. (1980). Test validity and the ethics of assessment. *American Psychologist, 35*, 1012-1027.

Messick, S. (1988). The once and future issues of validity: Assessing the meaning and consequences of measurement. In H. Wainer, & H. I. Braun (Eds.), *Test validity*. Hillsdale, NJ: Lawrence Erlbaum.

Messick, S., Beaton, A., & Lord, F. (1983). *A new design for a new era* (NEAP Report No. 83-1). Princeton, NJ: Educational Testing Service.

Metfessel, N. S., Michael, W. B., & Kirsner, D. A. (1969). Instrumentation of Bloom's taxonomies for the writing of educational objectives. *Psychology in the Schools, 6*, 227-231.

Millman, J. (1974a). Sampling plans for domain-referenced tests. *Educational Technology, 14*, 17-21.

Millman, J. (1974b). Criterion-referenced measurement. In W. J. Popham (Ed.), *Evaluation in education: Current Applications*. Berkeley: McCutchan.

Millman, J., & Greene, J. (in press). The specification and development of tests of achievement and abilities. In R. L. Linn (Ed.), *Educational measurement* (3rd ed.). Washington, D.C.: American Council on Education.

Mitchell, J. V., Jr. (1986). Measurement in the larger context: Critical current issues. *Professional Psychology: Research and Practice, 17*, 544-550.

Mitchell, J. V., Jr. (Ed.). (1983). *Tests in print III: An index to tests, test reviews, and the literature on specific tests*. Lincoln, Nebraska: The Buros Institute of Mental Measurements.

Mitchell, J. V., Jr. (Ed.). (1985). *The ninth mental measurements yearbook* (Vols. 1 and 2). Lincoln, Nebraska: The Buros Institute of Mental Measurements.

Muliak, S. A. (1972). *The foundations of factor analysis.* New York: McGraw-Hill.

National Research Council, Committee on Ability testing, Assembly of the Behavioral Social Sciences. (1982). *Ability testing: Uses, consequences, and controversies.* Parts I and II. Washington, D.C.: National Academy Press.

Nitko, A. J. (1983). *Educational tests and measurement: An introduction.* New York: Harcourt Brace Jovanovich.

Nitko, A. J. (1984a). [Book review of A technology for test-item writing]. *Journal of Educational Measurement, 21*, 201-204.

Nitko, A. J. (1984b). Defining "criterion-referenced test." In R. A. Berk (Ed.), *A guide to criterion-referenced test construction.* Baltimore: John Hopkins University press.

Nunnally, J. C. (1978). *Psychometric theory* (2nd ed.). New York: McGraw-Hill.

On Bias in Selection. (1976). Special issue, *Journal of Educational Measurement, 13*, 1-100.

Oosterhof, A. C., & Coats, P. K. (1984). Comparison of difficulties and reliabilities of quantitative word problems in completion and multiple-choice item formats. *Applied Psychological Measurement, 8*, 287-294.

Osterlind, S. J. (1983). *Test item bias* (Sage University Paper Series on Quantitative Applications in the Social Sciences, 07-030). Beverly Hill, CA: Sage.

Osterlind, S. J. (1986, Nov./Dec.). The question of tests. *Alumnus, 75*: 15-16.

Polin, L., & Baker, E. L. (1979). *Qualitative analysis of test item attributes for domain referenced content validity judgments.* (ERIC Document Reproduction Service No. ED 211 601)

Popham, W. J. (1975). *Educational evaluation.* Englewood Cliffs, NJ: Prentice-Hall.

Popham, W. J. (1981). *Modern educational measurement.* Englewood Cliffs, NJ: Prentice-Hall.

Popham, W. J. (1984). Specifying the domain of content or bahaviors. In R. A. Berk (Ed.). *A guide to criterion-referenced test construction.* Baltimore: Johns Hopkins.

Reckase, M. D. (1979). Unifactor latent trait models applied to multifactor tests. *Journal of Educational Statistics, 4*, 207-230.

Reckase, M. D. (1985). The difficulty of test items that measure more than one ability. *Applied Psychological Measurement, 9*, 401-402.

Reckase, M. D. (1986, April). *The discriminating power of items that measure more than one dimension.* Paper presented at the annual meeting of the American Educational Research Association, San Francisco.

Reckase, M. D., Ackerman, T. A., & Carlson, J. E. (1988). Building a unidimensional test using multidimensional items. *Journal of Educational Measurement, 25*, 193-203.

Rimland, B. (1960). The effects of varying time limits and use of 'right answer not given' in experiment forms of the U.S. Navy Arithmetic Test. *Educational and Psychological Measurement, 20,* 533-539.

Roid, G. H., & Haladyna, T. M. (1978). A comparison of objective-based and modified-Bormuth item writing techniques. *Educational and Psychological Measurement, 35,* 19-28.

Roid, G. H., & Haladyna, T. M. (1982). *A technology for test-item writing.* New York: Academic Press.

Rovinelli, R. J., & Hambleton, R. J. (1977). On the use of content specialists in the assessment of criterion-referenced test item validity. *Dutch Journal of Educational Research, 2,* 49-60.

Ruch, G. M., & Charles, J. W. (1928). A comparison of five-types of objective tests in elementary psychology. *Journal of Applied Psychology, 12,* 398-404.

Ruch, G. M., & Stoddard, G. D. (1927). *Tests and measurement in high school instruction.* Chicago: World Book.

Ruch, G. M., DeGraff, M. H., & Gordon, W. E. (1926). *Objective examination methods in the social studies.* New York: Scott Foresman.

Rudner, L. M. (1978). Using standardized tests with the hearing impaired: The problem of item bias. *Volta Review, 80,* 31-40.

Samejima, F. (1974). Normal ogive model on the continuous response level in the multidimensional latent space. *Psychometrika, 39,* 111-121.

Sarnacki, R. E. (1979). An examination of test-wiseness in the cognitive domain. *Review of Educational Research, 49,* 252-279.

Sax, G. (1980). *Principles of educational and psychological measurement and evaluation* (2nd ed.). Belmont, CA: Wadsworth.

Schmidt, F. L., Hunter, J. E., & Urry, V. W. (1976). Statistical power in criterion-related validity studies. *Journal of Applied Psychology, 61,* 473-485.

Schwartz, L. L. (1977). *Educational psychology: Focus on the learner* (2nd ed.). Boston: Holbrook.

Seddon, G. M. (1978). The properties of Bloom's taxonomy of educational objectives for the cognitive domain. *Review of Educational Research, 48,* 303-323.

Snow, R. E. (1980). Aptitude and achievement. In W. B. Schrader (Ed.), *Measuring achievement: Progress over a decade* (New Directions for Testing and Measurement No. 5). San Francisco: Jossey-Bass.

Stevens, S. S. (1946). On the theory of scales measurement. *Science, 103,* 677-780.

Sweetland, R. C., & Keyser, D. J. (Gen. Eds.). (1986). *Tests: A comprehensive reference for assessment in psychology, education, and business* (2nd ed.). Kansas City: Test Corporation of America.

Taylor, W. L. (1953). "Cloze-procedure: A new tool for measuring readibility." *Journalism Quarterly, 30,* 415-33.

Tenopyr, M. L. (1977). Content—construct confusion. *Personnel Psychology, 30*, 47-54.

Thorndike, E. L. (1904). *An introduction to the theory of mental and social measurements.* New York: Science Press.

Thorndike, R. L. (1949). *Personnel Selection.* New York: John Wiley.

Thorndike, R. L. (1982). *Applied psychometrics.* Boston: Hougton-Mifflin.

Thorndike, R. L., & Hagen, E. P. (1977). *Measurement and evaluation in psychology and education.* New York: John Wiley.

Tollefson, N. (1987). A comparison of the item difficulty level and item discrimination of multiple-choice items using "none of the above" and one correct response option. *Educational and Psychological Measurement, 47*, 377-383.

Toops, H. A. (1921). *Trade tests in education* (Teachers College Contributions to Education No. 115). New York: Columbia University.

Torgerson, W. S. (1958). *Theory and methods of scaling.* New York: John Wiley.

Traub, R. E. (1983). *A priori* considerations in choosing an item response model. In R. K. Hambleton (Ed.), *Applications of item response theory.* Vancouver, BC: Educational Research Institute of British Columbia.

Tuckman, B. W. (1975). *Measuring educational outcomes: Fundamentals of testing.* New York: Harcourt Brace Jovanovich.

Tversky, A. (1964). On the optimal number of alternatives at a choice point. *Journal of Mathematical Psychology, 1*, 386-391.

Tyler, R. W. (1949). *Basic principles of curriculum and instruction.* Chicago: University of Chicago Press.

Udinsky, B. F., Osterlind, S. J., & Lynch, S. W. (1981). *Evaluation resource handbook: Gathering, analyzing, and reporting data.* San Diego: EdITS.

Wainer, H., & Braun, H. I. (1988). (Eds.). *Test validity.* Hillsdale, NJ: Erlbaum.

Wainer, H., Wadkins, J. R. J., & Rogers, A. (1983). *Was there one distractor too many?* (Technical Report No. 83-39, Research RR-83-34). Princeton, NJ: Educational Testing Service.

Warm, T. A. (1978). *A primer of item response theory.* (Technical Report No. 941078.) Oklahoma City: U.S. Coast Guard Institute, Department of Transportation (NTIS AD A063072).

Weidemann, C. C. (1926). *How to construct the true-false examination* (Teachers College, Columbia University. Contributions to Education No. 225). New York: Bureau of Publications, Teachers College, Columbia University.

Weiss, D. J., & Davidson, M. L. (January, 1981). *Review of test theory and methods* (Research Report 81-1). Minneapolis, MN: University of Minnesota, Department of Psychology, Psychometric Methods Program, Computerized Adaptive Testing Laboratory.

Weitzenhoffer, A. M. (1951). Mathematical structures and psychological measurement. *Psychometrika, 16*, 387-406.

Wesman, A. G. (1971). *Writing the test item. In R. L. Thorndike (Ed.), Educational measurement* (2nd ed.). Washington, DC: American Council on Education.

Wesman, A. G., & Bennett, G. K. (1946). The use of 'none of these' as an option in test construction. *Journal of Educational Psychology, 37*, 541-549.

White, E. M. (1985). *Teaching and assessing writing.* San Francisco: Jossey Bass.

Wiersma, W., & Jurs, S. G. (1985). *Educational measurement and testing.* Boston: Allyn and Bacon, Inc.

Wilcox, R. R. (1981). A close sequential procedure for answer-until-correct tests. *Journal of Experimental Education, 5*, 219-222.

Wilcox, R. R. (1982). Some new results on an answer-until-correct procedure. *Journal of Educational Measurement, 19*, 67-74.

Williams, B. J., & Ebel, R. L. (1957). The effect of varying the number of alternatives per item on multiple-choice vocabulary test items. The Fourteenth Yearbook. *National Council on Mathematics Used in Education.*

Wood, R. (1977). Multiple-choice: A state of the art report. *Evaluation in Education: International Progress, 1*, 191-280.

Wright, B. D., & Stone, M. H. (1979). *Best test design.* Chicago, IL: Mesa Press.

Yalow, E. S. & Popham, W. J. (1983). Content validity at the crossroads. *Educational Researcher, 12*, 10-14.

Author Index

Subject Index[*]

---

[*] Throughout this index I.I. is used to abbreviate *Illustrative Item*.